Regent's Study Guide
General Editor: Paul S. Fi

C000296246

Theology from Three Worlds
*Liberation and Evangelization
for the New Europe*

TO Regent's Park College, Oxford, where I was taught theology.
TO Luther King House, Manchester, where I was helped to write it.
TO John Bunyan Baptist Church, Cowley,
Leamington Road Baptist Church, Blackburn,
and Dagnall Street Baptist Church, St. Albans,
where I have been freed to practise it.

Regent's Study Guides

Theology from Three Worlds

*Liberation and Evangelization
for the New Europe*

Michael I. Bochenski

Regent's Park College, Oxford
with
Smyth & Helwys Publishing, Inc.
Macon, Georgia

ISBN (UK) 0-9518104-4-8
ISBN (USA) 1-57312-168-1

Theology from Three Worlds
Liberation and Evangelization for the New Europe

by Michael I. Bochenski

Published by Regent's Park College, Oxford OX1 2LB
in association with Smyth & Helwys Publishing Inc.,
6316 Peake Road, Macon, Georgia 31210-3960 USA.

Library of Congress Cataloguing-in-Publication Data

Bochenski, Michael I.
    Theology from three worlds:
    liberation and evangelization for the new Europe/
    Michael I. Bochenski.
    p. cm.
    (Regent's study guides; 5)
    Includes bibliographical references and index.
    ISBN 1-57312-168-1   (alk. paper)
    1. Liberation theology.
    2. Baptists—Europe—History—20th century.
    I. Title.   II. Series.
    BT83.57.B593   1997
    230'.0464—dc21   97-14480
                                                           CIP

Contents

PART III: PRAXIS

Acknowledgements

I am grateful to the following publishers for their permission to reproduce copyright material:

SCM Press Ltd., London, for extracts from *A Theology of Liberation* by Gustavo Guttierez © 1974 SCM Press Ltd. Also Orbis Books, Maryknoll, New York, for extracts from the same book © 1973 Orbis Books, for rights in the USA and Canada.

SCM Press Ltd., London, for extracts from *The True Church and the Poor* by Jon Sobrino © 1985 SCM Press Ltd. Also Orbis Books, Maryknoll, New York, for extracts from the same book © 1984 Orbis Books, for rights in the USA and Canada.

Burns & Oates Ltd./ Search Press Ltd., Tunbridge Wells, Kent, for extracts from *The Holy Spirit and Liberation* by José Comblin © 1989 Burns & Oates Ltd./Search Press Ltd. Also Orbis Books, Maryknoll, New York, for extracts from the same book © 1989 Orbis Books, for rights in the USA and Canada.

Burns & Oates Ltd./ Search Press Ltd., Tunbridge Wells, Kent, for extracts from *The Bible, the Church, and the Poor* by Clodovis Boff and Jorgé Pixley © 1989 Burns & Oates Ltd./Search Press Ltd. Also Orbis Books, Maryknoll, New York, for extracts from the same book © 1989 Orbis Books, for rights in the USA and Canada.

Macmillan Press Ltd., Basingstoke, Hampshire, for extracts from *Ever Closer Union? An Introduction to the European Community* by Desmond Dinan © 1994 Macmillan Press Ltd., for world rights outside the USA and Canada. Also Lynne Rienner Publishers Inc., Boulder, Colorado, for extracts from the same book © 1994 Lynne Rienner Publishers Inc., for rights in the USA and Canada.

The Catholic Truth Society, London (Veritas), for extracts from *The Price of Love* by Jerzy Popieluszko © 1985 The Catholic Truth Society.

Church House Publishing, London, and The Central Board of Finance of the Church of England for extracts from *Faith in the City* © 1985 The Central Board of Finance of the Church of England.

Churchman Publishing Ltd., London, and The Archbishops' Commission on Rural Areas for extracts from *Faith in the Countryside* © 1990 The Archbishops Commission on Rural Areas.

Hodder & Stoughton Publishers, London, for extracts from Derek Worlock and David Sheppard, *Better Together. Christian Partnership in a Hurt City* © 1988 Hodder & Stoughton Ltd.

Hodder Headline PLC, London, for extracts from Stefan Cardinal Wyszynski, *A Freedom Within. The Prison Notes of Stefan Cardinal Wyszynski* © 1985 Hodder & Stoughton Ltd. Also Harcourt Brace Books, Orlando, USA, for extracts from the same book © 1985 Harcourt Brace Inc., for rights in the USA and Canada.

Hodder & Stoughton Publishers, London, for extracts from David Sheppard, *Bias to the Poor* © 1983 Hodder & Stoughton Ltd.

Quartet Books Ltd., London, for extracts from Jeremy Seabrook, *Unemployment* © 1982 Quartet Books.

The Baptist Missionary Society of Great Britain, Didcot, and David Quinney Mee for extracts from the newsletters of David Quinney Mee.

Quotations from Scripture are from the HOLY BIBLE, NEW INTER-NATIONAL VERSION. Copyright © 1973, 1978, 1984 by International Bible Society. Used by permission of Hodder & Stoughton Ltd.

Foreword

An interview with Karl Heinz Walter, General Secretary of the European Baptist Federation, held in his home in Hamburg, Germany, Autumn 1995.

Michael:

Thank you so much, Karl Heinz, for reading parts of this book and for agreeing to this interview. We have heard much from the Third World in recent years about liberation theology. As you know, the book I have written aims to build bridges between some of these theologians and the First World churches of Europe and North America. How do *you* think that will go down in the European Baptist family?

Karl Heinz:

If there has ever been a theology in the Second World, it is the theology of survival. East European Baptists have clung to doctrines of salvation, the deity of Christ, and the uniqueness of Scripture firmly against 'the world', especially in the Communist years. Their churches have been more places of refuge than bases for social action. This is not helped by the way they feel especially vulnerable right now in the face of the problems imported by First World missions and their influence. So many parachurch groupings from the United States and elsewhere are present across Eastern Europe now. Many Baptists are confused by the different voices they hear. Theology only changes with growing trust and confidence. Even students who have been to the West remain very wary of other theologies and of their influence. Issues of ecology, liberation, and justice are not often part of their world view or understanding of faith. Rather personal conversion and salvation are their main concern, that and the quest for recognition as Christians, not as a sect, by the majority culture. For them, the issue is more one of not being ashamed of being Baptist than of becoming 'citizens of the world'.

Michael:

And Western Europe. How do you view developments here in what some are calling the New Europe?

Karl Heinz:

Western Europe is full of unsolved problems. These affect far more than just Baptists. Secularization is not the main problem. Many Europeans have few answers to the basic questions of life, but our churches have failed to reach or communicate with them at all. One urgent need is for more exegesis of Scripture from our pulpits and less thematic preaching. There are also significant changes in attitudes and behaviour in the West that we must come to terms with, not least to do with sexuality and gender. The rôle of women is a major area of dispute. To be a 'citizen of the world' does not come readily to all. If anything, those Christians who see themselves as citizens of but one world are decreasing as individualism and nationalism take their toll. It is hard to see in national politics and in Christian leadership circles many with international vision. That is true for all the communication possibilities of the internet, e-mail, business connections, and so on. Those who are involved locally in social issues are often the ones who are the most world-mission minded. I hope before my General Secretaryship is over to convene a consultation for European Baptists to explore some of these issues together before the new millennium arrives.

Michael:
Thank you, Karl Heinz, for all you do and all you are for the family of Baptist Christians in Europe.

Introduction
The Three Worlds

During the remarkable autumn of 1989, as a New Europe was being born before our eyes, I enjoyed a time of sabbatical study leave under a scheme of the Baptist Union of Great Britain and based at Luther King House, Manchester. This opportunity enabled me to look back reflectively over what was then a decade of Christian ministry and to test a growing conviction that, through the theologians of liberation and through the Solidarity movement in Poland, the Living God had been speaking to the world-wide Church. During those weeks the conviction grew that we in the 'First World' local churches need to learn new ways of being church and of evangelization if we are to face the twenty-first century with anything like confidence. Some of the material that has become this *Regent's Study Guide* was drafted at that time. In 1995, my church released me for much of the summer to update and work further on the book that now you read.

The terms 'First', 'Second', and 'Third' World are used consistently throughout this book. They have their origins historically in the Cold War period following the Second World War, and since this guide deals in part with something of the history of that period and its aftermath it seems appropriate to continue to use them, even though the situation in Europe has now changed. I would, however, like to emphasize that the terms are not intended to carry any undertones of size, priority, or preference. Indeed one clear thrust of this study guide is the urgent need for church members in the First World to sit at the feet of those of the Second and Third Worlds and to learn from them. By 'First World' I mean to indicate economically advanced democracies, such as those in North America, Western Europe, and Australasia. By the 'Second World' I mean those former Communist nations in Europe currently coming to terms with First World Capitalism and democracy; this is, of course, an evolution of meaning from the original application of the term to the former USSR and its Warsaw Pact partners. By 'Third World' is intended the many nations where, for the majority of its people, acute poverty is endemic. It should not be forgotten, of course, that these Three Worlds all have elements of each other within themselves at one and the same time.

Theology from Three Worlds is about both liberation and evangelization, and is about the inter-relationship between them. The 'Declaration of Principle' of the Baptist Union of Great Britain includes the clause that 'it is the duty of every disciple to bear personal witness to the Gospel of Jesus Christ, and to take part in the evangelization of the world.' This book is the response of one local church minister to that ever-new challenge, and theological reflection upon it. North American readers will need to decide how cross-culturally relevant to their own First World context this study guide is. Not all the work of trans-Atlantic translation or interpretation is done for them!

Part I of the book is about liberation in three very different parts of the world. Chapter 1 introduces the Latin American Church scene in the decades after the Second World War; this sets the context for chapter 2 which is, essentially, a dialogue between myself as a First World local church pastor and some of the writings of the theologians of liberation during this period. Chapter 3 draws on my love for my 'other country', Poland, and describes its own liberation struggles in the 1970s and 1980s. The final chapter of this section considers Britain over much the same period of time.

Part II examines the main theme of this study guide: liberation. It does so with reference both to the New Testament and to the Law, Prophets, History, and Writings of the Old Testament. It draws out the recurring biblical theme of liberation—for a planet, a world, a continent, a nation, a community, a family, and an individual.

Part III draws on the already considerable corpus of European studies in seeking to discern something of the trends and issues that are creating Europe all around us as this decade, century, and millennium end. It also traces something of the exciting story of East European Baptist life in the early 1990s. The final chapter explores many of the themes of liberation introduced earlier in the book as well as describing local church praxis; the aim is to develop pointers towards what a contemporary First World theology of liberation, drawn from three worlds, might mean.

I am grateful to God and to so many people who have helped to make this writing and this book possible.

Michael I. Bochenski
St. Albans
May 1997

PART I
INTO ALL THE WORLD

Chapter 1
The Third World
Latin America, 1970–1990

Latin America might seem an unusual place from which to begin a study of the New Europe. But if we are to develop any kind of 'liberation theology' for Europe, the reason for choosing this starting point should be clear. 'Theology of liberation' is the name given to a movement that began among Christians in Latin America, and we have much to learn from their experience. By the term 'Latin America', the South American continent including the various Central American countries such as Nicaragua and El Salvador is intended. While the roots of this theology go back centuries, it was towards the end of the 1960s that what was to become the theology of liberation began to find clearer and more prominent expression.

Near its heart is the concept of *praxis*, with its insistence that right action and lifestyles (*orthopraxis*) are as important to God as orthodoxy or right belief. The dethroning of First World academic theology in favour of the priorities of acts of solidarity with the poor, the oppressed, and the marginalized was a hallmark of early understandings of praxis. The function of theology was to reflect critically on praxis and so to serve the cause of liberation. Two decades or so later, there has come to be a greater emphasis on the integration of Christian theology and right action, and the creative interplay between the two. But there is still no better definition of liberation theology than the one penned by Gustavo Gutierrez, a theologian from Peru, in his seminal work *A Theology of Liberation*:

> This is a theology which does not stop with reflecting on the world but rather tries to be part of the process through which the world is transformed. It is a theology which is open to the gift of the Kingdom of God—in the protest against trampled human dignity, in the struggle against the plunder of the vast majority of people, in liberating love, and in the building of a new, just, and fraternal society.[1]

To understand how and why this new way of doing theology happened we need, first, to understand something of the socio-economic policies and political changes that affected Latin America in the period after World War II. Telling this story will be the theme of this chapter. In the following chapter, key texts by some contemporary theologians of liberation will be introduced and reflected upon, taking our perspective from local Church life and witness not in Latin America, but in part of the 'First World'—Europe.

1. Development ?

Latin America is a continent rich in natural resources. It is probably the most deeply Christianized of all earth's continents. It is also, arguably, the most consistently abused and exploited continent of all from the time of the Conquistadors to our own day. Many people over the centuries have become rich through Latin American investments and business interests. The theologians of liberation remind us poignantly that little of these riches, over the decades or centuries, has percolated down to benefit those whose suffering and labour are largely responsible for this wealth: the poor majority.

Latin America became the focus of a concerted movement for development, inspired by Capitalist ideals, during the 1950s and 1960s. However, despite much investment and still more industrial expansion, the Latin America of the 1970s and 1980s remained for many a place of ingrained poverty, exploitation, misery, and oppression. Internally, a blend of often oppressive regimes and, externally, an exploitative brand of Capitalism combined to compound the plight of the majority Latin American poor. Many Latin American countries were in effect manipulated, throughout their 'Development' years, into supplying primary commodities at low cost to the developed nations of the First World. These commodities were used in the manufacture of expensive goods that were then exported back at considerable profit to the very same countries in Latin America whose labour and resources had made such trade possible in the first place. Such vicious trade spirals remain of course a continuing scandal of world scope, one that affects and bruises far more countries than those in Latin America alone.

In addition to these burdens, crippling interest charges and penalties from foreign loans exacerbated the situation: such is the Third World debt problem. At much the same time that it was becoming plain that this kind of industrialization was not the panacea for their socio-economic problems—and especially for those of their poorer citizens—many of the loans fell due. This, in turn, meant that a significant proportion of a nation's newly generated income had to leave the country. That is to say it was diverted back into the bank accounts, portfolios, and safes of the main financiers, the First World multinationals and banks. It went also into the treasuries of those First World governments that had provided the capital initially. Valuable 'hard' currency was thus leaving the country instead of being ploughed into alleviating something of the desperate poverty of the nation's majority population. As well as financial dependence on the developed nations, Latin America's problems were compounded by the existence of severe inequalities within a country, since a minority always did very well out of the situation.

The theologians of liberation reflected deeply on the failures of development for those they worked with and among: society's poor. They formulated a vision for both a New Society and a New Humanity that would be forged by liberating love. The goal of this struggle for liberation is powerfully communicated by Gutierrez in a classic statement in which we can hear echoes of the Chinese Maoist political philosophy of the time:

> The goal is not only better living conditions, a radical change of structures, a social revolution; it is much more: the continuous creation, never ending, of a new way to be man, a permanent cultural revolution.[2]

Humankind must learn to act in the present for the sake of tomorrow. That is to 'achieve an ever more total and complete fulfilment of the individual in solidarity with all mankind'. Unlike Maoist philosophy, the root of both this New Humanity and New Society is Jesus Christ:

> Christ the Saviour liberates man from sin—which is the ultimate root of all disruption of friendship and of all injustice and oppression. Christ makes man truly free; that is to say he enables man to live in communion with him; and this is the basis for all human brotherhood.[3]

2. Medellin, Columbia

In the 1960s and 1970s the Latin American Churches and their leaders, largely Catholic but also Protestant, became involved in what has become known as the process of 'conscientization'—the raising of social, biblical, and political awareness. In short, it was consciousness-raising. This was an awakening in two senses: first, the Church was to come to see its own rôle more clearly in the liberation process, to realize where it was hindering or assisting; second, the poor and marginalized were to come to understand their own situation more clearly and to realize God's love and support for them.

Thus Christian leaders began to expose and denounce the unjust economic and socio-political structures that, in reality, lay behind the oppression and poverty being so keenly experienced by those in their pastoral charge. In doing this, they were going beyond the traditional Christian response to poverty, which had been simply encouraging individual acts of charity and rescue. Now they were pointing the finger at the sources of the poverty themselves. Instead of constantly mopping up the water, they turned their attention to the plumbing system itself and wished to overhaul it.

Conscientization revealed many uncomfortable home truths. Most significant perhaps was that the Church's rituals and sanctions were often themselves used to legitimize unjust structures, to keep the poor 'happy with their lot', and to sanction an unfair status quo. The Church itself was part of the problem, not part of the solution. This fact led many Christians to a reassessment not only of the Church's rôle in society but also to a rethinking of the Scriptures and the Christian faith itself. At the 1968 Conference of Latin American Bishops in Medellin, Columbia, the theology of liberation was, in a real sense, born. As the final statement expressed it:

> In many places in Latin America there is a situation of injustice that must be recognized as institutional violence; a situation which calls out for far-reaching, daring, and profoundly innovating changes.[4]

Medellin also recognized the growing desire among many to employ violence to overcome violence, but urged that 'armed revolution generally gives rise to new injustices, throws more elements out of balance, and brings on new disasters'.

3. Into All the World

During the 1980s the various rivers and streams of liberation theology flowed into what is now—as this millennium comes towards its end—a very considerable theological sea. Though the generic term will continue to be used for convenience, the reality is that there are now many 'theologies of liberation'. As well as the numerous outpourings of such work from Latin America, there are now, for example, American Black, several Asian, a Jewish, a South African, feminist, and several First World theologies of liberation. The signs are that this mushrooming process will continue during the 1990s and will indeed play a powerful rôle in the understanding of Christian faith and the Church, which will obtain as we enter the next millennium.

Certainly the practice of Christian theology will never be the same again. The implications of this process for the First World are the real subject of this study guide. It is increasingly likely that the worldwide Church of the twenty-first century will be characterized and, in significant ways, formed by the Christianity of the Third World. The faith of this part of the world includes the challenge of the theology of liberation. It is perhaps harder for those of us locked into the thought forms of First World Christianity to acknowledge and accept this.

Those interested in understanding more of this phenomenon and, in particular, of its growing world dimension, will find the book by Theo Witvliet, *A Place in the Sun*, both helpful and very readable. He makes clear that something is happening in the worldwide Church that—refreshingly—has its origins in the rapidly expanding Churches of the Third World and not in, say, a Tübingen or a Yale or even an Oxford! In his book, which he describes as 'a guidebook . . . midway between a survey and an interpretation', Theo Witvliet provides both a historical and theological context for the theology of liberation. 'Theology must never lose sight', he writes, 'of marginalized people, of their struggle for the most basic human rights, and of the presence of the crucified and risen Messiah in their midst'.[5] Henceforward, he asserts, Christian thinking and living, reflection and involvement can never be separated. True theologians, and indeed all Christians, must have 'a fuller understanding of living in the Holy Spirit, for this also means being committed to a lifestyle of solidarity with the poor and the oppressed and involvement in action with them. Theology is not neutral'.[6]

Witvliet offers a kaleidoscope of liberation theologies throughout the world. As well as Latin American thinking in which the implications of liberation were first worked out, he shows us Black theology, with special attention to the writings of James Cone in the USA and South African theologians. African theology, he notes, is being done in a continent that was already 45 percent Christian by the end of the 1970s. Caribbean and Rastafarian theologies add other dimensions. Asian theology, including the Korean 'minjung' theology, is being worked out in the context of relationships with other religions and in experiences of persecution. Witvliet concludes his book with these stirring words:

> The Resurrection is the source of our hope that life-giving forces will finally triumph. To believe in this God of life is to believe in love, justice, peace, truth, and human fulfilment. . . . To proclaim a God who does not see the plight of the poor and does not act in their favour is to preach a God of death, a dead God. When the forces of death are free to kill, God's reality is not recognized. When life is ignored or cruelly crushed, false gods are set up. This is idolatry.[7]

The theology of liberation has, within three decades, developed into a worldwide Christian movement. I believe that through such Third World Christians, the Risen Lord is reshaping and building his Church for the twenty-first century. Is he expressing through them his outrage at the treatment of human beings in one hemisphere by those of us in another? Is he exposing the injustices and inequalities within particular nations? Perhaps God is, through this movement, expressing something of his prophetic anger with those First World Christians and Churches, whether North American or European, who fail to respond to the needs of the poor, hungry, and oppressed of humankind as this millennium draws to a close.

It needs to be said that if this movement really is the voice of the Spirit of God to our day and age then, like all similar moves of his Spirit, it will both unite many of his people and divide them as well. Some religious believers may, tragically, end up 'fighting against God', as the wise teacher Gamaliel called it, confronted as he was some 2,000 years ago by a radical Christian movement (Acts 5:38-9). The Gospel of the Kingdom of God often divides, as Jesus' own life—and murder—clearly demonstrates. We will, of course, need to turn to the biblical evidence for these claims, and we will do so in the second part of this book.

4. Base Communities

One response to Medellin after 1968 was the establishing across the Church of new ways of *being* the Church: the base communities. In his book *Ecclesio-genesis*[8], the Brazilian theologian Leonardo Boff makes the case that the base communities are, in fact, a reshaping by the Risen Lord of the kind of Church he always intended. The subtitle of this book is significant here: *The Base Communities Reinvent the Church*. Although Leonardo Boff has recently decided that he can no longer remain a Franciscan priest, he remains committed to the renewal of the Church as he has urged it in many books on liberation themes, sometimes written with his brother, Clodovis Boff. Like many other liberation theologians, he writes in Portuguese, and in this language 'liberation' is a fusion of two words: *liber* ('free') and *açao* ('action'). The term 'base communities' is an attempt to make another translation from Portuguese, in this case the phrase *Communidade de base*, which carries the ideas of 'base Church community', 'basic Christian community', or 'grass roots community'.

What are these communities? Essentially, they are small Christian groups all over Latin America. They meet weekly, sometimes more frequently, sometimes daily. They are usually led by lay workers or lay coordinators. They meet for Bible study, catechism, music, and worship. They meet for community purposes ranging from caring for the sick, sewing lessons, and literacy classes through to political action. They are characterized by deep mutual sharing and are rooted in the neighbourhoods they serve, rural or urban. The Bible again and again is used for reflection on current social issues in the locality and upon their experiences as a community.

The emergence of such Christian groups raises several important questions for the Church of our day. As Boff puts it, 'We may well anticipate that from this moment . . . a new type of institutional presence of Christianity in the world may now come into being'.[9] These communities have sprung into life for a number of reasons. One of the main ones is the scarcity of ordained priests to cater to the spiritual needs of Latin America's many Catholic Christians.[10] Among the consequences of this shortage of ordained priests is that the Eucharist cannot be celebrated at all in many areas on a regular basis. Christ is still present among Christians, Boff insists, even where there is no priest. 'The image of body and members or of head and members represents the relationship between Christ and the Church, not that between the universal Church and the local Church'.[11] The time has come, Boff pleads, to develop a new working model of the Church. It must be based on the community life of God's people within which the Risen Lord is present. This, he argues, is a superior model to the traditional, hierarchical model of Pope, bishops, and priests set over against the laity or the faithful. Just as the parish system came gradually to change the definition of the Church between the twelfth and fourteenth centuries, he suggests that the praxis of the base communities might, in fact, be God at work changing the face of the twenty-first-century Church.

A new definition of rôles and functions in Christian leadership is now called for. The bishops and priests must both serve and respect the gifts of the laity and so lead in the establishing of true community, true unity. Boff also argues that the scarcity of Latin American Roman Catholic priests demands similar flexibility in finding solutions, including that of lay presidency at the Eucharist. An extraordinary situation calls for an extraordinary solution. That some base communities are led by women was also recognized and affirmed by Boff:

> If a woman can be the principle of unity in so many communities, then theologically there is nothing to stand in the way of her empowerment through ordination, to consecrate, to render Christ sacramentally present at the heart of the community worship.[12]

Boff's own problems with the Vatican are well known to students of liberation theology. However 'Free Church' they may appear to a Baptist reader, it is perhaps not surprising that such views were not well received and that, in the early 1990s, after a decade and more of harassment, Boff felt obliged to leave the Catholic priesthood.

For a further account of the base communities, readers are well advised to read Margaret Hebblethwaite's thought-provoking introduction to this movement, *Base Communities*. This includes some information on Protestant base communities as well as the many Catholic ones. We are witnessing 'not a movement within the Church but rather the Church in movement', she writes.[13] Her conviction also is that God is doing something deeply significant in and through this movement. 'We must sit at the feet of the World Church', she writes, 'and discover how God is disposing his forces'.[14]

5. Puebla, Mexico

A second Latin American Bishops' Conference met in 1979 at Puebla, with Pope John Paul II in attendance. The base communities were now termed *cebs* ('sebs') from the Portuguese initials for 'basic ecclesial community'. Some say Puebla watered down some of the statements of Medellin, others that it developed them and only changed emphases. Since 1968, reactions within the Latin American Church to the theology of liberation had, in fact, polarized. Some who preferred to stress the Church's spiritual rôle in Latin America hoped that the new Pope (then only four months in office) would condemn it. Instead the Pope took a middle way. On the one hand, he defended the deity of Christ against those over-emphasizing his humanity. He attacked those who reduced the Christ of the Gospels to a political figure. But on the other hand, he endorsed the struggle for justice and insisted that commitment to the poor was based on the Gospels and not on any political manifesto. A tour of Mexico followed, with his every word scrutinized by both camps. After his return to Rome, the Pope spoke on Puebla again, developing the theme of evangelization. In his speech at a General Audience on February 21, 1979, the 'new' Pope said:

> It is necessary to call by their name injustice, the exploitation of man by man, or the exploitation of man by the State, institutions, mechanisms, or systems, or regimes, which sometimes operated without sensitivity. . . . Liberation in a social sense begins with knowledge of the truth.[15]

His words make interesting reading from the Second World perspective too, not least in the light of the collapse of Communism in Eastern Europe in the late 1980s. It is strange to see how the Pope could be so supportive of a liberation movement in one part of the world—his own—and be so diffident at times about one in another. The 1979 Puebla statements themselves spoke of the need for the whole Church to be converted to this option for the poor, of the poverty and wretchedness of so many on our planet, of the accumulation of so much wealth in so few hands, of the poor's lack of material goods, of the call to dignity for all, and of the importance of full participation for the poor in social and political life. Indigenous peoples, peasants, manual labourers, women, and marginalized urban dwellers were all specifically mentioned.[16]

Might these be the voices of God? Is God speaking again to the world-wide Church through the base community poor, through the Scriptures, through the social and political needs of this age? Is God calling people to adapt, change, develop, and build a new kind of twenty-first-century Church? Are we summoned to a new way of being Church? Or do the current mind-sets, the attitudes, the present Church structures, the traditions of past and present remain the only authentic word for the new century too? We must all decide.

6. Some Key Figures

During the 1970s some of the seminal works of the theology of liberation were written and published. We have already noted that in 1971 the Peruvian priest Gustavo Gutierrez published his foundational work, *A Theology of Liberation*. Other leading figures in the 1970s included the Mexican José Porfirio Miranda who concentrated especially on the relationship between the Theology of Liberation and Marxism, for example in his book *Marx Against the Marxists*.[17] The Uruguayan Juan Luis Segundo, the El Salvadorean Jon Sobrino, and the Argentinian Protestant José Miguez Bonino were also key exponents of the growing theology of liberation movement. Two leading bishops in the movement were the El Salvadorean Archbishop Oscar Romero, who was tragically assassinated in 1980, and the outstanding Brazilian bishop Dom Helder Camara. Other key theologians include the Boff brothers Leonardo and Clodovis from Brazil, José Comblin (also from Brazil), and the Baptist Jorgé Pixley in Nicaragua.

During the 1970s European and North American theologians such as Jürgen Moltmann, Hans Küng, Harvey Cox, and Langdon Gilkey realized that something of enormous significance was unfolding in world theology and, more important, in the World Church. Conscientization was beginning to embrace the First World also. This process was itself helped by a deliberate policy of international visits and speaking engagements undertaken by several key theologians of liberation from other parts of the world.

We return, in a different way, to the Latin American scene. What follows in the remainder of this chapter is an attempt to use a range of sources, pictures, and illustrations to illuminate the background against which the theologians of liberation emerged onto the international Christian scene. This section draws on assorted material that captures the realities of Latin America during the

1970s and 1980s. The theologians of liberation must be read—can only be read
—in the light of scenarios such as those that follow.

7. The Doctrine of National Security

A *New Society* magazine article from the autumn of 1980 powerfully evoked
the Latin American scene at the beginning of the then new decade. The article
was by David Stephen and was called 'South America's New Dictators'.[18] It
reminded us that 'Latin America is a land of military dictatorships'. The initially Brazilian policy of national government by military force had become the
norm for many Latin American countries during the 1970s. By the beginning
of the 1980s, below the Amazon, practically all the subcontinent was under
military rule: Brazil, Paraguay, Chile, Argentina, Uruguay, and Bolivia. In
Paraguay, for example, the strongman Stroessner had been in power since 1954.
Like the ousted Nicaraguan Dictator Somoza, Stroessner had been fashioned
in an older mould—that of the *caudillos* with a strong 'cult of the personality'
undergirding a paternalistic rule.

   These new-style Latin American regimes, David Stephen pointed out, had
adopted the 'Doctrine of National Security' first formulated by the Brazilian
Admiral Amarel Gurgel. According to this doctrine, the military rôle was first
to decree and then enforce a dose of social stability for the nation, freed from
all 'politics'. In practice, repression followed, particularly of Socialist or popu-
list supporters. Opposition political parties were banned. Universities were
'purged' and re-organized. The news media were steadily bought under State
control. Chile in 1973 was perhaps the starkest example of this process. The
Doctrine of National Security was, in effect, a total package for Latin American
social life. It sought to establish criteria and guidelines for all areas of activity,
from economic development to education and religion. Much emphasis was laid
on 'the nation' and 'the State'. Objectives for Society were set in terms of the
overall interests of the nation. Citizens and State became, in effect, fully
identified; the concepts of 'the people' or 'the individual' were correspondingly
eroded. This was against, of course, all the best Christian, democratic, and
humanist traditions of First World liberal democracies. Nonetheless, some supported these processes, not least by providing weapons, armaments, and even
equipment clearly intended for torture.

   With the National Security Doctrine went also a carefully thought-out
strategy for military counter-subversion. The main threat to the State was seen
as internal, and so a high priority was given to the armed forces' responsibility
to act on behalf of the whole nation's interests: these were, of course, as defined
by those in military power. This was in addition to preparations for

conventional warfare with foreign countries. There could be no peace while subversives were 'active', running the propaganda. Therefore, permanent, unrelenting war against them was necessary for the good of the nation. The minds of the people and the soul of the nation were judged to be at stake. Words and even thoughts were looked on as actual weapons of war. The scene of George Orwell's *1984* had arrived in some places a decade early. Billions of dollars were thus expended against rather than for people. Only when 'the enemy' was fully wiped out could the deeper problems of poverty be tackled or judicial niceties have a place in the system, the argument ran. Only then, for that matter, could the luxuries of parliamentary debate take place. All criticisms of the government or nation were seen as—quite literally—hostile acts of civil war. Such was the Doctrine of National Security that, Stephen writes, had taken hold of many Latin American countries during the late 1960s and 1970s.

By the beginning of the 1980s, there were some signs of this bankrupt, inhumane ideology beginning to break down—in Argentina, for example. Elsewhere in the Continent the process took considerably longer. Let us note the obvious here: there was little or no place for any Western kind of welfare state in such a doctrine. Opposition parties, human rights activists, spokespersons for the poor, and, indeed, all critics were dismissed in a variety of terms: 'subversive delinquents' (Argentina), 'Marxists' (Chile), and 'seditious elements' (Uruguay). Democracy was not openly rejected, merely shelved until 'the time is right'. Even then, any emerging 'democracy' would be obliged to work under some kind of National Security Commission.

It was in *this* Latin America that the Churches became increasingly involved in both protest and opposition in the name and for the sake of the neglected and abused poor. The result? Many Christians came to be viewed in the same ways as other opponents of the Governments and, often, received the same brutal treatment. They became 'the enemy within' as well. The prisons and torture cells of Latin America now contained Christians (priests, nuns, laymen, and laywomen) as well as political radicals and Opposition party members and trade unionists. Christians too were found dead on the roadside and in the death pits. In the Argentina of the 1970s, liberal schoolteachers and priests were dubbed 'the moral authors of terrorism' and were violently repressed. The fate of Argentina's many 'disappeared' in this period is only now becoming nightmarishly clear. Leading Chilean opposition figures were assassinated. The same was true in Uruguay. However, as history has often proved, you can rarely annihilate political or religious movements, but only contain them for a time. Peronism in Argentina, for example, as witnessed by its resurgence in the late 1980s, was only waiting in the wings for a comeback. The humiliation of the Argentinian generals in the Falklands War with Britain proved, of course, a further catalyst to change here, whatever we may think of the rights and wrongs of the actual conflict.

During the 1970s, then, some of the leaders of the Roman Catholic Church were increasingly reaching the conclusion that the social cost of the policies of the Latin American regimes had been to impose an excessive and unacceptable burden on the most defenceless sectors of society. A strike in Sao Paulo, Brazil, led by a Christian trade union leader, Luis Inacio da Silva, brought out some 250,000 workers in a protest, albeit unsuccessful, that lasted forty-two days. The Cardinal Archbishop of Santiago, Raul Henriquez, consistently condemned the Chilean government's repressive policies as harsh, brutal, and unchristian in their effects on ordinary people. In the words of one of the Chilean Church's fortnightly bulletins:

> Each time the Church has spoken out in recent years, a wave of attacks has been unleashed by small but powerful groups. . . . The Church's mission is, however, laid down in the Gospel itself, so it has been bound to speak out with increasing frequency and to act on behalf of the marginalized, the poor, and the oppressed.[19]

For such statements and acts of solidarity with the poor, the Chilean Church paid a high price. The Cardinal was vilified as a political bishop surrounded by 'Marxist priests' who did not have the support of the Vatican. Church buildings were raided; priests and nuns were searched and arrested. Even the graves of Church leaders' family members were desecrated.

In the early 1980s, as Stephen pointed out in his article, the Latin American policy of North America was undergoing change as Jimmy Carter lost office and was replaced by Ronald Reagan. He quotes a right-wing group policy statement of the time, which noted that 'the time has probably passed when the United States could have a single Latin America policy, applicable to nearly two dozen communities of unequal size, importance, and potential'. In practice, US Latin American policy in the 1980s seemed obsessed with two countries in particular during Mr. Reagan's presidency: Nicaragua and El Salvador. President Reagan's hostility to the Nicaraguan Sandinista regime or to the El Salvadorean FLMN seemed at times to be obsessive, and was to the minds of many (including those of many US Congressmen) a glaring aberration in his two terms of presidency, however popular those terms undoubtedly were among many Americans. Stephen's article helps us then to begin to piece together something of the prevailing conditions in Latin America towards the end of the 1970s. It is against such a backcloth of violence and repression that the theologians of liberation wrote, pleaded, suffered, . . . and sometimes died.

8. Oscar Romero

A look at El Salvador sharpens the focus here still further. On March 24, 1980, Archbishop Oscar Romero (originally considered a 'safe' Episcopal appointment) was murdered by a death squad. This was undoubtedly because of his identification with the poor and of his speaking out on behalf of the many victims of the army. His solidarity with 'the least of these' had led to his being labelled and condemned to death as a 'political priest'. A radio play by Bruce Stewart (*Incident at Devil's Gate* broadcast on BBC Radio 4 in April 1987) poignantly re-creates some of the decisions and life experiences that led to Romero's brutal death. In his small tribute booklet *Romero—a Martyr for Liberation*,[20] the liberation theologian Jon Sobrino includes Romero's last two homilies and analyses the impact of his life.

Romero's next-to-last sermon, broadcast live on radio across parts of Latin America, eloquently reveals the El Salvador of the late 1970s to us. It tells of four young women who were violated and their families beaten in Los Martinez. It recalls how in Candelaria a young reservist, Emilio Mejia, had been abducted from a bus and killed that afternoon. In San Juan Miraflores Arriba, Dona Pilar Raymundo de Mejia had been abused in front of his wife, abducted, and then decapitated. In Arcatao, four peasants—Romero names them one by one—had been recently murdered. On the Hacienda Colima, eighteen had been killed in a confrontation with the military. Four bodies had been discovered on a rubbish dump near Tecnillantas. As his sermon continued, he announced that an Amnesty International Report had documented some eighty-three political assassinations in just five days in March 1980 and an estimated six hundred at least in total—some of the victims murdered with thumbs tied behind backs and with corrosive liquid poured over them to hinder identification. 'In the name of God, in the name of this suffering people whose cries rise to Heaven more loudly each day, I implore you, I beg you, I order you in the name of God: stop the repression', Romero pleaded. On a recent previous occasion he had also said this:

> If they kill me I will rise again in the people of El Salvador. I am not boasting, I say it with the greatest of humility. . . . Can you tell them that if they suc-ceed in killing me that I pardon and bless those who do it? But I wish they could realise that they are wasting their time. A bishop may die, but the Church of God, which is the people, will never die.[21]

9. Baptists in El Salvador

In the 1980s, the Baptist Missionary Society of Great Britain (the BMS) appointed a missionary, David Mee (now after his marriage to Rachel, David Quinney Mee), to work for the first time in El Salvador. His missionary newsletters are among the most moving and powerful literature of missions I have ever read. David Mee saw his rôle as seeking to stand by some of the poor of El Salvador, no more and no less, in the nightmare of the political violence all around them. An estimated 70,000 people died in the bloodbath that was El Salvador in the 1980s. Three extracts from his late 1980s newsletters will make clear what all of this meant in practice for the then Baptist community among many others.

> The old corrugated iron roof is hopelessly pitted with holes but, as the family say, at least it isn't the rainy season. The family lost half of their maize crop last year due to late and destructive rains and that, coupled with even less land to hire due to expanding cattle farming, means this year is already harder than before in more ways than one. Little wonder that the man has several internal pains from time to time and is often pale and weak and unable to work. At the least he is likely to have some parasitic infection and, since the mosquitoes are now back there may also be a dose of malaria. What to do? They have no money for the customary examinations in the clinics—blood, urine, and faecal examinations could cost them more than 40 colones (£5). A visit to a cheaper clinic in the city could still cost £3 or £4 with bus fares, and after all that there is still the medicine to buy. 'Can't be done', they say. They stay sick and just hope it doesn't get too bad.

> On April 3rd Maria Cristina Gomez was snatched out of the city school where she was teaching. When she cried for help she was hit in the face and then thrown into a Cherokee Jeep. Three quarters of an hour later, near a cemetery on the far side of the city, she was dumped from the vehicle and shot five times. Her body had already been tortured with acid. Cristina was a founding member of Emmanuel Baptist Church and of an ecumenical Christian education movement here . . . (she) was an active member of the teachers' union (ANDES) and an advisor to a women's organization (CONAMUS). Her four children in their late teens and early 20s are all involved members of the Shalom Baptist Church. In Emmanuel and then at the grave side, her funeral was attended by hundreds of her friends from the Churches and organizations she has worked with. . . . Over 300 teachers have now been killed here. One ANDES member said, 'We have shed tears enough. We will not shed another until we see the justice for which all our companions have died. We will

transform our sorrow and danger into energy for the work that must be done to make that justice happen'.

Carmen lived her last weeks in the tiny house of her 17-year-old sister, the wife of a soldier usually drunk on leave; only there because her own family home lacked even the simplest resources—water, electricity—her sister could offer. We celebrated her 14th birthday with cake and balloons less than a fortnight before she died (of an untreated tumour in her foot and leg which spread). Cipriana, her mother, who had remained with her constantly, then, with help from her neighbours, dressed Carmen's body, placed her in the coffin, and decorated it with the flowers brought by those who came to keep the wake. The funeral held the following day was cold and impersonal. It was shared with another family who brought the body of 17-year-old Juan Roberto who had served 5 months with the National Guard before he was killed by shrapnel from a bomb which may well have been the army's own. Cold irony that Juan Roberto and Carmen should be side by side in that funeral, both victims of a war [i.e., civil war between the National Guard and the resistance movement] that is not their own; Carmen died because appropriate health care was stolen from her to pay for the toys of war that killed Juan Robert.

An article from the *Baptist Times* of the same period, headed 'Outrage at police torture—Pastor's daughter the latest victim', offers a further desperate vignette here:

A 28-year-old woman, Alicia Mendez Rosales, was beaten, hooded, and tortured as police tried to force her to admit links with freedom fighters. The police jeered when she responded by shouting the Lord's Prayer. They said they would wait and see if God came to her aid. Her face was cut and bruised from heavy beating. She told her father how a rubber hood was placed over her head and she was then beaten. Her crime was to be involved with the El Salvadorean Baptist Association which is heavily involved in human rights work and which has appealed for a worldwide reaction to the continuing atrocities in El Salvador.[22]

In November 1989 the government's militia (ARENA) tortured and then murdered six Jesuit priests, a housekeeper, and her daughter. A speaking engagement abroad saved Jon Sobrino, perhaps the most famous of El Salvador's Jesuit priests, from a similar fate. An *Independent* newspaper editorial of the time commented:

There were two immediate official responses from Washington to the grim news of the murder last week of six Jesuit priests in El Salvador: one was to condemn the murders as 'barbarous', a judgment with which few civilized people could quarrel. The second was to announce that the Pentagon was increasing arms shipments to the government of El Salvador, a government whose responsibility for this barbarous act is clear, however much Washington may deny it. . . .

While US officials privately acknowledged that the oligarchy of El Salvador was disposed to make almost no social or political concessions to the impoverished citizenry, in public the fiction was maintained that America's allies were amenable to democratic tutelage. Meanwhile with US aid the country was steadily militarized, the armed forces were quintupled, and $1m a day was spent to fight a guerilla force which at its peak, numbered 11,000 . . . The victims of the United States' lethal aid were not primarily the guerillas. They were the 70,000 civilians who have died in the last decade and the million more who have been forced to flee the violence. . . . The people of El Salvador continue to be sacrificed to Washington's ruthless and inane belief that this is how to win allies in Central America.[23]

10. A Violent and Desperate Path

During the late 1980s, Nicaragua and the off-on support of the Reagan administration for the rebel Contras featured prominently in international news. Argentina abandoned the doctrine of National Security in favour of civilian government—one of the political changes to which the Falklands conflict proved the catalyst. Strange and unconvincing 'elections' took place in Chile. Uruguay inched towards a measure of democracy again—bravely. Columbia also shot to prominence with news of the ongoing struggle to root out the drug industry barons (ironically based in Medellin itself), barons whose profits hinge on the broken bodies and withered veins of First World drug addicts, among many others. Brazil too shook off the legacy of the Doctrine of National Security and struggled towards a better future. It was not until the 1990s that anything approaching normalcy returned to El Salvador.

During these later years of the 1980s, parts of the Church of Latin America continued to work out the implications of a theology of liberation for lifestyle and pastoral practice. What this meant, for example, in Peru was well reported in an article in the *Independent* newspaper in September 1989, headed 'The Church takes on the shining path'. The article made clear that the theology of liberation had led the Church into conflict with Maoist revolutionaries. The Church in the Puno area was working closely with a legalized peasant movement, and was thus treading a delicate middle way between an unjust governmental status quo and the alternatives offered by active Maoist revolutionaries. Bishop Calderon had firmly rejected the way of the guerillas (*Sendero Luminosu*—'The Shining Path') who were, in fact, failing to gain support among the local peasants because the Church's own 'middle way' was already supporting and advocating their cause. A local priest, Father Hilario Huancai, was quoted as saying that 'boys and girls as young as twelve years old are being grabbed in the streets and taken away for a week. They are told they will be killed if they fail to cooperate afterwards. Sendero has the names on its lists and is picking on group leaders. It is a battle between the children's faith, their trust in us and our power to protect them, and the fear of Sendero'. The article reported that priests' houses had been bombed and some had received death threats. Masses had been cancelled for fear of guerilla attacks. An Aymara Indian peasant leader was quoted as giving this explanation: 'If the Church were destroyed, the peasants would lose a powerful instrument of support and would perhaps look to Sendero instead'. Bishop Calderon also pointed out that:

> Society itself has produced these youths. They have taken an honourable, violent, and desperate path because they have found no hope elsewhere. Sendero has a mystique; it is fighting for an ideal. Structural and repressive violence—the security forces never take prisoners or wounded—are just as evil as the violence of subversion.[24]

11. The Moving Image

Films and music afford further inroads into understanding Latin American society for those of us who live in—and only know—the First World. Several films of the 1980s brought home to First World audiences something of the ugly realities of contemporary Latin America.

Costa Gavras' film *Missing* (which won the Grande Prix at Cannes in 1982) opens with these words: 'Some names have been changed to protect the living and the dead'. The film contains harrowing images of butchery in the streets of Chile and in the Santiago football stadium, the latter piled up with the corpses of those 'terminated' by Pinochet's death machines. This slaughter was part of their determined destruction of the Socialism promoted by the former President Allende. The story portrays the anguish of a wife and a father as they seek the truth about what has happened to the missing Charles, and the All-American father becomes politicized, despite himself, by the growing realization of the enormity of the social crimes involved.

Roger Spottiswoode's *Under Fire*, with its portrayal of revolutionary Nicaragua, is another example of such moving images. What stands out in this film is the sheer brutality of these times in Latin America's history. The authenticity of the war scenes, the cheapness of human life to a dictator's forces, and the atmosphere of oppression are all terrifyingly evoked. The film helps us to visualize life for that country's Christians and others before the Sandinista victory. Oliver Stone's shocking film *Salvador* does much the same in evoking, for First World audiences, the hellishness of El Salvador in the early 1980s.

Hector Babenco's *Kiss of the Spiderwoman* gives us similar insights into the mechanisms of Brazilian politics. There, vividly portrayed side by side, is the Brazil of First World affluence alongside its Third World destitution. A trans-sexual prisoner (Molina) is used by the Security Police to win the trust of Valentine, a political radical, and then to entice from him some information about the opposition. The brutal torture scenes remind us harrowingly of the cost of political radicalism in Brazil as it then was.

John Boorman's *The Emerald Forest* paints another picture of Brazil, with its programme of industrial expansion in Amazonia. It portrays the effects of this on one Amazonian tribe, 'The Invisible People', who abduct Tommy, the seven-year-old son of an American working on a hydro-electric dam project. The exploitation of 'The Invisible People' when they are captured (by 'The Fierce People') and exchanged as prostitutes and as slaves for guns and alcohol is deliberately shocking. This film evokes the cheapness of human life to the big business interest groups in Latin America, whether national or international.

More recently the superb acting of Ben Kingsley and Sigourney Weaver in Roman Polanski's 1995 film *Death and the Maiden*, taken from Ariel Dorfman's play of the same name, has reminded audiences of the horrors of Latin American torture cells in the not-too-distant past. Nor is there any room for complacency about some of the present ones, as a look through Amnesty International's bimonthly journal sadly demonstrates.

Music, too, can help us to enter into something of the Latin American scene. In my own case, the music of *Incantation*, Paul Leoni's panpipes, and Ennio Morricone's soundtrack to the film *The Mission* accompanied the writing of these chapters.

The Mission itself is a particularly relevant film to our overall theme. It is ostensibly set in the 1750s, but let that fool nobody! I can think of no more accessible way for First World Christians to think through the implications of a contemporary theology of liberation than to watch this powerful film. The Church of the Poor is built by committed Jesuit priests. The poor are humanized; they learn crafts and practical skills; they discover liturgy and the beauty of Christian worship. Base communities are set up. Their future is threatened, nonetheless, by conflicting national and international (superpower) conflicts and by their various interest groups. The Vatican is trapped in the middle of these interests and is forced to decide between them. It opts for the affluent and powerful and not for the poor. A few Christians take up arms in order to defend the poor from massacre and slavery. The majority opt for the way of non-violent, peaceful protest. Many, irrespective of their stance, are brutally attacked and massacred with all the force of modern weaponry. The tormented face of the Cardinal, whose decision not to opt for the poor led to these injustices—and so to the catastrophe—lingers in the memory long after the Morricone soundtrack has played itself out.

To understand the issues that lie behind the theology of liberation and that confront the Church and world of today, one needs only hire one or two of these films on video. Then, reading the theologians of liberation after this experience, we begin to grasp the courage and daring of the stance they are taking.

12. Ten Precipitating Factors

These lives, books, articles, films, and writings set the context for the theologians of liberation. Their books can never be properly understood unless something of the pain and suffering and poverty they have emerged from has been at least glimpsed. In closing this chapter, some of the precipitating factors that gave rise to the theology of liberation are listed below by way of a summary.

- Pastoral concern for the poor and the victims, not least in the expanding great cities; anger over the abused and tortured, the disappeared and the dead
- The work of sociologists, social scientists, and economists in exposing the vested interests of international businesses and governments and the unveiling of the many inequalities within Latin American countries themselves
- The various papal encyclicals after Vatican II (notably *Populorum Progressio* 1967) and the 1968 Bishops' Conference in Medellin with their strong insistence on the importance of social justice; also the statements at and after Puebla in 1979
- The emergence of the Marxists and Maoists with their particular 'solutions' to Latin American problems and, therefore, the need for a Christian critique and response to them
- The failure of traditional Capitalist development programmes in the 1950s and 1960s significantly to reduce or eradicate poverty in Latin America; the concomitant Third World debt problems
- The unacceptableness and ineffectiveness of both competitive Capitalism and of Communism (whether Marxist or Maoist) in Latin America in the late 1960s and 1970s; the desire for a 'middle way' instead, and for Capitalism with a humane face

- The influence of some overseas 'political' theologians, including Jürgen Moltmann, Karl Rahner, and writers in the Marxist-Christian debate such as Harvey Cox in America and Bishop David Sheppard in Britain
- The 'martyrdom', as it came to be seen, of the guerilla priest Camilo Torres in the 1960s; the social and political radicalism of Brazilian Bishop Dom Helder Camara, Oscar Romero, and several others
- The experiences of military repression that we have glimpsed in nightmare images; the evils brought about by the Doctrine of National Security and by the concept of seeing all critics as 'the enemy within'
- The turning to the Scriptures by the Church and base communities to help them work out in praxis—theological insight integrated with action—a Latin American third way of 'revolution in liberty'

How long O Lord, how long?

Notes

[1]Gustavo Gutierrez, *A Theology of Liberation* (SCM, London, 1974), p. 15. A second edition of this book was published in 1988 (SCM, London), but I am deliberately using the first edition as the representative of a particular period in the development of liberation theology.

[2]Ibid., p. 32.

[3]Ibid., p. 37.

[4]From the Statement of the Second General Conference of the Latin American and Caribbean Bishops meeting at Medellin, Colombia, in 1968. The full, official text can be found in L. M. Colonnese (ed.), *The Church in the Present-Day Transformation of Latin America*, 2 Volumes (USCC, Washington DC, 1970).

[5]Theo Witvliet, *A Place in the Sun* (SCM, London, 1985), p. 22.

[6]Ibid., p. 27.

[7]Ibid., pp. 171-172.

[8]Leonardo Boff, *Ecclesiogenesis* (Collins, London, 1986).

[9]Ibid., p. 2.

[10]For the statistics, see ibid., p. 61.

[11]Ibid., p. 18.

[12]Ibid., p. 95.

[13]Margaret Hebblethwaite, *Base Communities* (Geoffrey Chapman, London, 1993), p. 15.

[14]Ibid., p. 138.

[15]Quoted in David Sheppard, *Bias to the Poor* (Hodder & Stoughton, London, 1983), p. 149. The full text can be found in *Reflections on Puebla* (Catholic Institute for International Relations, 1980), pp. 44-46.

[16]Bishop David Sheppard writes on both liberation theology and Puebla in chapter 9 of *Bias to the Poor*; see especially pp. 148-151.

[17]José Porfirio Miranda, *Marx Against the Marxists* (Orbis Books, Maryknoll, New York, 1978).

[18]David Stephen, 'South America's New Dictators', *New Society*, 16 October 1980.

[19]Ibid.

[20]Jon Sobrino, *Romero—a Martyr for Liberation* (CIIR, London, 1982).

[21]Ibid., p. 76.

[22]*The Baptist Times*, 16 November 1989.

[23]Editorial, *The Independent*, 20 November 1989.

[24]Simon Strong, 'The Church takes on the Shining Path', *The Independent*, 14 September 1989.

Chapter 2
Theologians of Liberation

1. A Bridge Between Two Worlds

In their introductory volume to a series of books about liberation theology,
Leonardo and Clodovis Boff (writing from Brazil) produce a catalogue of the
appalling misery of much of humanity, statistically quantified, in the world of
the late twentieth century.

- 1 thousand million people living in absolute poverty
- 500 million persons starving
- 1.5 thousand million people with no access to even the most basic medical care
- more than 1.5 thousand million people whose life expectancy is less than 60 years
- at least 500 million unemployed people
- 814 million people who are illiterate
- 2 thousand million human beings with no regular dependable water supply.[1]

As we have already seen, it is from this context of work among the world's
poor that the theologians of liberation write. In this chapter, several key writings and figures from liberation theology will be considered with particular
reference to a key theme of this study guide: the relationship between liberation
and evangelization. The term *evangelization* as I am using it incorporates both
evangelism—helping people towards an authentic personal faith in Christ—and
mission in its various forms, including social and community action. After an
introduction to a work from a liberation theologian, I shall add a reflection; this
comes from a First World local pastor seeking to enter into a dialogue with
theologians from the Third World, writing from the perspective of the Church
scene that I know best. For two decades now, while ministering in several First
World local Churches, I have read and been excited by theology from the world
of Latin America, though I have only travelled there so far in mind and spirit.
This chapter is an attempt to build a bridge between these two worlds.

2. Gustavo Gutierrez

Gustavo Gutierrez is a Peruvian priest who has done postgraduate studies in
Europe. He has been active in the social justice movement in Peru and has also
served as a consultant to the Latin American Bishops' Conference already
referred to. Gutierrez introduces his seminal work, *A Theology of Liberation*

(1971), as 'a theological reflection born of the experience of shared efforts to abolish the current unjust situation and to build a different society, freer and more human'.[2] A high emphasis is placed throughout this work on right deeds and action and on solidarity with those who are oppressed. It stresses *ortho-praxis*, or right action, as a companion to *orthodoxy*. Only after such *praxis*, such acts of solidarity and empowering the poor, Gutierrez insists, does the contemporary theologian have any real right to reflect or theologize.

Gutierrez insists that the privatizing of Christianity must be resisted. Biblically, God's people are called to be a community, a people. All are called to such community, not just the converted or saved. God expects humankind to co-operate in creating a just society—churched and unchurched, Christians and people of goodwill anywhere and everywhere, those of some faith, a different faith, or none. Gutierrez here affirms the value of all in God's sight and 'reaffirms the possibility of the presence of grace—that is of the acceptance of a personal relationship with the Lord—in all people be they conscious of it or not'.[3] This, he argues, is part of what the New Testament writers intend when they speak of Christ's universal lordship. Building a just society 'has worth in terms of the Kingdom of God . . . to participate in the process of liberation is already, in a certain sense, a salvific work'.[4]

Gutierrez analyzes clearly several of the options for the Latin American Church that, in the first place, he is addressing. He describes the process that has led priests and bishops and many ordinary Christians in Latin America to opt for in the way of liberation and evokes the climate of revolutionary ferment around in the continent at that time. In all of this, he explains, groups of priests have come together to commit themselves to the cause of liberation and to lobby for 'radical change within the Latin American Church both in terms of its internal structures and in its way of being the Church in this continent of revolution'.[5] He makes the case for a spirituality of liberation, or what we might call reflective action. He points out that not all Christians suffer under the existing Latin American order; indeed, some benefit from it. The challenge of liberation is also for them and to them. Latin America, he argues, is increasingly being called by God and the Gospel critically to analyze itself, to repent, and then to progress towards a better future: 'Not to speak is in fact to become another kind of Church of silence, silence in the face of despoliation and exploitation of the weak by the powerful'.[6] The Church must become genuinely proud of finding Latin American solutions, must slough off its colonial mentality in the process, and so learn to enrich the World Church.

This is not to say, however, that Gutierrez is unaware of the insights of First World theologians. He draws in particular on the work of Harvey Cox and Jürgen Moltmann, with evident appreciation. Gutierrez quotes approvingly

Harvey Cox's conviction in his book, *On Not Leaving It to the Snake,*[7] that the only future theology has is to become a theology of the future. He also praises the German theologian Jürgen Moltmann's *Theology of Hope*[8], especially for its analysis of the Christian contradiction that exists between present and future realities. With Moltmann, Gutierrez argues that because of the Resurrection we can be liberated from the narrow limits of the present and learn to view present realities from the perspective of the new creation that is coming. Moltmann's work, he argues, 'is one of the most important in contemporary theology'. It offers 'a new approach to the theology of hope and has injected new life into the reflection on various aspects of Christian existence'. Indeed, it is probably not exaggerating to claim that Moltmann's theme of *contradicting reality* has emerged as a key one in the whole liberation theology movement.[9]

Gutierrez draws inspiration especially from the example of Jesus. He pleads for a respect for the historical Jesus and (happily) rejects any concept of him as some kind of revolutionary Ché Guevarra or political militant figure. That would be to misrepresent both his life and witness. Gutierrez's analysis of Jesus' ministry and the political world of his time is masterly. He notes, for example, Jesus' criticisms of Herod 'the fox', of the Sadducees and the Pharisees, and of the rich and powerful. Jesus preferred the company, we are reminded, of publicans, collaborators, the poor. What is more, he died at the hands of the political and religious authorities of the day. 'To preach the universal love of the Father', he concludes from the life of Jesus, 'is inevitably to go against all injustice, privilege, oppression, or narrow nationalism'.[10] Gutierrez seeks to re-define salvation itself from the perspective of a theology of liberation. In doing so, he draws on the Old Testament and especially the tradition of the Exodus from the slavery of Egypt. Most explicitly, Gutierrez asserts that 'the struggle for a just society is, in its own right, very much part of salvation history'.[11] Consequently, he also pleads for a broader concept of sin: 'Sin is evident in oppressive structures, in the exploitation of man by man, in the domination and slavery of races and social classes'.[12]

In the section of this work entitled 'The Christian Community and the New Society', we find a strong and passionate appeal for the Church to reassess its rôle in *evangelization* as the future unfolds. Here Gutierrez defines poverty as experienced by millions in Latin America. As well as criticising the present social, economic, and political order in Latin America, the contemporary Church must also learn to criticise itself, insists Gutierrez. The Church must now preach a Gospel with a clear political dimension to it: 'the annunciation of the Gospel precisely insofar as it is a message of total love, has an inescapable political dimension, because it is addressed to people who live within a fabric of social relationships which, in our case, keep them in a sub-human condition'.[13] To know God is necessarily to work for a New Society. 'To know him is to work for justice. There is no other path to reach him'.[14]

This kind of Christian witness is needed to authenticate not only the evangelization of the Church, but also its very existence and integrity. In his conclusion Gutierrez puts this still more strongly. By acts of genuine solidarity with exploited social classes (*praxis*) and only then by reflection on them, the Church must prove its worth.

> The theology of liberation attempts to reflect on the experience and meaning of the faith based on the commitment to abolish injustice and to build a new society; this theology must be verified by the practice of that commitment, by active, effective participation in the struggle which the exploited social classes have undertaken against their oppressors.[15]

By this test, the theology of liberation, and indeed all theologies, must be judged.

Reflections

There is much here that should challenge and excite Christians who call themselves 'biblical'. Gutierrez's case for the importance of acts of solidarity with the poor and oppressed in the name of both our faith and of our common humanity is incontrovertibly backed up by his use of the Old Testament and of examples from Jesus' ministry. We cannot escape the question, 'Whose side are we on?' We shall be examining this biblical evidence more closely in the second part of this study guide.

Likewise the insistence that any mature concept of Christian salvation must incorporate progress towards a more humane society, and that sin needs to be more broadly defined to include unjust social structures, is vital in any contemporary proclamation of the Gospel. This message is perhaps especially needed in those local churches that define understandings both of sin and salvation in highly individualized ways. Gutierrez points us to part at least of what the rounded Old Testament concept of *Shalom* means: wholeness and right relationships with God and all humankind. This involves naming and resisting structural sins as well as individual ones.

Gutierrez expresses the hope that Latin American theology of liberation will contribute significantly to the universal Church. There can be little doubt, re-reading his book in its original edition in the mid-1990s, that this has indeed been happening over the past few decades. Perhaps, too, the best is yet to be. This powerful book surely raises important biblical questions for evangelization in our First World national and local churches. Authentic Christian evangel-ization must embrace a commitment to social justice and action, along-side winning people to the personal liberation that comes from discovering a rela-tionship with the Risen Christ for themselves. Any comparisons with Latin America are, of course, relative in the sense that the scale of injustices in the First World cannot normally be equated with those that gave rise to the the-ology of liberation. Nonetheless, as part of the universal Church, do we not need to be criticised and examined just as fiercely as the Latin American Church has been in Gutierrez's pages? Are we silent before unjust or repressive structures? Do we keep quiet about inequalities and injustices in our interna-tional relations, in our nations and our local communities? Are we legitimizing an unjust status quo by our privatizing of religion? Are we proclaiming a brand of salvation that is, in effect, only narcissistic and inward-looking? Indeed, is the Church and—if we still belong to one in the unchurched 1990s—is our local church seen as only for certain types and classes of people and for no one else? Is it so homogenous as to be unrecognizable biblically?

Again, this book raises for us in the First World this question: How effec-tively are we opting for the *poor* in our churches? This involves other questions such as: Where are our priorities? What do our lifestyle and our 'image' com-municate as denominations? Put another way, how far are we opting for the *underprivileged*, by our giving and by where our resources and buildings and personnel are mainly to be found? How committed are our local churches to service and work for liberation in and with the local communities that make up our particular context for evangelization? How far do our First World churches reflect a bias to the poor? To these issues we will need to return towards the close of this book.

On the other hand, I believe that some aspects of Gutierrez's writings can-not go unchallenged. In the first place, his language is irritatingly sexist—*man, brotherhood, fraternal, mankind*, and so on. We are, of course, all creatures of our time, and I recognize that these archaisms have been corrected in a later revision of his book. Such language does both date the book and, to a limited extent, mar it.

More fundamentally, a doctrine that God is unquestionably 'in' every woman and man must be examined carefully from a biblical perspective. Here there seems to be an ambiguity as to what Gutierrez means when he says that all are 'graced'. If this means, in practice, that we neglect the importance of personal conversion and of enabling humankind to encounter and be trans-formed by the Risen Christ, then something has gone awry. To take just one example from the New Testament, the letter to the Church at Laodicea assumes that God in Christ only enters *fully* into the life of an individual or a local community after invitation (Rev 3:21). Not all received or welcomed Christ in the Israel of the first century A.D., as John's Gospel reminds us (e.g., 1:10-13). If, on the other hand, Gutierrez intends to say that God's gracious activity in human beings extends a long way beyond the confines of the Church and local churches, then this must certainly be affirmed. God's Kingdom activity mercifully is far bigger than what goes on inside the Church. Few cannot be moved by the commitment to social justice and the poor that is demonstrated by many who do not name the Name of Christ. Nor can we miss seeing that there are qualities of love, good deeds, and community care achieved by many unchurched people that are sometimes *far* more effective than those of many Christians put together. A local councillor or national politician who is committed to empowering the community for social justice will achieve much for the purposes of God's rule in the world. God's Kingdom *is* bigger than the Church.

Some biblical questions also need to be set against the idea that social justice is the *only* path to God. It is indeed one of the most important, but never the only one. According to scripture, salvation can be received and experienced even if its full implications are (alas) neither fully understood or practised, and church history surely demonstrates this. The Gospel is all about forgiveness and grace for flawed people. Many Christians play no part at all in the struggle for social justice except when they vote—and that may be counterproductive anyway! Certainly, such Christians need to be clearly challenged by a theology of liberation or, rather, by the biblical passages that lie behind its truest insights. We cannot deny, however, that such people are still receiving salvation; they just have much more to learn about living out that salvation more biblically. In the witness of scripture, salvation hinges on Christ's death for humankind on Calvary, understood in the context of the whole of Christ's life and his resurrection. In the historic tradition of Christianity, this *Christ event* is the ultimate way to God; it may be entered upon *through* the experience of social justice, but it cannot be collapsed *into* social justice and political action alone.

In stressing salvation for the poor, moreover, we must not forget that humankind also includes the rich and the oppressors. The Bible makes clear that the call to conversion has particularly strong implications for them. Jesus spoke much of loving and caring even for enemies. Does that not include even rich oppressors, too? Matthew the tax collector and Zacchaeus the cheat experienced change and then made restitution. One real test of the new humanity and of liberation for all must surely be the Christian way that past oppressors, even torturers and assassins, are treated. How are they to be re-educated? What form should punishment take? In the Argentina of the 1990s and the debate on show trials of the former torturers there, this has been far from an academic question.

Nor is it a theoretical matter in the Poland of the 1990s. How extensive is liberation in such circumstances? It is easy, of course, to say this from the comfort of a study in England without the pain of Latin America all around. In terms of the teaching and lifestyle of Jesus, however, even on the cross, the question remains a valid one.

3. Dom Helder Camara

From one of the seminal books of the Latin American Church in the 1970s, we now turn to one of its seminal leaders. What follows is drawn from a series of interviews held between Christmas 1975 and Epiphany 1976 as transcribed by José de Broucker. These were published as *Dom Helder Camara: The Conversions of a Bishop.* Dom Helder Camara, a widely travelled international speaker, then aged sixty-nine, was effectively a nonperson in Brazil at the time. His book, *The Desert Is Fertile,* had been banned. Camara can surely be described as a Brazilian bishop with a difference; wearing a plain black pectoral cross and one simple episcopal ring, with no car, and living in three furnished rooms as his 'palace' in the outbuildings of a parish church, he was a friend to both rich and poor alike.

In eighteen hours of taped interviews, Dom Helder Camara's words range over his early life in Brazil and over the pre- and post-war history of his country. They describe his growing concern for the poor all around him, not least in the *favelas* or slums of Brazil. That is to say, they describe his personal 'conversion' to the poor. They also explain the emergence of the concept of liberation after the failures of the Brazilian Development Movement. They illuminate the Christian faith, the cause of nonviolent protest, the nature of aging, and the hope of heaven. Indeed it is no exaggeration to say that they shed light on the whole of the twentieth century. There is no better way to commend this remarkable Christian leader than to allow him to speak for himself and for his Lord, as de Broucker skillfully does:

> Very soon in Brazil, as with everywhere else, Development came to mean simply economic growth; people didn't see that it brought profit only to the privileged classes, and that it was achieved at the cost of the proletarianization of the masses. . . . Without wanting to, we (the Church) merely added to the burden of oppression, reinforced the unjust structures under which the people suffered. That's why we must think now about liberation and help to bring about the liberation of the people.[16]

> What God does not want is a world torn between an excess of money and mortal hunger, between loveless pleasures and appalling suffering, between

soaring palaces and tumbledown shacks, between those who give orders and those who bend the knee.[17]

We must not forget that the rich countries in the world, the countries that are constantly becoming richer and who maintain their wealth by keeping poor countries in misery, are all—at least in name and origin—Christian. What have we done with the Gospel?[18]

If the rich countries had the courage to trace the roots of their wealth they would see that they were buried deep in the misery of the Third World.[19]

The Communists are very impressed when they meet the Christians in prison. They thought religion was a thing of the past. They never imagined that Christians, priests, nuns, and laymen might be prepared to suffer torture for a love of justice, the poor, and the oppressed.[20]

Suggest, teach, persuade: the day will come when all the world's minorities will unite to construct a world that is more just and more humane, the day when we shall finally discover the nuclear force of Love![21]

Reflections

Critique? Who would dare! In Dom Helder Camara we find a life that exposes by contrast our insularity, our compromises, and our mediocrity. Here is a citizen of the twenty-first century (as well as a citizen of heaven) speaking a quarter of a century before it has even begun. To read his words is to glimpse some of the possibilities for the future and to believe them afresh. There are lives, and Dom Helder Camara's is among them, that are in themselves an indictment of our own in the First World, and of the only world humankind has yet managed to build: a Babel full of injustices, poverty, hunger, and oppression; a place of violence, torture cells, abuse, suffering, and sadness for many.

4. Jon Sobrino

Jon Sobrino is Professor of Philosophy and Theology at the Centre for Theological Reflection, University of José Simeon Canas, San Salvador. In his book, *The True Church and the Poor*, written in 1985, he attempts a theological reflection on the very basis of the Church and dedicates it to 'all the men and women of El Salvador who have given their lives for the Kingdom of God'. As we have seen, in 1989, he was very nearly among them. This section will focus on what Sobrino writes on evangelization, but not exclusively.

As Sobrino reminds us, European theology—and we might add more to the point Europe itself—is no longer the focal point of the world, if ever it once was. Theology today needs the social and political sciences to accomplish its goals: 'For they analyze the concrete misery of the real world, the mechanisms that create it, and consider possible models of liberation from it'.[22] At the same time as seeking to transform the real world, the theologians of liberation are also seeking to recover the meaning of the faith. Praxis informs good theology.

The proclamation of justice is emphasized as an essential requirement of a full Gospel message. 'The practice of justice is a basic material demand of the Gospel. Without it, the Gospel would be substantially mutilated'.[23] The very nature and character of God cries out for justice: 'A God of life does not call for justice as simply one of the many possible demands he might make, but as the demand without which his own reality would be empty and his will for the world and history would be meaningless'.[24] The ways of faith and justice are inseparable. It is Sobrino's conviction that the Risen Christ is currently re-defining the whole nature of the Church in Latin America: 'The Spirit of Jesus is in the poor and with them as his point of departure, he re-creates the entire Church'.[25] This was, of course, exactly the case in the Early Church—slaves, peasants, fishermen, and women were the first converts and disciples. Now the Church must reflect this after centuries of deference to the earthly authorities and powers that be, to the rich and the influential: 'the entire Church should migrate to the periphery and share the powerlessness of the poor, at the feet of a crucified God, so that it might there cultivate Christian hope and develop effective activity'.[26]

Jesus the Lord followed the way of humiliation and self-emptying—*kenosis*—and so, now, must the Church. Poverty is the human experience of the majority of humankind. The Church must, therefore, become a Church of the Poor. This is not to say that such a Church has a monopoly on the experience of God or on an understanding of Jesus. Only such a Church, however, can be true to the experience of God revealed in Jesus.

> [Christians should be] able to learn to change and be converted and thus to be honest with themselves; persons whose values are those of the Sermon on the Mount, whose eyes and hearts are pure, who show mercy, are devoted to justice and are ready to run the risk that this devotion entails, who prefer peace to needless struggle, those who are ready to forgive their enemies, are generous in victory, and always give their adversary another chance. They are, finally, disposed to be thankful for life and to celebrate it; they believe in life and continue to hope.[27]

It would be hard to find a better description of what 'life to the fullest' means anywhere in Christian literature. For parts of the Latin American Church in recent years this has meant a rôle of prophetic denunciation; the defence of basic human rights; demands for structural changes at social, economic, and political levels; fighting for trade unions and for the organization of the people; a call for a more humane exercise of power; and finally, for some, martyrdom. Such a Church and such a Gospel will not appeal to all. Sobrino records that while some accept the theology of liberation, others fight against it; some prefer 'a more or less tidied-up version of traditional theology' or even 'a watered-down version of the theology of liberation itself'.[28] He urges us never to forget, in the face of such divisions, that the Church and the Kingdom were never synonymous in the teaching and ministry of Jesus. A Church that fails to follow the way of Jesus is a corrupt Church. Sobrino powerfully throws out this partic-ular challenge in words that need to be heard way beyond Roman Catholicism and Latin America: 'Does the Church seek only to proclaim Christ, or does it seek also to do what Jesus did and in this way declare him to be the Christ?'[29]

Sobrino devotes a chapter to the ugly realities of oppression in El Salvador as it was at that time. He documents, for example, the expulsion of foreign priests; the imprisonment, torture, and maltreatment of priests and accusations against them for 'falsifying' the faith of the Church; hurtful accusations against Church leaders; accusations against an entire religious order; the murder of many lay Christians; attacks on the Church's communications media; the obstruction of catechetical meetings; the imprisonment, torture, and mockery of lay ministers; profanation of the sacramental bread and wine; and the prohi-bition, in some places, of liturgical gatherings.[30] In and through all of this, the Church is rediscovering its real mission. 'The Church, finally, is restoring hope to the people. Without indulging in triumphalism and recognizing that the Church still has a long way to go, we may say that the Church has given the people a voice and opened a way for them'.[31] It is little wonder that the concept of a Suffering God, prominent in modern theology since the event of the Holo-caust, finds such resonance in the writings of Jon Sobrino, drawing as he does on the experience of Christians in the land of El Salvador—which means 'The Saviour'.

In a chapter called 'Evangelization as Mission of the Church', Sobrino wrestles with the task of the Church and with the nature of the Good News that the Church is called to proclaim. 'We must not assume that every good news that is proclaimed is Christian or even that the good news that has been proclaimed throughout the history of the Church has been fully Christian'.[32] It has been well said that the problem with preaching half a Gospel is that it might be the wrong half! Sobrino's Gospel vision here is a global one. It is for a world divided between atheism and theism, for a world where many have rejected the Christian faith and many have no concept at all of God as revealed in Jesus Christ, but also for a world where many other faiths exist that are theistic. In such a world, Sobrino asks what sort of Church should Christ's people be and what Gospel must they proclaim. 'This problem is a serious one; its resolution calls not simply for a new way of evangelizing but for a new way of existing as the Church'.[33]

This means, urges Sobrino, that the Church's rôle is never merely to keep itself in existence—to perpetuate its own systems—but constantly to carry out its mission. Mission in all its dimensions is always evangelization:

> Any action—education, conscientization, organization, political work that effectively leads to the creation of a world more in accord with the Gospel ideal is evangelization. I thus reject a concept of Christian action as an ethical requirement of evangelization (merely) as a preparation for the acceptance of the Gospel.[34]

The Gospel is for all, however, and not just for the poor and oppressed:

> Depending on the case, therefore, the emphasis in evangelization must be either on offering hope or on calling to conversion. In both cases the purpose is to humanize human beings and to bring them the good news in an effective, not an idealistic, way. At every point in the process of evangelization we must bear in mind that the oppressed need conversion and that oppressors (too) may be being deprived of the proclamation of the good news.[35]

The Church today needs itself to be converted to such an *evangel*. Sobrino pleads that we must all come to hear the Word of God again without 'the death of a thousand qualifications'.[36]

Reflections

In his writings Sobrino covers theology, justice, the Church, and evangelization in a magnificent broad sweep. In particular, I regard *The True Church and the Poor* as still the finest work to emerge from the theology of liberation to date. Will the twenty-first-century Church be such a one as Sobrino portrays and so a Church that will regain and, in some places, acquire for the first time credibility among other theists and among the atheists of the world? What kind of local church do we need to become to serve the poor and vulnerable in our own societies and to attract some from the vast armies of the unchurched? Our traditional local church models have, largely, failed to impress—never mind save—

the millions. Will it be, in the last few years of this century, the mixture as before in our churches with some authentic examples of Jesus' faith and praxis to be found among some churches while the rest of us remain trapped in our mediocrity, our individualism, our narcissism, and our compromise?

What of the wider Church? Will it too remain trapped by regional, national, and international Church structures that we are all, in effect, powerless to either reform or transform? Sobrino's is a message for far more than El Salvador. Our First World regional, national, and continental Churches desperately need the kind of conversion he pleads for. It is instructive to note that the Reformation in sixteenth-century Europe began among Roman Catholics such as Martin Luther and Desiderius Erasmus. They spoke prophetic words to the Church of their day. The Church, then, was slow to respond to what millions now realise to have been the clear voice of God. A voice then was using the Holy Scriptures in new and fresh ways, and a voice was echoing the popular thoughts and needs of the ordinary women and men of the period. Schisms and bloodshed resulted from a deep-set failure really to listen. Sobrino and the theologians of liberation speak like this to both Catholic and Protestant Churches alike in our day. They challenge the status quo we have drifted so comfortably into. Their appeal to us all is both simple and shattering: redefine the Church, change, be transformed. The cause of evangelization depends on it. Is it possible that the Church is missing a new Reformation as the twenty-first century approaches?

The issues are already very clear for Catholic and Protestant alike: the redistribution of wealth and other resources, the rethinking of priorities in evangelization. What are the ethics of the Church in preserving and maintaining vast treasures of culture, architecture, sculpture, art, and libraries in a world and in societies where many are hungry, thirsty, lonely, needing clothes, sick, and in prison? How can the vast and mighty Roman Catholic Church serve Jesus by helping to change unjust structures so as to feed the world's millions and help to release the oppressed? The theologians of liberation have been issuing such prophetic challenges to the Church in Latin America. But their significance goes way beyond Latin America. There is a powerful scene in Zeferelli's memorable film about Francis of Assisi, *Brother Sun, Sister Moon.* Francis and a few followers—all but scarecrows in dress—are granted an audience with the Pope, splendidly attired as Solomon in all his glory in opulent surroundings. Slowly you see the beginnings of recognition and awe in the Pope's face and manner. The scene is splendidly done. He has met with Christ in the face of the 'poor' through Brother Francis. Might the base communities be a late twentieth-century repeat of Francis of Assisi before the Vatican?

Nor, of course, is the impact of the theology of liberation any the less challenging for, say, the Orthodox Churches of Eastern Europe or the worldwide

Anglican Community or the Free Churches. As for those of us who belong to the British Baptist family, it is fascinating to ponder the implications of this book for us. In England, our Home Mission grant system makes possible ministry in the inner city and in neglected rural and socially deprived communities. More recently the *Against the Stream* initiative has targeted a small proportion of Baptist income to key social action projects. Third and Second World mission happens through the Baptist Missionary Society. Industrial mission, community projects, and solidarity with the marginalized all feature strongly in some parts, at least, of the British Baptist family. But we are bound to ask: Is this enough in a world and society of such misery and inequality? The question becomes even more urgent and shaming when for several years there has been talk—and experience—of cutbacks, inadequate giving, and of a potential crisis unless support increases.

In Eastern Europe, as we shall see in the third part of this study, life is often much tougher for Baptist life and witness—in Romania, the former Soviet Union, Bulgaria, or Poland, for example. These have known something more, in recent decades, of the furnace of persecution and of social and economic deprivation; that is, they have known more of what it is to be a Church of the Poor. We need to hear and listen to their voice and take care that it is not stifled or blunted by the traditional Anglo-American dominance within the Baptist World Alliance. For British Baptists, the programme of international exchange visits organized by the BMS provides one way in which we can sit at the feet of our Third World sisters and brothers in Christ and learn the Gospel afresh from their lips and lives. We in the First World local churches need to think, pray, and act more globally. We need to hear the voice of God from the Second and Third World Church far more than we do.

American readers will surely draw the parallels with their own church and missionary structures. But might a British Baptist dare to suggest that they do so? An outside observer sees a huge socio-economic range within the Northern American Baptist family, from poor Baptist communities to enormous Baptist empires owning land, property, and vast wealth and resources. The Scriptures are plain enough. How many affluent and powerful Baptist churches will be able to look the Lord of the poor in the face on the day they appear before his judgement throne? The Baptist principle of the liberty of the local church means that in the end each Diaconate and Church Meeting will need to answer to God for the sort of church we are, the image of the Gospel we present, and for our fidelity to the Gospel of the Christ who came from and lived for the poor of his day. Answer we all must, however. Sobrino's words and challenges are ones for far more than the Latin American Roman Catholic Church.

Far from offering us an alternative Christian faith, the theologians of liberation are really pointing us towards what has always been the traditional faith of the Church. The baggage of centuries, sadly, has buried or at least submerged it. Perhaps through the theology of liberation we really are now being helped to re-discover and re-affirm a truer biblical faith itself.

5. José Comblin

José Comblin has been described by Dom Helder Camara as 'a living example of the committed theologian'. A Belgian Catholic priest, he has worked in Latin America since 1958. In 1972 he was expelled from Brazil for his commitment to the Church of the Poor. He was allowed back in 1980 when he went to work in a poor peasant community in the northeast of the country. He has written more than forty books. The one we are considering in our present study is *The Holy Spirit and Liberation,* in which he writes: 'The experience of God found in the new Christian communities of Latin America can properly be called experiences of the Holy Spirit. The aim of this book is to show how this is.'[37]

At the heart of this book is a concern for evangelization. Comblin seeks new ways of winning the atheists and the unchurched back into a dynamic Christian faith. He suggests that it was the church models of the past that often contributed to the rise of atheism and to the unchurching of many in the World. Now God calls us to build 'a new era of Christianity and a new face for the Church'.[38] Words alone will not bring our contemporaries to Christ, but experiences of God and of lived realities will. The Holy Spirit is showing this way through the base communities. They are rediscovering the Bible: 'The Bible is read in an atmosphere of enthusiasm and joy; it sheds the light of truth on the contemporary world, clarifies the present situation, shows people how they need to act'.[39] Worship, too, has been renewed among the base communities and reinvigorates them for the programmes of community action God has called them to be involved in. The dumb are learning to speak again as

> the poor are beginning to face up to the authorities, demanding their rights, demanding accounts of public spending. They are forming associations and unions to speak out and publicly take the side of the oppressed. They have learned not to worry about their grammatical mistakes, not to be ashamed of the way they speak . . . they no longer accept that speech is the exclusive property of the powerful.[40]

Church planting is also a result of this miracle of new speech. 'When someone who has always been silent begins over the course of a few weeks to proclaim the Gospel and found new communities, there can be no doubt: the Spirit is there.'[41] Individuals are being transformed, families are more united, children are more carefully brought up, people are more neatly dressed. Such money as they have is better spent; converts look healthier and better. *Being* more is of greater importance than *having* more. Comblin contrasts this life-style with the acquisitiveness of the First World that 'does not produce life, but just consumption, excitement, and the satisfaction of desires, and, above all, isolation and individualism'.[42]

In these communities God is seen not as a paternalistic dictator, powerful and fearsome above the clouds, but as a friend and liberator. To contain the Spirit in the inner lives of the faithful is impossible. Where freedom, speech, action, community, and a fuller life emerge anywhere in the world we may trace the activity of the Spirit of God, humanizing and making people more whole: 'The Kingdom of God embraces the whole world; it is not confined to the community of the faithful'.[43]

Not only the poor, however, are responding to this move of the Holy Spirit. There are those among the privileged who are learning how to give up their privileges and to take part in the struggle of the poor for their liberation. Effective evangelization thus needs new models, and Comblin suggests three approaches here.

(1) Praxis is a wiser first step than mere words. Christianity is better communicated through deeds, actions, changed attitudes, and lifestyles than through sermons or religious language.
(2) Dialogue will be necessary. Dialogue means genuinely listening to those of other faiths or none, as well as proclaiming to them.
(3) The supremacy of Christ must still be affirmed. 'Religions divide, but liberating action unites. . . . The hope is that a liberating praxis will show the superiority of Christ and Christianity over other world religious figureheads and teachings'.[44]

In all this we need the Holy Spirit's help. 'There was one Easter', Comblin says memorably as his book nears its close, 'but there are millions of Pentecosts'.[45]

Reflections

Comblin may well be showing us all the way forward for the evangelization of our local communities by our local churches, in the world of the new century. In his own cultural setting he is holding together a belief in the supremacy of Christ with engagement in genuine dialogue, and the key is a praxis shared with others. In an increasingly multi-faith and pluralist Britain with a relativistic 'each to his own' world view prevailing, effective evangelism will not come easily. A praxis inspired by the Holy Spirit, co-operation towards making a New Society, and dialogue in this context are needed here desperately. We must, however, never lose sight of the importance of personal conversion and of the supremacy of Christ in the process. In the final chapters of this book, we will need to return to these insights as part of a model for contemporary evangelization.

Comblin shows us ordinary people doing the evangelization in place of the over-educated priests. Where have we heard that before? 'When they saw the courage of Peter and John and realised that they were unschooled, ordinary men, they were astonished, and they took note that these men had been with Jesus' (Acts 4:12). If the First World unchurched are to be won by the Gospel of Christ in the coming decades, it will surely be mainly by a new army of 'ordinary' Christians involved in their local communities in a praxis that both impresses and challenges. The Latin American base communities have been paving the way.

The charismatic renewal movement has been truly worldwide in its effects and influences. The Holy Spirit has been restored to a rightful place within the Christian faith of the late twentieth century. The gifts of the Spirit (*charismata*) are in evidence across many of the world's churches—whether they be the essential gifts of hospitality, administration, and generous giving, or the more high-profile gifts of prophecy, healing, and glossolalia. It is not within the scope of this book to detail the phenomenal growth of the Pentecostal and other evangelical Protestant Churches in contemporary Latin America. That too is a remarkable story and is another example of the new forms of Christianity coming to life in that bubbling continent. In Latin America there has been a major move of the Holy Spirit of God that, as in the First World, has embraced both Catholics and Protestants. Comblin's book captures something of this movement; for me, it glows with a sense of God's Spirit.

6. Jorgé Pixley and Clodovis Boff

As this chapter draws to a close, we will finally consider an example of ecumenical liberation theology at its finest: *The Bible, the Church, and the Poor* by Clodovis Boff and Jorgé Pixley.[46] This book is the fruit of co-operation between a Baptist pastor and a Brazilian Servite priest. The Baptist, Jorgé Pixley, has ministered and taught in Puerto Rico, Argentina, and Mexico, and now teaches at the Baptist Theological Seminary in Managua, Nicaragua. Clodovis Boff is a Roman Catholic priest who has worked in Amazonia and in the *favelas* of Rio de Janeiro. Both write out of their direct experience of service amongst Latin American base communities. Both conclude that traditional models of caring for the poor have failed such people: 'The whole huge and inspiring effort to help the poor ended in failure. Poverty has not diminished; it has increased'.[47] Individual and collective charity are still needed, but these barely scratch the surface of this worldwide problem. Nor are these problems limited to the Third World. First World industrial societies, as well as the more developed industrial centres of Latin America, also have their poor. The 'poor' include physically and mentally handicapped people abandoned to the streets, immigrant workers, the homeless and the unemployed, the suicidally depressed, old people dependent on a meagre state pension, and young drug addicts.

The book is divided into three parts that explore different aspects of the option for the poor. Part one considers the biblical aspect, and insights are drawn from Old and New Testament material. They survey the liberation of the poor in the Exodus, the defence of the poor through the instrument of the Davidic monarchy, legislation to protect the poor in the Torah, the protest of the prophets against existing conditions on behalf of the poor, the petitions of the poor in the Psalms, and expressions of God's favour to the poor in the Wisdom literature. Similarly the writings of Paul, John, and Luke (including Acts) are considered against the background of the Jesus who proclaims Good News to the poor. Boff and Pixley are refreshingly original both in the new material they discover and in their treatment of familiar passages.

The second part of the book considers the theological aspect of the theme, re-examining doctrines of the incarnation, the nature of the Church, and 'spiritual poverty'. This is a section full of quotable passages. Consider for example this warning against a concern for the poor that excludes other sectors of society:

> A church of the poor is a church in which the poor are privileged, a church in which the poor occupy the first rank. This means that there is also a room in it for the rich, but only to the extent that they are converted and fraternize with the

humble. It is not true that the church of the poor is against the rich; what it is
against are the privileges, illegitimate interests, and anti-evangelical pretensions
of the rich.[48]

Or reflect on this description of many a First World society: '(these) with their
sad-faced, over-fed people, their hearts emptied of hope and meaning, cannot
serve as an adequate model for the utopia of the Gospel'.[49]

The third part of the book deals with the 'pastoral aspect' of the option for
the poor. This wide-ranging section sweeps through church history to discover
examples of the Church over the centuries as it grapples with being the Church
of the Poor. Whilst Boff and Pixley find much to admire; their overall conclusion is that all the charity, relief, and almsgiving that has been undertaken has
failed to get to the root of the problems of world poverty. The Church, too, has
usually held back from attacking the social, political, and economic injustices
that undergird and cause poverty. As it was then, so it is now. The pastoral
dimension to the option for the poor has many implications. Peaceful means
must be the means to any worthy end; there must always be respect for adver-
saries' rights as well; there must be an openness to the non-poor whilst proclaiming the Gospel to them; the goal must be a full and rounded life, not just
economic liberation; resentment must be resisted, and the whole process of
liberation must be seen as an ongoing one of permanent conversion.[50]

The book contains a delightful chapter on the culture of freedom. Christian
freedom will embrace the cultivation of beauty, humour, human love, convivi-
ality, festivals, celebrations, and leisure; it will also respect popular religion.
This is how true Christian communities will be recognized. There is an attractive inclusivism in the writing and vision of the two authors:

> Together with pastoral action on behalf of the poor, then, and in association
> with it, there can be pastoral action on behalf of the non-poor: the middle
> classes, the rich, the intellectuals, politicians, those working in the communi-
> cations media, doctors, university professors, and so on.[51]

Finally, Christian teachers and leaders seeking a cogent and well-argued agenda
for world mission in the 1990s need look no further than the splendid final
chapter of this book—'Looking Ahead, the Future of Humanity.' In a world of
hunger, repression, the arms race, debt, unjust economic structures, racism, and
the oppression of women, what sort of a church should there be, and what sort
of a Gospel should we be proclaiming? Are there any more important questions
than this for our world and Church? The authors conclude with a warning: 'Out
of sheer instinct for survival, humanity has to make a preferential option for the

poor. If it does not succeed in doing so, all the indications are that we shall all perish, rich and poor alike'.[52]

Reflections

As a minister who has helped a little to advocate Baptist involvement in the British *Inter-Church Process* in the late 1980s, in the interests of more effective evangelism and mission to the unchurched, I am excited to see this partnership between a Baptist minister and a Jesuit priest. What a striking book has emerged as a result! My hope is that similar partnerships and fruit may be seen as the *Inter-Church Process* unfolds in the Britain of the 1990s between Free Church, Catholic, and Anglican partners in the Gospel.

My only reservation with this outstanding book is the way that the campaign against poverty is, at times, identified totally with the Gospel. Of course, there is no question that the Gospel truly is good news of liberation for the poor. Action against poverty is not, however, the whole Gospel, and we must beware any movement towards a collapse of the Gospel into a social and poverty action package alone. I would like to see more stress laid on such aspects as discipleship, forgiveness of sins, the gifts and fruit of the Holy Spirit, 'growth in grace and in knowledge of the Lord Jesus Christ' (2 Pet 3:18), eternal life now, and the promise that death is not the end. These too belong to the theme of liberation!

Whilst written from a Latin American perspective, however, this book is full of insights for those of us seeking to work out in praxis something of a First World liberation theology. It analyses the failures of the First World as thoroughly as it does those of the Third World. How good it is to be brought to realise through this book—and through the others mentioned in this chapter—that the Third World poor have at last found a voice. They no longer need so desperately the relief agencies' glossy magazines and photographs to plead their cause. They are now doing this for themselves.

Perhaps this is an apt point at which to end this survey of several of the key works of liberation theology over the period we have concentrated on—the 1970s and 1980s. Here is an author's plea to the reader as this chapter closes: seek out some of these writings for yourself. Read and hear the voices of Third World Christians speaking to you directly. Your Christian faith and life will never be the same again.

Notes

[1]Leonardo Boff and Clodovis Boff, *Introducing Liberation Theology* (Burns & Oates, London, 1987). This grim scenario is described fully on pp. 1-4; American billions have been converted into British 'thousand millions'.

[2]Gutierrez, *A Theology of Liberation*, p. ix.

[3]Ibid., p. 71.

[4]Ibid., p. 72.

[5]Ibid., p. 105.

[6]Ibid., p. 139.

[7]Harvey Cox, *On Not Leaving It to the Snake* (Macmillan, New York, 1967).

[8]Jürgen Moltmann, *Theology of Hope, On the Ground and the Implications of a Christian Eschatology* (SCM Press, London, 1967).

[9]Gutierrez, *Liberation Theology*, pp. 216-218.

[10]Ibid., pp. 225-32 for a fuller analysis of this theme.

[11]Ibid., pp. 168.

[12]Ibid., p. 175.

[13]Ibid., p. 270.

[14]Ibid., p. 272.

[15]Ibid., p. 307.

[16]José de Broucker, *Dom Helder Camara. The Conversions of a Bishop* (Collins, London, 1979), pp. 90-91.

[17]Ibid., p. 125.

[18]Ibid., p. 141.

[19]Ibid., p. 173.

[20]Ibid., p. 198.

[21]Ibid., p. 222.

[22]Jon Sobrino, *The True Church and the Poor* (SCM, London, 1985), p. 19.

[23]Ibid., p. 53.

[24]Ibid., pp. 57-58.

[25]Ibid., p. 93.

[26]Ibid., p. 98.

[27]Ibid., p. 188.

[28]Ibid., p. 199.

[29]Ibid., p. 205.

[30]Ibid., pp. 229-230.

[31]Ibid., p. 252.

[32]Ibid., p. 253.

[33]Ibid., p. 254-255.

[34]Ibid., p. 271.

[35]Ibid., pp. 273-274.

[36]Ibid., p. 334.

[37]José Comblin, *The Holy Spirit and Liberation* (Burns & Oates, London, 1989), p. xi.

[38]Ibid., p. xvi.

[39]Ibid., pp. 11-12.

[40]Ibid., pp. 26-27

[41]Ibid., p. 27.

[42]Ibid., p. 30.

[43]Ibid., p. 45.

[44]See the section, 'Christ and the Spirit in Evangelization', pp. 159-62.

[45]Ibid., p. 184.

[46]Clodovis Boff and Jorgé Pixley, *The Bible, the Church, and the Poor* (Burns & Oates, London, 1989).

[47]Ibid., p. 3.

[48]Ibid., p. 137.

[49]Ibid., p. 155.

[50]Ibid., pp. 210-215.

[51]Ibid., p. 228.

[52]Ibid., p. 242.

Chapter 3
The Second World
Poland, 1945–1990

1. War and Love: Autobiography

On December 4, 1948, my mother and father married. How much lies behind that simple statement! My father's story begins in Stolin, which was then in Poland and which is now in Belorussia. He was born on September 2, 1922, the only son of Wlodzimierz and his second wife Mary (née Chropowska). He grew up on a farm in Luniniec in the Pripyet Marshes territory. Our surname Bochenski—we have Anglicized it over the years and pronounce it B-hen-ski —may have its origins in the southern town of Bochnia. Or it may be the equivalent of something like Baker in England—'bochen' in Polish means 'loaf'. My father's education was through the gymnasium system. He seemed destined for university, perhaps the ancient and renowned one at Krakow, the Polish version of Oxbridge. His father was a landowner and a veterinary surgeon. Little surprise that he doted on his only son, Jan Edward, the apple of his eye. His marriage to his former wife, now dead, had given him daughters but no son. Now he had one. Wild boar hunts, peasants bringing their sick animals to his home for help, and the delicious Polish stews and salamis were among my father's childhood memories, as the privileged son of a well-to-do father.

Hitler's invasion of Poland in 1939, which marked the entrance upon war with Britain also, ended an era for Poland and for many families, our own among them. At the beginning of the war, Stalin's Soviet Union operated a non-aggression treaty with the Third Reich. In practice, for Poland, this meant being carved up by two invaders and not just one. My grandfather Wlodzimierz was too wealthy to be left alone for long. His land in the east of Poland was expropriated by the occupying Soviet army, he was taken off to prison in Stolin, and he was never seen again. Even a protest by local peasants, whom he had helped in the past, failed to save him from death in mysterious circumstances. Like many other deaths, it was probably a bullet in the back. We still do not know. The young Jan Edward, aged just seventeen, was exiled to Siberia with his mother Mary. They were soon separated, and it was only much later that he heard of her death—aged just forty-two—which had resulted from the harshness of the conditions.

Jan became part of the mammoth slave labour force in Stalin's Soviet Union. He was taken to Karaganda in Kazakhstan. His work included labour on a collective farm; snow clearing—'there was a lot of it', as he said, laying a mountain railway track, and—much to his frustration— having to transform a church into a club house. His escape came when the Russian leader Stalin joined the Western Allies, and Generals Anders and Sikorski intervened on behalf of the Poles then in the Soviet Union. Jan Edward enlisted with the Polish army within Russia. The Polish were perhaps intended as Western front tank and artillery fodder. For Jan, a long journey began instead. Crossing the Mongolian border, he went over desert terrain to Krasnovodsk, then to Pahlayi in Iran (then Persia), and over the Caspian Sea. By way of Tehran, Baghdad, Damascus, and Jerusalem, he arrived in Tel Aviv. After training with the British Royal Air Force in the Middle East, he returned to Syria and Iraq, and then in June 1943 took a long ship's journey to Britain by way of Egypt, the Suez Canal, the Red Sea, the Indian Ocean, Durban, Rio de Janeiro (to avoid the U-boats), and so finally to Scotland. By the age of twenty-two, my father had experienced more than many could in several lifetimes, and he, of course, was one of the fortunate ones who survived. Millions did not.

In England, my father worked as a wireless operator and was billeted in Nottingham. There he met and courted Phyllis—clandestinely, since at first the family objected. As he once told me, the postwar racial prejudice was strong and real. There were many who tried to put them off, but their love won through. Their courtship and marriage centred upon Radford in Nottingham. Phyllis had grown up in more prosperous times, relatively speaking, for her older sisters were at work by the time she was in school. The family was nonconformist with Baptist roots traceable back to Baptists in Derbyshire. So here were two nations, two families, and also two Christian heritages—nonconformity and Catholicism. Mass movements of people in the terrors and traumas of war were the backcloth to many a courtship. Love often flowered against the odds and probabilities. All came together in a Saturday wedding in the postwar Britain of 1948, with Christmas only weeks away: 'Many waters cannot quench love; rivers cannot wash it away' (Song of Songs 8:7).

It was in 1953 that the priest came. My mother was carrying me. Many years later she told me the story of how the priest came to their home and told my father that he was not 'properly married' as they had made their marriage vows in a Protestant church. He threw the priest out of the house and for years to come never went to any church again. That priest, I now think, is the real answer to the question why my brother and I were not brought up as Catholics as most second-generation Polish children were. Also it explains why I never came to learn the language of my father's homeland. Instead, doubtless for some peace on a Sunday afternoon, my mother used to send me and my brother to the small Baptist church down the road for Sunday School, just as she had been sent as a girl. I owe much to that little congregation. There I was taught the Gospel stories of Jesus and was nurtured in the Christian faith. There I first learned to love and respect the Bible. There, too, I came to a personal faith, was baptized, and learned to preach. There I was married, and there, in 1980, I was ordained to the Baptist ministry in the presence of family and friends. This autobiographical interlude explains something, then, of how and why I have two nations in my bloodstream.

2. A Christian Nation

I have ventured to tell my family's story in a book of theology that is also full of stories. In the first two chapters we traced the experience of Christians in Latin America and their witness to the meaning of liberation and evangelization. I now want to turn to the experience that occurred in these same years of the two nations I know best through my own story, and first to the movement for liberation in a 'Second World' country, Poland. Might the rôle of the Church and the people of God in Poland—always a very Western-looking East European country—offer clues to us all as we seek to unravel something of the mysteries of contemporary evangelization. Can we discern the hand of God in the struggles towards freedom of contemporary Poland in the postwar period?

An atheist or agnostic will interpret the remarkable revolutionary events in Poland and elsewhere in Eastern Europe during 1989 and afterwards in different ways. For many Christians, the interpretation is both simpler and yet more profound: the hand of the God of liberation was at work answering the cries and pleas of his people. The God of the Bible is a God always active in *human* history and not, let it be emphasized, only in *church* history. The Christian God is One who is sovereign and, therefore, active way beyond, as well as within, the confines of the Church. What if the liberation of Poland in the 1980s could be seen as just one visual aid of what the Living God wishes to do with all who will cooperate with him? It would provide some clues for individuals, communities, churches, and nations as the twenty-first century approaches.

Poland has been a European State since Prince Mieszko adopted the Christian faith in A.D. 966. For all the inroads that Western Capitalism and its multi-faith options have made in 1990 Poland, Poland remains one of the most deeply Christian nations on earth. It offers a remarkable example of a country where the Christian faith has played a major rôle for more than a thousand years in a nation's history, culture, struggles, and liberation. As the historian Norman Davies puts it, 'The history of the Roman Catholic Church provides one of the very few threads of continuity in Poland's past. Kingdoms, dynasties, republics, parties, and régimes have come and gone; but the Church seems to go on forever'.[1] In his book *Discretion and Valour*,[2] Trevor Beeson has done much to bring home to Christians in the West the trials, the spirituality, the persecution, and the incredible strengths of the Church in Eastern Europe. His chapter on Poland, though written in the early 1970s, remains helpful in seeking to understand something of the heart of this deeply Christian nation.

Beeson noted what is in a real sense the Polish national motto: *Polonia semper fidelis*—'Poland will always be true to the faith' or 'will always be faithful'. In 1931 the Roman Catholic Church had the loyalty of some 65% of the population. At the end of the second world war and its genocide, that figure was nearer 97% of the survivors. For 1971, Beeson quoted the following figures for the Roman Catholic Church in Poland: 25 dioceses; 6,376 parishes; 18,151 priests—1 for every 1,750 people; 13,392 churches and chapels; and 30,162 monks and nuns. Some of this growth can be attributed, of course, to the acquisition of the eastern territories in the former German lands. By 1979 Richard Davy, writing in *New Society* about the then new Pope's visit to his homeland, gave estimated figures of 30,000,000 Roman Catholics, out of a total population of 35,000,000; 20,000 priests; and some 14,000 churches.[3] Norman Davies helps to complete this picture for us:

> Churchgoing is normal. The entire population of the villages and of working class districts in the towns walks to Mass and kneels submissively for long periods. The singing is rich and lusty. Religious processions are scrupulously observed. On Catholic feast days, fields and factories are deserted. Annual pilgrimages to Czestochowa or to Kalwaria Lanckorona attract hundreds of thousands and perhaps millions. The Marian cult flourishes as never before.
> . . . The parish priest, 'God's deputy', enjoys great social prestige. He both expects, and is expected, to make clear pronouncements on all issues of public concern.[4]

It would be very wrong, however, to assume that Poland was ever an entirely Catholic country. As Beeson points out, the Russian Orthodox Church in the early 1970s had some 460,000 adherents. Any visitor to eastern Poland will soon witness the strength of the Russian Orthodox Church if only from seeing the many churches on the skyline. The Polish Old Catholic Church had 25,000 communicants. The Methodists, who had in 1972 just celebrated their golden jubilee in Poland, had 4,133 worshippers. The Polish Lutheran Community was then some 80,000 strong. As for the Polish Baptist Church scene in postwar Poland, the Baptists had some 10,000 members before 1939, many of these German-speaking. The war decimated them too. Their standing in Poland ecumenically was significantly enhanced by the (Baptist) Jimmy Carter presidency in America and by the visits of evangelist Billy Graham to several venues in Poland in October 1978. Under the leadership of the then President Konstanty Wiazowski and now of General Secretary Ryszard Gutkowski, the Polish Baptist Union has made many advances in the post-Communist era.

There were and are, as Beeson notes, some smaller evangelical causes also. On a sadder note, he draws our attention to the persecution experienced especially in the 1940s by the (Ukrainian) Uniate Church whose members were often forcibly resettled into the now Russian western territories. More terrifying still are the figures Beeson quotes of the decline of the Jewish Community. In 1939 this was 3,250,000 strong; but 2,900,000 died in the hell that Poland became in World War II. Nor were the Nazis the only enemy. Anti-Semitism has long been a sorry feature of Polish nationalism. It does no objective observer any good to deny this. Sad indeed that a race so persecuted itself should treat another persecuted race so cruelly, but the evidence here is overwhelming.[5] As late as 1967, the then Polish leader Gomulka spoke of the few remaining Polish Jews as a 'fifth column' and actively encouraged their emigration to Israel. Beeson estimates that by the early 1970s only 7,000 Jews were left in Poland.

3. Stefan Wyszynski

When the full history of the twentieth-century Church comes to be written in the next few decades, one name at least deserves to figure far more prominently than is currently the case. It is that of Cardinal Stefan Wyszynski (1901–1981). Norman Davies, in his magisterial two-volume history of Poland, describes him thus: 'the war horse, the doughty champion of his cause, a man of simple patriotism, of radiant piety, and of total integrity'.[6] Cardinal Wyszynski died in 1981. For three full decades he had led the Church in his country. Like Moses of old, he was never to see the outcome of his labours for the liberation of his country. He may never even have imagined the events of the autumn of 1989 to be possible. For instance, back in 1981, who could have anticipated the changes Mikhail Gorbachev, the Soviet leader, would bring? The wilderness wanderings were all Cardinal Wyszynski was ever to know. Soon after his death, the cruel military suppression of Solidarity occurred, and it was only some eight years later that any sign of light at the end of the tunnel appeared. Through three desperately hard and difficult decades, this Christian leader, under God, bore much of the strain of the fight for the soul of the Polish nation. He was a prophet of liberation long before others arrived on the scene.

In 1985 the prison notes of Cardinal Stefan Wyszynski, entitled *A Freedom Within*, were published in English.[7] These chronicle the three years during the 1950s when he was imprisoned and kept incommunicado by the Polish Stalinists under the then President Boleslaw Bierut. In Rywald, Stoczek, Prudnik-Slaski, and finally Komancza, he was kept from his diocese—Warsaw and Gniezno—and from people. Komancza is in the Bieszsczady not far from the

Soviet Union itself: 'Couldn't you take me any further?' he joked with his captors. Poland he loved devotedly. 'The forest stood long before you came—you will be gone, and the forest will remain.'[8] While under arrest, Wyszynski read Henryk Sienkiewicsz's book *The Flood* about the brave defence of the Jasna Gora monastery by monks, led by Father Augustyn Kordecki, under attack from some 9,000 invading Swedes in 1655. This experience led Wyszynski to develop a sense of the need for Poland once again to defend a 'Jasna Gora' of his own day:

> The defence of Jasna Gora is a defence of the Christian spirit of the nation, a defence of our native culture, a defence of the unity of human hearts within God's heart; it is the defence of man's right to breathe freely, of a man who wants to trust in God more than he wants to trust in people and to trust people in a godly way.[9]

His diary abounds with meditations of profundity and insight:

> *On the Church's chains over the centuries*: The cause of Christ has existed almost 2,000 years and people are still in prison for it today. The cause has survived. It is alive, fresh, young, full of allure. How many guards have changed, prisons have fallen into ruin, keys have rusted, locks and chains been removed—yet the cause endures. . . Paul's chains clank not only in historical recollections; their living current reaches all the way into my prison cell.[10]

> *On sin*: Beware of one sin, for one alone can start the avalanche.[11]

> *On love*: Love is the most important treasure we take with us from this world; all other virtues and accomplishments, however great, we leave at the threshold of our new life. There is as much happiness and glory for one in heaven as there was love in that person's heart on earth.[12]

> *On evangelism*: You must diminish me Lord even more, so that I may know how to lead souls to you.[13]

> *On Christ's resurrection*: When Christ rose from the dead he revealed so many possibilities to men that we no longer even care about our present situation. We know that all possibilities stand before us.[14]

Such was the faith that was to sustain Cardinal Wyszynski and, indeed, much of Poland, over the next three decades and beyond. Here the faith, the vision of liberation, the hope for a better future for Poland was both born and kept alive. Wyszynski's spiritual vision, I believe, actually helped to keep that hope alive.

In the late 1980s it helped to transform entire nations. Wyszynski's spiritual roots went down deep—they were fed by contemplation, study, Scripture, adoration, discipline. His spirituality stretched to embrace a whole nation and has helped to change our contemporary world. Much contemporary Protestant and Catholic spirituality will be found wanting when compared to that found in this journal. Our superficiality should shame us. This is not a book for the speed reader. Rather it is one to read slowly with many pauses and prayers. It was one of my father's last gifts to me.

4. The Gomulka Years, 1956–1970

Soon after Cardinal Wyszynski's release, with the Stalin years now behind people, things looked better for Poland. Inspired by his confinement vision of a new defence of Jasna Gora, Cardinal Wyszynski called the nation to a programme of spiritual renewal that would lead up to the Polish millennium celebrations. Between 1957 and 1966, special sermon outlines for Sundays and Holy Days were provided. So was study material for catechism groups. Special conferences were called for Lent and Advent, and the overall momentum was successfully maintained up to the millennium celebrations themselves. It is hard to conceive of any other country in the world where a religious programme of such intensity and range could be undertaken over almost a decade—and that in the Cold War 1960s! The forces of Communism and of Catholicism remained in active struggle throughout that decade. The President then was Wladyslaw Gomulka. In 1959, the police invaded Poland's most sacred shrine —the monastery of Jasna Gora at Czestochowa—seeking illegal publishing equipment. Police and pilgrims fought with each other. Licences were refused for many new churches. In Nowa Huta, in 1960, these intimidatory policies led to a street riot.

As the 1966 celebrations for the millennium of Polish Christianity approached, further acrimonious State-Church disputes marred the entire proceedings. The Polish bishops earlier that year had attempted a rapprochement with the West German bishops. There were longstanding disputes about the so-called 'western territories' and whether they came under the jurisdiction of the Polish or the German cardinals. The Vatican had sat on the fence on the issue for several years. The bishops' appeals for reconciliation and for the past of World War II to be put behind the nation was now exploited by the State: 'We shall not forgive, and we shall not forget', it said. The bishops were in fact, as we can now see, playing for higher stakes: full recognition of the Oder-Neisse line. The government used the bishops' stance, however, to stir up anti-Church feeling. The tactic backfired, especially when the Pope was refused permission to visit Poland. The mutual propaganda battles that ensued were bitter. The result was that the millennium events became an ill-tempered affair with Church and State holding separate programmes of ceremonies. In 1966, as part of these celebrations, the British and Foreign Bible Society helped to publish a modern Polish New Testament.

In 1968, a purge of intellectuals was attempted. A production of the nineteenth-century play *Forefather's Eve* by Poland's greatest poet Adam Mickiewicz—which deals provocatively with Polish-Russian relationships—was banned. A brutal campaign against 'revisionists' and 'Zionists' was instituted, and many students were arrested and intellectuals purged. There are clear parallels here with the Doctrine of National Security implemented in Latin America. There were several student protests. Censorship tightened still further. The Cardinals Wyszynski and Wojtyla and the Polish bishops wrote an open letter defending the students. By 1970, when a misguided attempt to put up food prices caused mass popular unrest, strikes resulted. Some Poles died in protests against the security forces. The Gomulka régime was discredited and, as popular protests grew to fever pitch, Gomulka himself was justly ousted.

5. The Gierek Years, 1970–1980

The 1970s in Poland are crucial to our book's theme. One cannot read or write about them without drawing comparisons with what was happening in Latin America at much the same time. Development had a devastating effect in the Second World just as it had in Third World Latin America.

Edward Gierek came to power on a tide of revulsion after the killings that marked the Gomulka régime. He also came with a fund of goodwill behind him. This was to have been the decade for re-establishing contact with the working classes, for raising consumption and living standards, for rapid industrialization, for increasing technology to Western standards, and for encouraging agriculture and reform in the countryside by investment. By the end of the decade and by summer 1980, however, quite the reverse had happened on almost all these fronts. Workers were deserting the Party in droves to join *Solidarity*. The Polish people had come to know the grim realities of queues for even basic commodities such as butter, meat, and sugar. Some even travelled to East Germany regularly to buy their food and basic commodities. Poland's foreign debt was a despair-ridden sum of at least $23 billion. There was an enormous gap between food supply and demand. On top of all of this, some 40 percent of the state budget was going to retail food subsidies alone. The serious charge of economic illiteracy against the Gierek regime is incontrovertible. Still today, it can be argued, Poland and its people suffer for the mistakes and mismanagement of those years, not least in their current national debt burden.

At first, the import-led investment boom had gone well. Links with Polonia —Poles in exile abroad—were encouraged and brought in some Western currency. So too did a growing tourism market. The need for such hard currency meant that many foods were constantly being exported to the West but were rarely available in Poland. By 1976 strikes were again a growing phenomenon. The post-war Poles have never been afraid to take to the streets in non-violent demonstrations. In doing so, they have taught the whole of the Second World and indeed others a lesson in how to achieve democratic goals without inflicting violence on other people. What had they to lose? Two thousand people were detained in Radom after street demonstrations and riots that led to an estimated million dollars worth of damage. More than 200 workers at the Ursus tractor factory near Warsaw were severely beaten by riot police. Some had earlier torn up the rails on a nearby stretch of railway track. Attacks on Party offices also occurred. Many of those arrested were summarily imprisoned, though most were later released, not least after appeals by priests and the Church. The riots were as much about work conditions as they were about food prices. The special pay and conditions that obtained for the Party élite particularly rankled with them also. It was an all too familiar case of the circumstances satirized brilliantly by George Orwell in his modern classic, *Animal Farm,* one of the most popular of all underground books in the Second World of that time. The Polish film maker Andrzej Wajda portrayed the corruption of post-Stalinist Poland mercilessly in his 1977 film *Man of Marble.*

By early 1977, Gierek was forced to shift his economic policy significantly. The emphasis was now to be on providing consumer goods and foods for the domestic market. Subsidies to hold down the price of food soon amounted to an estimated 70 percent of the retail price! Poland's economic 'miracle' had led, in the end, to negative economic growth and to a stagnating economy. Some of the many loans entered into were rescheduled. The foreign debt problem was clearly now directly related to the experiences of poverty among the poor majority of Poland's population and to their deprivation. Money that was desperately needed to feed people was being repaid, instead, to Western and other banks. There were just not enough funds left to invest significantly in the domestic economy any longer. Neal Ascherson summarizes the effects of all this in ways that will, again, bring Latin America to mind:

> Poland was now caught fast in a trap which awaits all backward economies attempting rapid industrial transformation. Imports of advanced technological goods financed by hard-currency loans have to continue, if for no other reason

than that they are now required for the production of export goods that alone can raise the hard currency needed to service the previous debts.[15]

The whole Polish economy had effectively become geared to financing foreign creditors whose claims nonetheless increased, not least due to compound interest rates and charges.

As for the Church in the Gierek years, it continued its rôle of being, in effect, the only opposition in postwar Poland. Wyszynski saw the fight as one against the secularism and atheism that were being imposed everywhere. Towards the end of these depressing years, an event of enormous implications for what was to happen in the 1980s took place way beyond all Polish (or Soviet) influence and borders. On October 16, 1978, a puff of smoke announced the election of a non-Italian Pope! Cardinal Wojytla of Krakow had become Pope John Paul II. Wojtyla had been Archbishop of Krakow since 1967. An actor, poet, sportsman, philosopher, and university chaplain, Norman Davies dscribes him as 'a figure of scintillating talents and of profound spirituality who had given proof of his mettle by protecting intellectual dissidents'.[16] The Polish people rushed to their phones, opened bottles, hung out Polish flags, and openly wept in front of television screens. A great source of authority in Polish Society was now no longer confined to Poland nor, of course, constricted by the pervasive influences of its government and secret police.

In June 1979, Pope John Paul II revisited his homeland for the first time since his election. The scenes were extraordinary by any standards. Millions turned out to greet him all over Poland. Two million gathered for the farewell on Krakow meadows. The Church oversaw all the organization and policing both professionally and, by all accounts, superbly. The Party could only look on as 'its country was dominated and looked after by the Church and people for eight very hot days in June 1979. The television recorded the meeting of Gierek and the Pope. It was not hard to see whose future position was the more secure! Poland could never be the same again. It was not.

6. Solidarity Is Born, 1980–1981

In the summer of 1980 the Polish government was taken by surprise, and so was the world. A working-class revolt challenged the very existence of the Polish State itself. This would have been 'pure Marx', except that the State being challenged was itself a Communist one! It was not the Church or Party reformers or even dissident intellectuals who took the lead. All were to play a part later, but the lead was taken by the *proletariat,* specifically, working-class leaders, and notably by the charismatic electrician Lech Walesa, earlier victimized and then made redundant. In July 1980 a rash of strikes protesting the worsening food and social situation began in several places. By mid-August 1980, these had spread to the Lenin shipyards at Gdansk. 'Workers of all enterprises unite', the slogans ran. During the weeks of the sit-in that followed from time to time, the conspicuously robed figure of Father Jankowski could be seen hearing confessions and leading Mass in the very heart of the shipyards. Mass was celebrated in the presence of hundreds of kneeling workers. They were not the only ones on their knees! Slowly but surely government investigators were forced to accept a number of previously unheard-of concessions: the right to strike, the right to establish independent trade unions, the erecting of a monument to those murdered in the 1970 protests, a relaxation of censorship not least in Church matters, the re-employment of dismissed workers, and the release of certain political prisoners.

Solidarnosc was born. Another Wajda film, *Man of Iron*, bravely told its story, which was also Lech Walesa's story. In retrospect, many factors had led to these momentous days:

- The 1970 food riots and the June 1976 popular protests
- The moral and intellectual bankruptcy of the official Communist ideology
- The existence of continuing corruption and of the gulf between Party and people
- Low industrial productivity and concomitantly poor living standards
- The failure of government to support peasant agriculture and the resulting food shortages
- The collapse—generally—of the Party's economic strategy
- The strength and background support of the Roman Catholic Church reinvigorated by the recent papal visit
- The ambiguous stance of the Polish armed forces
- The steady growth of a dissident opposition, much of it Catholic in its sympathies

One of the key figures here was Tadeusz Mazowiecki. Remarkable though it was, Solidarity did not 'just happen'. It was the culmination of a long and painful process. Its early survival was helped by a number of factors. Like the Church, it was prepared, at first, to work within the system, specifically, with and not against the Party, however different their ideologies. Solidarity also gladly welcomed support from other social groupings, for example, students and intellectuals, as well as from the priests. The theologians of liberation, it will be remembered, argue for just such solidarity in praxis among all people of goodwill. The consistent background support of the Church was always something the government needed to take into account. So too was the fascination of the Western media with these events. These factors clearly helped Solidarity's early survival.

Two main dangers remained at these delicate times: over-reaction by Party hard-liners or, worse, a Czechoslovakian 1968-type invasion by the Soviet Union and others. One enterprising tourist shop at the time displayed a poster that said it all: *'Visit the Soviet Union before the Soviet Union visits you'*.

Poland's debt crisis, meanwhile, had not vanished. The Soviet Union stepped in with some credit and, with other Comecon countries, provided an emergency package of food exports to Poland after the summer strikes. West German bankers made more loans—$670 million in October 1980. The Polish government was even pressing America, inexcusably, for a further $3 billion loan at this time it seems. By 1979–1980, Ascherson estimates that Poland had already paid out some $8.4 billion in interest alone.[17] The government was by now dragging its heels over keeping its promises to Solidarity. It does not take much to imagine the regular phone calls and visits to and from Moscow going on at the time! Despite a long and frustrating legal battle, Solidarity was never fully registered. Nor was Rural Solidarity, an agricultural equivalent with strong Church backing behind it. And all this time the strong, clear evidence was of Soviet manoeuvres on Poland's borders. Worse. It seemed there was a 'creeping invasion' already underway, unit by unit of the Warsaw Pact.

The Church played its hand on the whole superbly. With Russia in mind the episcopate warned:

> None may act in such a manner as to drive our fatherland into danger of losing its freedom or its existence as a sovereign state. . . . A decisive act of will is needed to counteract all attempts to slow down the progress of national renewal, to inflame society, or to exploit our present difficulties for aims alien to the interest of our nation and our State.[18]

Very popular rumour had it that the Pope had single-handedly prevented Soviet invasion with a simple threat: 'Invade my country and I will land my plane at Warsaw Airport and sit there until you leave'. Food queues lengthened. In April 1981, some rescheduling of debts at a foreign creditors' meeting in Paris was allowed, and $2.5 billion was saved in an eight-year deferred repayment package. American hard-liners prevented this from being extended significantly further however and, according to Ascherson, Poland's total hard currency indebtedness at this time stood at about $25 billion.

7. The Jaruzelski Years, 1981–1989

In December 1981, the 'national tragedy' so long feared actually took place. As Neal Ascherson graphically describes it:

> In the snowy darkness of Sunday 13th December . . . General Wojciech Jaruzelski launched a military coup on a scale and with an efficiency and ferocity that nobody had anticipated. Almost the entire leadership of Solidarity were arrested within hours at Gdansk, where the Union's executive had been meeting, and thousands of union militants, intellectuals, journalists, and individuals suspected of liberal views followed them into prison and into detention camps. All trade unions were occupied by security forces, and the Union's property and files were confiscated.[19]

Jaruzelski launched his Military Council of National Salvation, a Second World equivalent of those we have glimpsed at work in Latin America a decade or so earlier. Poland was declared to be in a 'state of war'. Civil liberties were suspended; some public services, for example transport, were conscripted; civil disobedience was classified as 'mutiny', and offenders against martial law faced punishment by military courts empowered to apply the death penalty. Protests continued nonetheless in factories, shipyards, coal mines, universities, and colleges. Military police commandos were sent in to storm many such places of work or protest. On December 17, the deaths of seven miners were announced at Wujek colliery near Katowice. That there were many other killings in those grim days seems beyond doubt.

The Church refused to counsel submission. The workers often resisted suicidally. Lech Walesa refused to co-operate or negotiate in any way. Polish blood had again been spilt by Poles for the first time since 1970. These days were emotively captured in Andrew Carr's BBC Panorama special broadcast in December 1982 of *Two Weeks in Winter* to commemorate the grim anniversary. This 'docu-drama' was based on eyewitness reports, smuggled documents, and secret films. The terrifying Zoma (secret police)—some perhaps Russian and some perhaps drugged—were portrayed with their riot shields, clubs, and guns. Solidarity leaders were rounded up and treated like cattle, while Warsaw Radio broadcast only glib platitudes. The machine gun killings of the seven miners in Katowice were harrowingly portrayed. The sense in the whole nation at that time of not knowing what was really going on permeated this powerful film.

Some of the bravery of those interned and threatened were communicated to Western journalists:

- 'They are fools if they think they can win; we are used to working underground.'
- 'Even if we are defeated, now we have shaken the whole system.'
- 'Tell the world not to recognize this illegal junta, not to send us aid through it, but please to send us aid against it.'
- 'Tell them to support the moderates in the Party as well as Solidarity.'

The grim world of internment and of social correction centres was experienced again in the land of Oswiecim and Majdanek. At Radom, 2,000 men were kept in below-freezing conditions in unheated tents, and deaths from exposure occurred. People returned to work only after intimidation or threats of violence.[20] Z. A. Pelcynski captured the present conditions in the Poland of that time in an article, 'Poland looks for a way forward from martial law'. Lech Walesa appealed to General Jaruzelski to abolish martial law, to declare a general amnesty, and to permit pluralism among trade unions. The Roman Catholic Church played a major part in moves towards restoring normalcy. A strike at the shipyard at Gdansk was stopped only by militarizing the plant. 'It will be years before the current mood of despondency and alienation lifts and the Solidarity generation becomes integrated into the system', Pelcynski concluded.[21]

BBC reporter Tim Sebastian's book *Nice Promises* captures something of the early 1980s in Poland. He describes the new Polish Cardinal Glemp's reactions after visiting an internment camp thus:

> Do you think it is easy for the Primate to go to such places and administer the sacrament and give out New Year wishes? It's terribly difficult. God's peace is needed to visit imprisoned people and bring them a beam of freedom, to try to make what happened at Bethlehem happen there. We know that many of our brothers have been dismissed because they refuse to resign from a legal trade union. It doesn't happen without violating human rights, without harm, without some kind of humiliation. A man has a natural right to his conscience and views.[22]

Or consider the following anecdotes Sebastian tells. At one Warsaw school, pupils marched around their playground in protest at the sacking of a pro-Solidarity teacher. At another, a military commissar told a class that Solidarity members 'were criminals and opposed the will of the State'. 'That's not true', said a child. 'My father was in Solidarity, and he wasn't a criminal.' The child was summarily ordered out of the classroom. As he went, the entire class got to its feet and walked out into the playground![23] No force can win, in the end, against such deep and widespread resistance.

8. Jerzy Popieluszko

Consider, too, the sermons of the remarkably brave Solidarity priest and martyr Father Jerzy Popieluszko, Poland's Oscar Romero. He typified the explicit support among many radical priests for Solidarity long after the repression. In 1980, at Cardinal Wyszynski's request, he had given Mass to striking steelworkers in the Warsaw steelworks. In February 1982 in the parish church of St. Stanislaw Kostka in Zoliborz, Warsaw, he conducted a monthly pro-Solidarity Mass for the Fatherland, attended by thousands. Poetry and religious and patriotic songs all featured at these defiant Christian pro-Solidarity rallies. When a young student, Gregorz Przemyk, was savaged to death by policemen on duty, it was Father Popieluszko who conducted his funeral and also spoke up for the imprisoned lawyer who had been employed by the murdered boy's mother. Thousands of mourners attended Gregorz's funeral. Father Popieluszko was eventually framed by the secret police and accused of harbouring an immense illegal arsenal in December 1983. He was later amnestied, but an intense campaign had already been stirred up against him in the media.

Death threats were received, and he was provided with a bodyguard laid on by the steelworkers themselves. On October 19, 1984, he fell into the hands of a group of secret policemen, functionaries of the Department for Religious Affairs. His brutally battered corpse was dragged from the river Vistula a few days later. In the church where he was a priest, set in a suburb of modern Warsaw, his grave and the church crypt remain a place of pilgrimage and a grim reminder of the real cost of the Solidarity years in Poland. When I visited it, a photograph of the mutilated and tortured body of this Christian leader, taken soon after his death, could be seen. The New Europe was bought with blood, and we should never forget this. A successful play on the trial of those responsible, *The Deliberate Death of a Polish Priest,* was televised early in 1987 on British television. The play was based on the 1,000-page transcript of the resulting trial. Slowly the court functionaries draw out from the thugs involved how Father Jerzy was hijacked, clubbed, trussed, gagged, beaten, dumped in the boot of a car, and then tipped, living, into a local reservoir weighed down by a lump of concrete. The reconstruction of the trial of his killers and the horrors of his killing come grippingly alive. So, at the time, the First World was given a glimpse of the horrors of events in the Poland of the 1980s.

There is in print a collection of Popieluszko's brave and highly political sermons entitled *The Price of Love.*[24] These reveal more of the courage of this man:

We must not remain silent when our culture, our art and literature, is treated with contempt by those responsible for the education of our children, when Christian morality is replaced by dubious Socialist morality.

Let us remember that a civilisation based on purely materialistic principles turns a man into a slave of production and robs him of his true and intrinsic value.

Let us have the courage to acknowledge Christ in public, to profess our loyalty to the Church, our faith in everything that makes up the glory of our nation; the courage to speak about it openly in the school, in the university, in the workshop as well as in the office.

The trial was a farce. This travesty of justice hurts deeply. It appears that it took more than a year to find those who, whilst on duty, savaged Gregorz, causing his death.

We stand here with a hope in our hearts that a rightful place will be found for God in our schools, offices, and factories; that truth, justice, and charity will become the uppermost values in the life of the State and nation.

Some may accuse me of involving myself in politics, but in a country where politics endeavour to penetrate, unhampered, all walks of life, then there is an additional reason why we should examine some matters from a moral point of view.[25]

With Christian leaders like Popieluszko around, it is little wonder Solidarity was never allowed to die.

9. Non-Violent Change

An interesting perspective on these years, and indeed on the whole Solidarity movement, is given by Paul Keim in an article he wrote for the Keston College journal *Religion in Communist Lands*. He entitled it 'A Polish strategy for non-violent change'. In it he quoted the Polish philosopher Leszek Kolakowski: 'Solidarity was not a peace movement, but it was a supremely peaceful movement'. Keim claims that, in Poland, non-violence

has emerged as a liberation movement using truth as a weapon and the overcoming of fear as a shield. It emphasises the importance of inner freedom, personal integrity, and sacrifice for others. The renunciation of violence as an effective and ethically justifiable means of bringing about social change is a central tenet of the movement.[26]

Keim quotes, in a similar vein, the Polish Youth Oasis or Light-Life Movement to good effect here:

> In choosing this way we unite ourselves with the world-wide movement for liberation through non-violence, which is engaged in the great work of freeing all people from all bondage and violence following the example of Christ as shown in the Gospels.[27]

Keim's perception into the nature of liberation is a deeply important insight:

> It must be emphasized that the primary focus of Poland's present struggle is liberation—personal, social, political, national. It has been in this context that a method of liberation has been developed which embodies the ends as part of the means. Peace and justice are won by peace and justice.[28]

Kolakowski himself, a one-time critic of Catholic philosophy in the 1950s who rejected his earlier Marxism, was 'purged' in the events of 1968. He reviewed the rôle played by Christianity in Poland in an article he wrote in 1979:

> The Church . . . has managed to preserve its independence from the State. Not surprisingly, it provided an outlet for all sorts of social and political discontent and, though it never encouraged any violent expression of opposition, it naturally absorbed . . . both the feelings of national humiliation that resulted from the forcible incorporation of Poland into the Soviet Empire and the people's passive resistance towards so oppressive and mendacious a power system.

> It cannot print what it would wish to, but (the Church) does not lie. In the atmosphere of all-pervading mendacity which poisons and distorts the public language of the entire Communist world, the language of Christianity has remained honest. We all know that the Catholic press is muzzled, but when we read it, we get the feeling of a breath of fresh air.

> This kind of coalescence of Christianity in its worldly aspects, with the human rights movement and democratic values, has never before been achieved. It might herald dramatic changes throughout the entire Christian world.[29]

The concerns of the Church for human rights and in the struggle for democracy, non-violently achieved, can also be traced as we have seen in the Latin America of the 1970s and 1980s. I believe, therefore, that Kolakowski is wrong in assuming that such a coalescence was unique to Poland. God had been leading others of his people in this direction also. We are clearly returning here to the central contention of this book, that the cause of liberation is a major call and move of the Living God across the world in the late twentieth century in all Three Worlds. The parallels with the non-violent resistance and protest of the theologians of liberation in Latin America are once again quite clear. And yet the Pope was only able to give unequivocal support to the liberation movements of the Second World and not to those in the Third. This seems an inconsistency to say the least. Strange, too, how some First World Christians consider this social and political action to have been dangerous and wrong in Latin America and yet hail proudly the same processes in Poland or elsewhere in the Second World. Who can fathom the human heart?

10. Poland Enters the New Europe

In August 1989 the next phase in Poland's postwar history began. Anne Applebaum earlier in that month had reported for *The Independent* from Warsaw and had pointed out that prices remained bizarre for Polish people. The average monthly salary was then approximately £9. Some pensioners were struggling to live on just £2.50p a month. Imported vodka cost £1.26p, bananas 60p, a kilo of ham—still heavily subsidized—50p with queues at butchers lasting up to four hours and with their shops empty by midday. Such was Poland at the beginning of the 1990s.[30] Bierut, Gomulka, Gierek, and even Jaruzelski were leaders of the past. The Soviet Bear was no longer the threat it had been, or at least not as long as *perestroika* and *glasnost* (reconstruction and openness) remained the order of the day. Foreign debts were enormous, making a Third World economy in the Second World. The Party was bankrupt in more ways than one. A new Solidarity-led government was imminent, with a hopeful, courageous, dignified, but battered and bruised people to lead. This was the Poland that Tadeusz Mazowiecki inherited on Wednesday, August 23, 1989.

'Poland enters democratic era', read *The Independent*'s front page. Steve Crawshaw and Anne Applebaum went on to report:

> Finally yesterday it came: the brave and fearful leap into the unknown that breaks all the rules of the post-war anti-democratic game. Poland became the first country in East Europe to end the era of one-party rule that the region has suffered for four decades. Today the country has a new prime minister: Tadeusz Mazowiecki, the Catholic editor who advised Lech Walesa in 1980 and who was interned by General Wojciech Jaruzelski for a year under martial law.
>
> Mr Mazowiecki told parliament that changes had come about because 'society does not agree to live as it has done until now'; he spoke of the critical

state of the economy and pleaded with the West to look kindly upon Poland's attempts at painful economic reform. 'The friends of Poland should realize that they cannot wait until we start drowning'.[31]

Stirring and true words these. Within a year it was Mazowiecki who had drowned in the sea of Poland's social and economic difficulties in the post-liberation process. The rush to democracy had created so many political parties that the Sejm, the Polish Parliament, had become almost ungovernable except through unlikely Party coalitions. Mazowiecki's disagreements with the incoming president did not help either. This chapter ends with the declaration of Lech Walesa as Poland's next president after a landslide victory in the second ballot held on the 10th of December 1990. A Nelson Mandela kind of story this—the one-time prisoner comes back to lead his country. His presidency, as we now know, was not a happy one.

The contention of this book is that the *evangel*, the Good News, must be for the individual, for the family, for the community, for the people of God, for the nation, and for the world. In the postwar liberation struggles of the deeply Christian country of Poland, we can see perhaps more clearly than anywhere else in the world the full implications of what that can mean in practice. Post-war Poland is, I believe, an inspiring visual aid to the world. I dare to affirm that God was at work through her, so bringing about the collapse of an ideology that had held much of the world in political, economic, and spiritual bondage for more than seventy years. The *domino-collapse effect* of the Eastern Europe Communist régimes in the late 1980s began in Poland. God worked through trade unionists, journalists, academics, students, and working people to undermine and then overturn a bankrupt ideology and régime. God used the Church and its bishops and priests for nearly five decades in Poland as the principal Opposition Party and as the conscience of a whole nation. The consequence was the liberation of Europe.

This too is evangelization. Here, surely, we see as clearly as anywhere in twentieth-century history the interplay between Church and Kingdom, between God active in history creating a New Society and God active in and through the Church's history in a partnership to help secure these ends. The Christian God is *out there*, active in 'the world', and not just *in here* gathered with the faithful few or even the many. Had we but the eyes to see as Christians, we would discern God to be as active in community, regional, and national politics as in our prayer meetings, evangelistic events, and sermon preparations. How sad that we continue instead so often to compartmentalize these two worlds as sacred or secular. But God mercifully defies all our attempts to categorize and contain him.

Poland is a fascinating nation. My wish is for the twenty-first century to see it happier and beginning at last to prosper: 'Long Live Polska', and long may it remain faithful to the Christian faith, whatever the end of one century and the beginning of a new millennium may bring.

Notes

[1]Norman Davies, *God's Playground. A History of Poland. Volume II: 1795 to the Present* (Oxford University Press, Oxford, 1981), pp. 207-208.

[2]Trevor Beeson, *Discretion and Valour* (Fount Paperbacks, Collins, London, 1977).

[3]Richard Davy, 'The Pope's Poland', *New Society*, 24 May 1979.

[4]Davies, *God's Playground*, p. 224.

[5]Davies instances several examples in *God's Playground*, chap. 9.

[6]Ibid., p. 615.

[7]Stefan Wyszynski, *A Freedom Within. The Prison Notes of Stefan Cardinal Wyszynski*, with an introduction by Malcolm Muggeridge (Hodder & Stoughton, London, 1985). See Michael Bochenski, 'Notes from prison which point us to freedom', *The Baptist Times*, 11 April 1985.

[8]Stefan Wyszynski, *A Freedom Within*, p. 51.

[9]Ibid., p. 124.

[10]Ibid., p. 24.

[11]Ibid., p. 71.

[12]Ibid., p. 147.

[13]Ibid., p. 253.

[14]Ibid., p. 163.

[15]Neal Ascherson, *The Polish August* (The Viking Press, New York, 1981–1982), p. 118.

[16]Davies, *God's Playground*, p. 615.

[17]Ascherson, *The Polish August*, p. 192.

[18]Quoted in Ascherson, *The Polish August*, p. 222.

[19]Ibid., p. 278.

[20]Michael Yardely, 'They call it war', *New Society*, January 1982.

[21]Z. A. Pelcynski, 'Poland looks forward for a way from martial law', *New Society*, December 1982.

[22]Tim Sebastian, *Nice Promises* (Chatto & Windus, London, 1985), p. 195.

[23]Ibid., p. 132.

[24]Jerzy Popieluszko, *The Price of Love* (Veritas, Catholic Truth Society, London, 1985).

[25]Quotations are from sermons recorded in Popieluszko, *The Price of Love*, pp. 9, 30, 33-34, 42, 50.

[26]Paul Keim, 'A Polish strategy for non-violent change', *Religion in Communist Lands*, 11/2 (1983), p. 162.

[27]Cited in Keim, 'A Polish strategy', p. 162.

[28]Ibid., p. 166.

[29]The full text of Kolakowski's article can be found in K. M. Olszer, *For Your Freedom and Ours: Polish Progressive Spirit from the 14th Century to the Present* (Ungar Publishing Co., USA, 1981), pp. 335-341.

[30]Anne Applebaum, writing in *The Independent*, 2 August 1989.

[31]Steve Crawshaw and Anne Applebaum, writing in *The Independent*, 24 April, 1989.

Chapter 4
The First World
Britain, 1970–1990

1. The Two Britains

None of us are given a choice as to where we are born. If we were, I would choose Britain again. I love the beauty of its countryside, its cities and towns, its sense of history, its culture, and its character. Why though such an introduction? Because it will give balance and an alternative perspective to what follows. There is a good and healthy Christian patriotism that is not the same as the xenophobic nationalism with which it is often—pitifully—confused. I am glad, very glad, that my father chose these shores to make his home and that this country received him and gave him a home and a future. I am proud to have been born here and, prouder still, to have found Christ here. I am proud to be British as well as European. There is, however, another Britain. Some wake up to its agonies and pain each day, each month, each year, even as others of us wake up to a very different and—probably—more Comfortable Britain. What does the Gospel have to say to these two Britains: the Other Britain and Comfortable Britain? What does the Gospel of the Risen Christ have to say to us as one nation as we move through the 1990s and approach the new century and millennium?

As we have already seen from our studies of Latin America and Poland, we can be helped by the tools of social and political description and analysis as we begin to discern the situation around us. We need in Britain to experience *conscientization*. What follows, drawing on a variety of sources, is an attempt to paint a picture of this Other Britain. Some readers will not need to picture it. You are it, and it is you. Others of us in Comfortable Britain may find the process more shocking.

2. *Unemployment*

One of the finest books on the Other Britain of the 1970s and 1980s was a book called *Unemployment*, written by Jeremy Seabrook. My copy was bought in memory of a member of the church in Cowley, Oxford, where I then ministered —Sid Joseph. A Welsh miner, Sid was eventually killed by the coal dust he had breathed in in the valley pits in earlier life. Sid had made Cowley his home and built a family there in the decades since he had left Wales, like so many, in search of work. Parts of Cowley were known as 'little Wales' in the 1930s and 1940s. Sid talked to me, when we had opportunity, of Wales in the 1920s and 1930s; of the humiliations of the means test; of the grinding poverty many knew then and of the indignities of unemployment. His stories moved me then and still move me now. A life-long Socialist, Sid died an unhappy man. He could see all around him, as the unemployment figures soared, history repeating itself. He had given his whole life to the Church, the Trade Union, and the Socialist Movement, to fighting against the conditions and politics that had bred such misery for him and for many in earlier decades. 'What has it all been for?' he would ask, sometimes with tears in his eyes. His widow, Grace, and daughter, Mary, gave me a book token after I had conducted his funeral. I had grown to respect Jeremy Seabrook's writings in *New Society* magazine very much. His book had not long been published. It was an obvious choice.

This is a tough, aggressive book. Its prose—often using the words of the other Britain uncensored and undiluted—may well be considered shocking by some. Sanitizing the vocabulary may make some readers more comfortable but only renders the account less authentic, less passionate, less effective. The Bible writers knew how to use such descriptive, coarse realism also.[1] In *Unemployment* Jeremy Seabrook describes and contrasts unemployment in the 1930s with that of the early 1980s; in fact, his writing is at times reminiscent of George Orwell's *The Road to Wigan Pier* (1937).

We should note the date of this book's publication: 1982. It is interesting to see that Seabrook saves most of his anger and criticism not for the then 'new' prime minister, Mrs. Thatcher. She, as we now know, had calculated that unemployment was the price many in the nation would have to pay if her administration's policies to tackle inflation and regenerate the economy were to succeed. But it is, rather, against the Labour Party and the failures of post-war Socialism that Seabrook most strongly inveighs. His claim, quite simply, is that the British Labour Party had failed its most loyal supporters and had left them a broken and defeated force, ill-equipped to face the ravages of unemployment and the new monetarism sweeping then through the economy. He wrote as much with former Labour Prime Ministers Callaghan and Wilson in mind as with Heath or Thatcher.

Before writing, Seabrook spent months living with different families in areas hard hit by unemployment. In an earlier book, *City Close-Up* (1971), he had done similar participant journalism in Blackburn. Seabrook talked in pubs, in homes, on council estates, in job centres, and in shopping precincts. He talked to the redundant; to frustrated school leavers; to many angry, bitter, hope-less people. His writings point beyond the propaganda, the party-political games with unemployment statistics, the politicians' use and abuse of facts and figures. They point us unequivocally to the realities of the lives affected by those times. Some of the First World poor find here a voice and a writer. Indeed Seabrook dedicates his book to 'the warmth and resilience of people, temporarily discarded by a society that does them the injury of not knowing where its real resources lie'.[2] The whole book is a painful, provocative, alarming answer to one basic question: What happens to people in a society based on the necessity for work when work ceases to be available? It transcends a concern with unemployment alone in the process. As the writer tells the tales, we hear people's pleas and their desperation. Their words may sound again in our ears at the parting of the sheep and goats:

> It is the context that gives poverty its definition. To see a child doing his homework by the light of a street lamp on a freezing December evening because the electricity in his home has been cut off; to hear the half-sad, half-proud voice of a mother saying of a handicapped three-year-old child, 'He's just had his first clothing grant', as though it were a rite of passage from infancy to childhood; to listen to the woman whose husband has been out of work for five years, and who allows herself one pot of tea that has to last all day—all this would not be shocking if you felt it served some other purpose than the humiliation of those who suffer it. But it doesn't. As one poorly paid railway worker said, 'Poverty has become a crime'.[3]

> A man of about forty and a woman some ten years younger were eating out of the dustbins behind the Commodore cinema and gnawing at detritus from a nearby Indian restaurant. The man was wearing a tattered, greasy suit; the woman was disheveled and dirty, without stockings, wearing odd shoes and a man's gabardine raincoat. She was opening up the plastic sacks, thrusting her arm inside and retrieving a half-eaten bone, some handfuls of saffron-coloured rice still with its sprinkling of peas. It's no use saying that there is no need for people to have to live like that: for some—those who have no address from which to claim Social Security, those on the run, those too far corroded by alcohol, those who despair—there isn't a choice.[4]

Seabrook's outstanding book is full of anecdotes that do far more than bring home the grim realities of unemployment to us. They paint a picture of the Britain of the 1980s for Europeans. The recurring theme of the book is that, in return for the many consumer goods of capitalism, the working classes have allowed themselves to be effectively depoliticized. Now, they serve the political purposes of others.

> It seems that the purpose of the poor now is more nakedly ideological: Their purpose is to be poor. Not to produce, but simply to serve as a contrast, a defining edge for wealth and success, a warning and example to the rest.[5]

These same consumer goods now mock the unemployed through their television screen adverts. The best of working class culture, he argues, has been denuded: unity, community, solidarity, frugality, dignity, caring. Fragmented communities living private lives in private homes and experiencing much misery is the end product

The restlessness, anger, bitterness; the elasticity of time; the stretching to breaking point of family love; neighbours informing on neighbours to 'the Social'; a nation and the working class itself divided into two groups defined by whether or not they work; redundancy settlements that meant, in effect, the selling of children's and grandchildren's jobs and those of a whole community; the struggles of trade unionists; race tensions and the uglier sides of British racism; suicides. These are all described, documented, and communicated. Noted, too, are what the writer feels to be the platitudes and the naivety of the political left, ignorant so often of what was really happening: 'The emotional withdrawal of people from the Labour Party has come about because Labour has presided as serenely over these losses as the Conservatives'.[6] Yet the uncaring insensitivity of too much of the political right does not escape either. This is not the whole Britain of course. It is a significant part and a story that First World Christians need to listen to, again and again, if we are to take at all seriously the praxis of the historical Jesus and the Bible's message of liberation.

3. Eyes Half-Open

Similar in tone and style is the work of Pat Barker. So often it is novels, films, and plays that bring home the conditions of deprivation and poverty that still obtain in contemporary Britain. Steinbeck's *Grapes of Wrath* did this for the American poor. J. M. Coetzee's *The Life and Times of Michael K* or Nadine Gordimer's *Burger's Daughter* did so for South Africa. Dickens' novels did much the same for Victorian England. Pat Barker's novels are stories of the Other Britain, the one that many never see or never want to realize exists. *Union Street* (1982) describes life in the 1970s for several women in a northern town. This is life as it is, painted with coarse realism, and not for the squeamish. Her book *The Century's Daughter* (1986) is in a similar vein, superbly crafted and highly memorable. It concerns Liza Jarrett, born on the stroke of midnight 1899/1900 and now recounting her life story to a pre-occupied social worker whose attention wanders.

Why do so many of us go through life with our eyes only half-open? Why are so many of us blind to the Other Britain? Farrukh Dhondy's collection of short stories, *Come to Mecca* (1978), captures life in multi-ethnic Britain of this period more effectively than countless government statistics and reports. Writings by disabled people, similarly, give us a very different perspective on the Britain we live in. Christy Nolan's *Under the Eye of the Clock* (1987) reminds us powerfully of the secret knowledge and creativity that might so easily never have surfaced were it not for the belief in Christy of his mother Nora.[7] Or consider Jack Jones' autobiography *Union Man* (1986) with its vigorous campaign for the cause of the elderly among the First World poor. The First World's casualties are all around us . . . if we would but open our eyes.

4. The World of Work

The Other Britain to which many Christians are blind often includes the realms of industry and commerce. Peter Mayhew, whom I met during my Oxford years, ploughed an often lonely furrow trying to open Christian eyes to parts of society we were prone to ignore, neglect, or dismiss as 'secular', and therefore as not so important as worship or Bible study! Peter had traveled the country to visit our industries and to listen to and record the views of trade unionists, managers, and factory workers for his book *Justice in Industry*.[8] This account, too, opens eyes.

When I interviewed Peter on his concern that Christians should understand more about where so many people spend their working lives, he shared his impression that too many companies were cursed with bad management. When pressed, he unpacked that statement: in some places there were poor communication skills, little care for the work force, a failure to value it properly, and so a distance from the very people on whom the company's future depends. Peter felt strongly that one way forward was training in company time for the leaders of industry, especially managers and shop-stewards. All leaders needed some training in economics, human psychology and relations, industrial law, and workers' rights. When it came to the Church, Christian concern for industry was often the 'Lazarus at the gate' when it came to using denominational resources. 'Theological training itself needs revolutionising', he said. 'It is almost all too middle-class orientated'. In a later book, *Unemployment Under the Judgement of God,* which he was struggling to get published when I met him, he reflects on the importance of work from a psychological, spiritual, and theological perspective. Anger against the indignities of unemployment breathes through its pages. It also calls for determined attempts to eradicate unemployment entirely, naive as this still sounds in the late 1990s:

> We need now to persuade people that the cause of removing the scourge of unemployment is a good cause and one worthy of sacrifice. I am arguing for a drastic and radical manner of dealing with the cancer of mass unemployment. I am asking all sorts of people—trade unionists and employers, MPs, Christians—to consider very seriously whether work sharing on a big scale may not be far better for society as a whole than a system which is seemingly resigned to mass unemployment for years to come. I am asking for thorough

research, for education for both sides of industry, for painstaking thought for all who have any sort of social conscience within the community.[9]

Unemployment is seen as a disease, a cancer. He argues that construction and reconstruction work, in providing housing and investing generally in the infrastructure of the country, is part of the solution. So are work sharing, tax penalties upon overtime, thirty-five-hour weeks, and no inevitable annual pay rounds for those privileged to have work. All of this and more must be done, Mayhew suggests, in order to redistribute the work more equitably.

It may seem strange that an Anglo-Catholic Socialist should be more concerned to attempt to redefine work and to eradicate unemployment than many workers, trade unionists, and the government of the day. Perhaps it is ever thus that God speaks and challenges through people who go on speaking his Word even if they are persistently ignored. As Mayhew pleads:

> For the community's sake, for the individual's sake, and for God's sake, mass unemployment must be eliminated. Because it is evil, God must surely be concerned, and he will truly be served by the curing of it.[10]

5. The Experience of Struggling to Survive

Bob Laken tried also to open Christian eyes in his book *More than a Friend*.[11] This funny and sad book is the account of his work as a community-based social worker who was motivated and sustained on a housing estate by his Christian faith. He writes of work with young people's clubs, broken families, teenagers in borstal, single mothers struggling to survive, and petty crime rife everywhere. He also writes about the little chapel they adopted, open house, and countless cups of tea. He charts the dependence/rejection syndrome that social workers and other counsellors will recognise and describes conversions to a faith that not only changed individuals but had some impact on the community as well.

The literature of the Other Britain is all around us, in frequent television screenplays and in the pages of the newspapers. There *are* none so blind as those who will not see. It is in this Britain and its other European equivalents that we should be 'doing theology'. Here—especially but not exclusively—we shall find the Lord Christ. It is the concerns of such people, such communities that should be setting the agenda for our churches and our evangelization. The Other Britain is all around each one of us. It is there in the experiences of the 5 percent of our nation who are not white and in their attempts to be integrated in this nation that belongs as much to them as to those of us with white skins:

On the coffee table, Mr. Khan lays out a newspaper, and from a carrier bag he takes out some of the bricks that have been thrown through his window in recent months: two half-bricks, green with lichen, and two pieces of concrete studded with pebbles and stones. Mr. Khan sits in the armchair, nursing his oldest daughter, a handicapped twelve-year-old, with her dark hair swept up into a cockade on top of her head and tied with a silver lurex ribbon. He rocks and kisses her, stroking her face as he speaks. . . . You hear the little ones chanting 'Paki, Paki', even children of eight or nine. . . . I had fireworks through my letter box. I had to seal the letterbox each night because I was afraid the house might catch fire. The worst was when a brick came through the bedroom window and was within six inches of my wife. We began to sit up half the night. . . . You have no idea of what it can do to you, how badly it can affect you. My wife was pregnant at the time. She had a nervous break-down and had to go to the hospital, and, as a result of that, she had a miscarriage.[12]

The Other Britain also includes many elderly people who have poured their lives into rebuilding postwar Britain and are now on the margins of society, struggling to pay their bills. It is there in the single parents' tightening the belt again as child benefit is effectively frozen a few more temperature points. It is there in the mentally ill people 'decanted' back into the community, bewildered and afraid, years of institutionalization suddenly undone after a policy whim from on high. Some will survive, and some will thrive in such a Britain, but what of the others? The Other Britain is there in the hospital waiting list, in the person released prematurely from the hospital because 'throughput' is all important now and because beds are short as the Area Health Authority's ability to purchase services runs out. It is there in those desperately struggling at home so as not to bother the hard-pressed community nurse again. There too is the nagging pressure to pay into the private health sector and 'get it done more quickly'. It is there in a teenager still unable to read or write after years of poor 'education' behind him or her. It is there in the handicapped person's dignified struggles to make his or her way against the obstacles placed in the way of employment.

The Other Britain is exhausted from paper rounds or weekend work in the shop, daydreaming in schools on a Monday. It is working seventy hours a week to pay a mortgage and being told 'not to be greedy', whilst senior executives' expenses claims alone amount to what others earn in a month. It is bored kids vacantly offering their veins to the crack dealers and their bodies to the punters so as to stay on the move and fill the stomach or the vein. It is the mother and several children in a bed-and-breakfast hostel, crammed into a damp space twelve feet square to sleep, play, work, and furtively eat. It is on the dole queue, rejection slip in the pocket, and no bike to get on, nowhere to go.

These are the First World 'poor'. We just pretend not to see them. Many of us hide in our homes and our churches and offer our prayers for Her Majesty's government, whatever its hue. Life goes on 'as normal' for those of us who are the comfortable of Comfortable Britain. The two nations exist side by side in our churches; they co-exist but rarely meet.

6. *Bias to the Poor*

In 1983, Hodder and Stoughton published David Sheppard's book *Bias to the Poor*. It was perhaps the first major British book of the 1980s to begin to try and transpose into the British scene some of what the theologians of liberation were saying. It was also backed up by a lifetime's praxis. The book draws on Bishop David's experiences in London and Liverpool and directs the Church's attention to a number of the problems of the inner city. It points to the desperate housing needs of Britain in the 1980s, to the ugliness of racism and its debilitating effects, to the issues of unemployment and the future of work, and to the importance of industrial mission and to the value of wealth-creation but only if backed up by a just and fair welfare state:

> Christians should take a lead in a public campaign to change the assumption that everyone pays their taxes grudgingly and unwillingly. Taxation is a proper way by which wealth is distributed more fairly and by which the poor and the whole of society are given better opportunities. A scheme of international taxation is needed if the enormous gap between rich and poor nations is to be lessened.[13]

We shall return to this Christian view of taxation when we consider, in the final part of this guide, the new internationalism that will be needed in the twenty-first century.

Again this is an eye-opener of a book. It draws on much biblical material to make the contention that God has a divine bias to the disadvantaged. It also appeals both to Church and to nation to transform their structures so as to reflect this divine bias more in their priorities, lifestyle, and action:

> More affluent Christians must be seen to stand for justice on behalf of the poor, even when that may be to the disadvantage of themselves and of their families. Only then will many of the poor believe that the Christ whom the churches preach could be for them.[14]

Bishop David Sheppard devotes a whole chapter in this book to liberation theology. He emphasizes a central insight, that those currently on the margins must become the focal point of the Church's mission. Occasional acts of charity are not enough: 'If the concerns of the Christian community are to reflect those of its founder, [the Church] must put the needs of the poor at the centre of its worship and of its study and activity'.[15] Christians must work and pray both for the change of the individual and the system. Suspicion and anger from the poor themselves, at least initially, may be experienced. So may harsh criticisms from those who find it easier to blame the alienated themselves for their plight. Accusations of undermining society may also follow. Ours, he points out, must be the way of reconciliation in all this.

His appeal in this book to Mrs. Thatcher and her Cabinet of the early 1980s was clear and forthright: 'It is not more surveys or speeches about concern that are wanted. The needs of the urban poor are well-known. What is wanted is the political will to act'.[16] The government should actually act upon the considerable research evidence it already has before commissioning any more, he argued. The Incarnation also makes our priorities as Christians clear. We must seek, as Christians, to live like 'God taking flesh in the Person of Jesus, living out his life in a special relation to the poor'.[17]

7. Faith in the City

Faith in the City—a Call for Action by Church and Nation was published in 1985 by Church House Publishing. This report, commissioned by the archbishops of the Church of England, was a powerful piece of conscientization in itself. The following extracts will serve to bring this call to the nation to mind and life for us. For some, they will be a reminder of the report itself; for others, perhaps a further awakening to the Britain we still all live in a decade or so later. The tone is well set in the report's introduction:

> We have to report that we have been deeply disturbed by what we have seen and heard. We have been confronted with the human consequences of unemployment, which in some urban areas may be over 50 percent of the labour force, and which occasionally reaches a level as high as 80 percent—consequences which may be compounded by the effects of racial discrimination. We have seen physical decay, whether of Victorian terraced housing or of inferior system-built blocks of flats, which has in places created an environment so degrading that some people have set fire to their own homes rather than be condemned to live in them indefinitely. Social disintegration has reached a point in some areas that shop windows are boarded up, cars cannot be left on the street, residents are afraid either to go out themselves or to ask others in, and there is a pervading sense of powerlessness and despair.[18]

Some of the nations' housing estates are tellingly described:

Huge impersonal housing estates, many post-war, can be found in all our cities. They are often spoken of as being monochrome—that is, drab, dreary, and depressing, with no vitality, colour, or beauty. Many outer estates are nothing less than the architect-designed, system-built slums of our postwar era. They suffer from poor design, defects in construction, poor upkeep of public areas, no 'defensible space'; with packs of dogs roaming around, filth in the stairwells, one or two shuttered shops, and main shopping centres a twenty-minute expensive bus journey away. Unemployment rates are typically 30-40 percent and rising. Bored, out-of-work young people turn to vandalism, drugs, and crime—the estate takes the brunt, and the spiral of decline is given a further twist.[19]

Equally vividly recorded is the world of bed-and-breakfast hostels:

Well over 10,000 families a year are being placed by local authorities in this kind of accommodation, often in a single room. Environmental health officers have found appalling conditions—gross overcrowding, cockroaches, bathrooms without hot water, dangerous fire risks. A large number of the hotels inspected have been classified as unfit for human habitation.[20]

Elderly people are among the most vulnerable in the Other Britain:

The evidence we received from Age Concern spoke of 'the particular complexities generated by increasing political conflict, the breakdown of traditional employment and living patterns, and the lurking tensions between different races and cultures' which characterise the special needs of elderly people living in urban areas.[21]

British children also suffer neglect and deprivation:

Poor and inappropriate housing, unhealthy surroundings, and lack of play space in Urban Priority Areas (UPAs) make life for young children less than satisfactory and sometimes hazardous. In UPAs they will more often than in other areas be the children of single parents and may lack stimulation and amenities. They are likely to reach primary school at the age of five already considerably disadvantaged in comparison with their contemporaries. To say this is not to say anything which is not widely recognised.[22]

Some from within the so-called ethnic minorities also experience the pain of the Other Britain daily:

Black people continue to receive humiliating and discriminatory treatment from their white fellow citizens in many areas of daily life. Manifestations of racial prejudice are liable to occur in every branch of society and in every institution (including the Church) in Britain today. Such treatment is stoically endured by the great majority of black people.[23]

Some of the problems faced by British youth are similarly and painfully outlined:

[Youth unemployment] has a particularly damaging effect on teacher and pupil morale in certain UPA secondary schools where, for the majority of pupils, the prospect of finding employment is remote. Teachers in UPA schools throughout the country have told us how difficult it is to sustain motivation, especially with their more senior pupils. The pupils we spoke to were friendly and articulate, but in general had little optimism about finding employment. Their apparent acceptance of the situation gave us great cause for concern.[24]

Drugs remain a growing menace in the various youth cultures:

What has caused this kind of drug addiction to invade our cities? Doubtless the sheer availability of drugs and the activity of drug pushers are a major cause; but we cannot doubt that the social deprivation and level of unemployment particularly among young people which we have seen in the UPAs is a crucial factor. Vigilance by customs officers, severe sentences for grave offenders, specialised school and medical care, and responsible education on drugs in schools all have a part to play in responding to drug abuse; but we are convinced that the underlying problem must be the conditions of the UPA themselves.[25]

Faith in the City is a moving document. It presents an agenda for this country for the twenty-first century and for Europe too. God was speaking, I believe, to the Britain of the mid-1980s through it. We may dare to suppose that it was part of the Risen Lord's strategy for the evangelization of Britain—the God we have discerned at work in the Poland of much the same period of time—for God is as much concerned for the world of work and politics as for that of the baptismal class and candlelight carol service. A choice of two ways was offered to our nation and its churches. We could continue the move towards two Britains with the wedge between them created in the 1970s and early 1980s pressed in ever more firmly, or we could return to 'One Nation' thinking and make our priority the First World deprivation all around us. *Faith in the City* with its challenge to church and nation offered this choice as clearly, as irenically, as passionately as any document could possibly do. That it has been largely ignored by successive governments and by large parts of the British Church scene does not make it any the less God's voice. The Bible is full of the words of prophets ignored, of lessons learned too late if at all. The commission asserts in one place in the report that we have lost one decade already. Now it is two.

8. *Faith in the Countryside*

In 1990 the companion volume to *Faith in the City* was published, entitled *Faith in the Countryside*. This second Anglican Commission sought to integrate insights about God, Creation, and Wholeness (*shalom*) with the concerns of rural Britain. This book was published at the height of the Green Movement with its cornucopia of environmental concerns. The report expresses this as well as painting a far-from-idyllic portrait of rural Britain in the 1990s:

> For some, the countryside can be a limiting and narrow existence, especially for those who have no transport of their own, whose children have left the village or who live in inaccessible areas or in villages where the 'community spirit' is a hollow sham.[26]

A contemporary scenario of the Other (rural) Britain is painted:

- Resentments against 'incomers'
- Tenant farmers unable to retire and so lose their tied cottages
- The absence of small businesses in rural areas
- Village shops undermined and closed by superstores
- Projected figures of as few as 60,000-70,000 professional farmers only by the end of the 1990s
- Rural road systems under threat from the increase in traffic
- The plight of elderly and low-paid workers in rural areas
- The sale of rural council houses on a one-off basis piling up housing problems for the next generation
- Post office closures
- Longer drives to hospitals as more and more National Service ones are 'rationalized'

All these issues are considered before this conclusion is reached:

> There is much goodwill in rural areas, but it needs to be focussed politically and with an understanding that rural life needs a proper share of resources even if deprivation is hard to see and the lot of a minority. . . . the government must govern in the interest of the whole community and not just for those who brought it to power.[27]

In its address to the rural church, the Archbishops' Commission appealed for more flexibility and creativity of approach in evangelizing rural Britain. The parish system is not the only viable model, it asserted. Ecumenical partnership and co-operation between parishes may be the way of the future. Speaking both to rural and urban churches, the Commission recognized that a majority of the population has some kind of religious faith, but that the Church as a whole in Britain has generally failed to inspire. The British people have become largely disconnected from us all. The challenge to reverse these trends remains a priority for us all and not just in the Decade of Evangelism.[28] *Faith in the City* and *Faith in the Countryside* provide us, it can be argued, with many of the materials upon which a fully Christian evangelization of part of the New Europe—Britain—will need to be built.

9. *Better Together*

David Sheppard and Derek Worlock, respectively the Anglican Bishop and Roman Catholic Archbishop of Liverpool, were surely two of the most outstanding Christian leaders of the British Church to emerge in recent decades. I see them as men raised up by God to challenge and speak to a whole nation and to the many Christian communities it contains. To them we must certainly add the names of some northwestern Free Church leaders such as the Baptist Area Superintendent, Trevor Hubbard,[29] and especially the Methodist Superintendent, John Newton, who formed a 'third' in the team in Liverpool. The Liverpool Diocese has, more successfully than perhaps anywhere else in Britain, seen the coming together of the three great Christian traditions of these islands—Anglican, Free Church, and Roman Catholic—in partnership and in a commitment to serve a whole city. The process is described in *Better Together—Christian Partnership in a Hurt City* (1988), which received the ultimate accolade for a religious book: being reprinted in a popular 'Penguin' paperback edition. The episcopal team has now, sadly, been broken by the death of Derek Worlock in early 1996.

In Merseyside, some of the principles that inspired *Faith in the City* had been first put into practice. Here an ecumenical evangelization with a vision of a New Society for the 1990s had begun. As the two church leaders put it,

> On our appointment to Liverpool it seemed right to both of us that, given Liverpool's sectarian history, it must be right for us to give higher priority than ever before to ecumenical relations and the work of reconciliation which must be involved.[30]

In words that echo one of the key themes of this study, they write that the renewal and unity of the Church and the renewal and unity of the human community are closely linked:

> It is our belief that often it has been the common concern of the churches for the real problems of how people in Merseyside live, which has led to a lessening of the old sectarian hatreds and to the beginning of a desire for Christian unity.[31]

Social problems too are tackled better together:

> There is nothing directly denominational about social problems. The challenge is to all people of good will. For Christians the response is more effective when it is undertaken ecumenically. The need is immediate.[32]

As a docker put it when asked the meaning of ecumenism: 'I suppose it's them two bishops standing up for our jobs'! The bishops wrote soon after the Swanwick ecumenical breakthrough that, as we now know, was to result in the death of the old-style British Council of Churches (BCC) and the birth of new national Ecumenical Instruments in 1990, Churches Together in England (CTE), and the Council of Churches in Britain and Ireland (CCBI), which included for the first time Roman Catholic and black-led churches as full members within the British ecumenical movement. The questions they put to themselves again and again in Merseyside are the very ones that the Risen Lord is surely addressing to all his people in the Decade of Evangelization:

- What activities could you effectively do together that at present you do separately?
- What does your church still wish to do separately and why?
- What areas of Christian work might you carry out on behalf of other believers?
- What can all of you do together, which should be done, but that, as yet, none of you are doing?

Here is a very practical ecumenism, a living out of the high-priestly prayer of John 17—'that they may all be one'—rather than stale arguments about what it *really* means. Here, too, is a Christian faith that is for individual, community, city, nation, continent, and world. The Liverpool story over the past decade is well told. We live imaginatively through its key moments: the joint Church leaders' meetings; the reduction of Catholic/Protestant sectarianism, at least in places; a higher Christian profile in both the community and the media; prayer and worship together, and growing friendships; the Toxteth riots; Michael

Heseltine's visits as a Tory Government minister concerned with urban renewal; the 'Militant' crisis in the Labour Party; the bankruptcy of a city; the housing problems; the indignities of unemployment; the Heysels Stadium tragedies and the act of contrition the bishops and other civic leaders undertook in Turin; the flower festival; the Pope's visit and the Queen's visit. In this process David Sheppard and Derek Worlock became known to local councillors, to Cabinet ministers, and to the local and national media. That story remains the main challenge to the new ecumenical instruments midway through the Decade of Evangelization, and the rationale for them. Here is ecumenical praxis at its finest and a glimpse of the kind of Christianity that deserves to survive the transition into the twenty-first century. We have seen the future . . . and it works:

> All the efforts to achieve Christian unity will add up to no more than a busy, highly-organised, institutional amalgam of Christian communities and churches unless there is at the same time an inward journey towards the mind and mystery of Christ through prayer and the Christian life. On the other hand, the result will be inward-looking, pre-occupied with our own church's experiences, unless there is also an outward journey into God's world. The journey Christians are to make together must continue in the context of mission, with a consciousness of God sending us out into the world.[33]

10. Individual Standards

In February 1988, Douglas Hurd, who was then the British Home Secretary and later became a most distinguished Foreign Secretary, spoke to a fringe meeting of the General Synod of the Church of England. 'I do not agree with those who say that the Church should not comment on political and social problems', he said. 'It has always had that right and will continue to exercise it.' He went on to urge that when Church leaders use that right they must regard themselves as having come down from the pulpit and must be prepared to engage in the 'rough and tumble' of political debate with politicians. He then proceeded to enter into the 'give and take' of the debate himself. Below is a little of what he had to say. His remarks clearly come from a different Christian perspective from the one I have been developing myself and give a somewhat different assessment of the Thatcher years in the Britain of the 1970s and 1980s. He emphasizes individual values and responsibilities, and while this cannot be the whole story, I believe it is an aspect that also offers a considerable challenge to the Britain and Europe of the next century. Here are some extracts from his address:

The content of politics shifts all the time, and it is our job as politicians to come to terms with this. In contrast, the Church's message is timeless and should have a stronger foundation than these shifting sands. That, it seems to me as a layman, is the weakness of the liberation theology. That, no doubt, is why our Lord, when offered a political rôle by those who wanted a political messiah, so clearly refused it.

It often strikes me that many of those who commit violent crimes seem genuinely to have no sense whatsoever of the consequences of their actions. To them, it is as if the old lady whom they assault, the young boy whom they abduct, the rival whom they stab is simply a target, a stuffed doll without human emotions. There is no sense in many of them of the suffering which their violence can cause. This can only be because from neither their parents, nor their school, nor from any television at which they goggle hour after hour, nor from any influence upon them have they gained the simplest inkling that every human being is worthy of respect and that the infliction of suffering is a sin whether or not the offender is caught. The only moral principle to which they respond is the comradeship of the jungle. It is as if, for them, neither the Old nor the New Testament had been written.

The nation has pulled itself out of the cycle of defeatism. Confidence has returned. Individual citizens are regaining power over their own lives in fields like education, trade unions, and housing. But we are agreed that the most prosperous of societies can be impoverished by crime, by violence, and by selfishness. We need to work together, in Church and State, to rebuild the moral standards and values which should form the sure foundations of a cohesive and united nation. We shall sometimes differ on individual issues. That is inevitable. I hope, nonetheless, that where we disagree, those questions will be aired intelligently. But if we are to restore cohesion and acceptable standards of behaviour, we need to look to the churches—and here I include religious leaders of other faiths in Britain—to speak and insist and insist again on the individual standards which are the foundation of a healthy society.[34]

Our reactions to these passages will quickly reveal our personal politics. The previous chapters of this study guide will, hopefully, have made it clear that four sentences to dismiss all that the theologians of liberation are saying just will not do! No one political party or, for that matter, branch of the Christian Church holds all the truths. As Dom Helder Camara once said: 'Truth is so vast that each one of us can see only one angle, one aspect of it. If only we could piece our little glimpses together, instead of fighting one another'.[35] Our current political leaders and their parties could transform Britain together had they only the courage to adopt Camara's philosophy.

11. Seeds of the Word

In the First World, evangelization must increasingly be done in a multi-faith and multi-racial social context. Britain is already a living visual aid of this. It is perhaps also uniquely placed, once again in its history, for the tasks of world evangelization. In a relatively small country, with excellent communications, almost all the countries of the world are represented, many by sizeable communities. These are some of the appropriate population statistics for multi-ethnic Britain in the late 1980s:

300,000 Irish
900,000 Indian
700,000 Pakistani/Bangladeshi
700,000 Afro-Caribbean
200,000 Italian
200,000 Greek
150,000 Arab
125,000 Chinese
100,000 Polish
90,000 African
55,000 Turkish
50,000 Iranian
35,000 Egyptian
30,000 Ukrainian
20,000 Vietnamese
15,000 Baltic Peoples (e.g., Lithuania, Latvia, Estonia)
10,000 Libyan
10,000 Moroccan
5,000 Yemeni

With regard to the numbers of those adhering to major non-Christian religions, the figures in Britain at the end of that decade were:

900,000 Muslims
400,000 Jews
300,000 Hindus
300,000 Sikhs

Many, of course, within these ethnic communities are Christian in their religious allegiance, such as the Irish and Polish Catholics. There are many thousands of black and Asian Christians in Britain. Some are in traditional denominations, others in black or Asian-led churches. Asian Christians may number at least 50,000 already and perhaps more. In some places, they have not been able to 'come out' and join local churches for a number of reasons.[36]

The prayer of the great American pioneer William Penn is an important one here: 'O Lord help us not to despise or oppose what we do not understand'. Too many Christians by far fail to heed that healthy advice. Their proclamation of Christ is sadly bound up with appalling ignorance, rudeness, and an insidious racism. There are still far too many First World Christians, for example, who will arrogantly dismiss all other faiths as 'of the devil'—as if that ends all discussion of the matter. Such a position is not borne out when you take the trouble to read carefully some of the great sacred books of other faiths. These are readily available now in translation—for example, in the Penguin Classics series that offers *The Koran, The Buddhist Scriptures, The Bhagavad Gita,* and *The Upanishads.* Any First World evangelization in countries such as Britain that is not prepared to take into account the undoubted spirituality of people of other faiths will be both insincere and ineffective. Let me try to illustrate something of what I mean by that statement.

I wish that we approached God with the same awe, or our prayer times with the same discipline, as the Muslim. I wish that the meditation and self-control of the Buddhist, redirected in Christ, might work their way into more Christians' lifestyles. I wish that we acknowledged more generously our enormous gratitude to the Jewish community who gave us, under God, both Jesus and our Old Testament. I wish that the colour, richness, and liveliness of Hinduism—refocused in Christ—might be reflected more in the often dull Sunday hour of 'worship' in too many of our churches. Dangerous talk? Perhaps. All I ask is that before any Christian readers succumb to the temptation to 'criticize what you don't understand'[37]—especially if they are Christian leaders—they make the time at least to read, with an open mind, some of the holy scriptures of other faiths. Any Christian believer who does this cannot help but be often impressed as well as, of course, at times being disappointed. The *Koran* contains many wise words alongside those passages that sadden us as Christians by reducing our Lord Jesus to a prophet, even though a great one. The Buddhist Scriptures echo in places the Old Testament Wisdom literature and, also, many a modern-day Christian preacher's denunciations of materialism. There are some hauntingly beautiful prayers in the Hindu *Vedas.* The former Archbishop of Jerusalem, George Appleton, has gone to print often on this subject. Anyone who has used his splendid volume *The Oxford Book of Prayer* (1985) will know of the section towards the end where the Archbishop draws on the prayers of other faiths. He writes,

> There is enough available to give Christians the taste or feeling of the prayers
> of other religious people and to perhaps provide evidence that if others can pray
> prayers of such beauty they must have some experience of the transcendent
> reality. . . .[38]

If we are not prepared or able to read more, then at the very least we should
keep silence on these matters lest we betray only our ignorance and closed
minds by our words

How, though, do we seek to reconcile our deep and passionate commitment
to Christ as the Way, the Truth, and the Life at the same time as respecting all
that is good and indeed very good in the faiths of others? The particular question for this study of the relation between liberation and evangelism is this:
How do we interpret what we discern of God's liberating Spirit at work in the
Kingdom in those who do not name the name of Christ nor have any dealings
with the Body of Christ, the Church? In my account of liberating forces in society I have been affirming that God is at work in unchurched people of goodwill
and among those committed to justice and mercy. How do we relate this to the
witness to Christ that we make in our evangelism?

We are not the first Christians to wrestle with this question, of course. In
the days of the Early Church Fathers, the Greek Apologist Justin Martyr struggled to understand how such great wisdom could be found in the poets and
philosophers of Ancient Rome and Greece—Aristotle, Plato, and Socrates, for
example. He hit upon the idea of 'the seeds of the Word' to help explain this.
Jesus Christ, he asserted, is the living embodiment of the Divine Word—the
Logos. Over the previous centuries, however, Christ had been liberally sprink-
ling 'the seeds of the Word' among humankind, like the sower in the parable
of Jesus. Wherever we then discover truth, justice, wisdom, beauty, and insight,
Christ has been there before us.[39] Might this not help us as we think of those of
other faiths, and none, who are committed to the cause of liberation? Might not
this too be the influence of the Risen Christ among them? The risen and
ascended Christ, now returned to the Father, has spread his truths widely. His
glorious activity, as Lord of the Cosmos, is surely not confined to the Christian
Church only. In the Christian faith, however patronising or arrogant this must
seem to some, Christians *unashamedly* affirm that the fullness of the Word has
come in Jesus. As the apologist C. S. Lewis put it in his own quest for God:
'The question was no longer to find the one simply true religion among a thousand religions, simply false. It was rather "where has religion reached its true
maturity?" '[40]

Augustine approached similar issues along the lines of truths and Truth. All
Truth he argued came from the Trinity. Wherever it may be found, whatever the
immediate source of a truth may be, its ultimate source is the One God made

known in Jesus Christ. Such truths though must always be tested against the fullness of truth disclosed in Christ.[41] In the seventeenth century, the Christian poet and priest John Donne took another tack altogether, stressing the unsearchable ways of God and human humility, which we would do well to reflect upon:

> To me to whom God hath revealed His Son, in a Gospel by a church, there can be no way of salvation but by applying that Son of God, by that Gospel, by that church. Nor is there any foundation, nor any other name by which any man can be saved, but the Name of Jesus. But how this foundation is presented and how this Name of Jesus is notified, to them among whom no Gospel is preached and no church established, I am not curious in enquiring. I know God can be as merciful as these tender fathers present Him to be; and I would be as charitable as they are. And therefore humbly embracing that manifestation of His Son which he hath afforded to me, I leave to God His unsearchable ways of working upon others, without further inquisition.[42]

12. Evangelization in Britain

The 1990s were hailed in Britain and in many other places of the world as a 'Decade for Evangelization'. Perhaps 1997 is a good time to reflect on what—frankly—for many of us went wrong. Whatever happened to the Decade of Evangelism? Here are some suggestions that draw upon the link between evangelism and liberation, which is our concern in this study.

(a) *It got lost in all the routine maintenance.* The conflict between maintenance of church structures and systems over against mission has become a cliché in Baptist and other circles. Clichés usually have some truth however. Too many Christians at national, regional, and local church levels spend too much of their time trying not to drown under the tyranny of the urgent, the important, and too often the frankly unnecessary. In the process, restructuring our churches on Sundays and in midweek to focus on prayer, social action, and appropriate evangelism gets relegated to the pending file.

(b) *It is a casualty of the spiritual battle.* The experience of many of us has been that most attempts to mobilize local churches into direct evangelization are met with unexpected obstacles, opposition from unlikely places, surprising circumstances not anticipated, and the emergence of a pre-outreach hurdle and assault course that not all succeed in negotiating. We can dress this up in all the theological language we like. The apostle Paul's warning in Ephesians 6:10-20 offers, to me, the most plausible explanation. The spiritual battle in a darkened world is real, unmistakably personal, and at times quite frightening. If, as Christians, we believe the New Testament, then we are actually seeking to redeem people and communities from the kingdom of darkness. The liberation theologians rightly point out that these hostile powers also take a structural form in ideologies, bureaucracies, and oppressive authorities. All these problems should not really surprise us. But they often do. It is far easier to stay in the securities of our local church ghettos than to venture out in mission.

(c) *It has been undermined by a crisis of confidence in the faith handed down.* There is a crisis of confidence in many of our First World Christians. The constant onslaught of media bad news, the presence all around us of alternative world views and perspectives, and the failure of still too much preaching and teaching to face up to people's doubts and sufferings as well as to their certainties all contribute here. Some exciting examples can be found of local churches committed to liberation and evangelization, to constructive participation with God's work in the local communities, and to personal conversions. Too many, however, have lost both their evangelistic nerve and their Kingdom vision.

(d) *The culture gap has widened.* Christian churches are ministering now at a time in Britain when some 95 percent of those in their twenties attend no church of any label. It is a generation whose parents did not hear the stories of Jesus and whose children probably will not either. It is a period when the growing army of 'Third Agers' (those aged fifty-plus) has still largely not been recognized by the Church as a priority area for evangelism. We are ministering in an age when much of life has become individualized and when the idea of belonging to families and communities and groups no longer means what once it did. Perhaps the politicians will return to an emphasis upon communal life (there are some hopeful signs in 'New Labour'), and this will provide the context for socially active churches to engage in meaningful mission and to demonstrate true community in Christ. Perhaps the Church will learn to communicate in a decade of Euro News, CD ROM, internet, modem, and naicam stereo. Perhaps the Church will break through into the very different world of the Other Britain, especially the 'tower block culture' of truancy, racism, drug cocktails, graffiti, and teenage pack warfare. Or perhaps not.

(e) *We have not worked hard enough on an apologetic, backed up by an authentic Christian lifestyle.* Depressingly, that expert in the 'Gospel and culture' debate, Bishop Lesslie Newbiggin, once concluded that 'post-Christian' Britain is uniquely resistant to the Gospel. An increasingly marginalized Church that no longer speaks the same language as dozens of the subcultures to be found in contemporary Britain clearly has an uphill struggle to evangelize effectively.

Hit-and-run excursions from our churches will carry little authority and make few converts. Evangelization, as we have seen in Latin America, is a whole lifestyle and not an occasional optional extra for the very committed Christians only. Nor is the problem *just* evangelizing the Other Britain. Comfortable Britain too presents us with many problems of strategy and approach. It is not just materialism or the vagaries of youth culture that we must discover a new apologetic for, but also for our encounter with alternative religions, philosophies, and world views. These range from the postmodern to the subtleties of New Age thinking and practice, from an Islamic presence stronger in our country now than that of Methodism through to the new foci of Sunday worship for so many —the nation's shopping malls. *Tesco ergo sum!*[43]

This context for evangelization is increasingly true of much of First World Europe also. Perhaps our calling then in Europe will remain one to evangelize without much fruit to be seen for a while for all the prayer and enterprise, the creativity and energy. The command to disciples in the New Testament is to share the Gospel faithfully and not to think we are responsible for the responses. Elsewhere in the world the 'Decade' has had some remarkable effects upon people's lives. Less nationalism as well as less denominationalism may be part of the answer to this question for us all. An ecumenical forum of *Churches Together in St. Albans* in 1995 heard the St. Albans Diocesan Missioner remindng us all that the decade was an international initiative as well as an ecumenical one. He gave portraits of church growth and conversions to Christ in places as far apart as Nigeria, Nepal, and South India. My own contacts with Baptists in post-Communist Poland also suggest that exciting things are happening in the Second World this decade. As we struggle, as we must, with new and appropriate ways of being church in the First World, perhaps it really is in Second and Third World Christianity that our destiny and at least some of our answers lie. Such, of course, is the conviction of this book.

13. Themes from Three Worlds

We have explored the world of Latin America, especially as it is perceived by the theologians of liberation. We have entered the world of Central and Eastern Europe in the postwar years, especially that of Poland in its quest for a liberation that was to change the face of Europe. We have tried to look with open eyes at the Britain of the 1970s and 1980s and to see the prophetic models of *Faith in the City* and the so-called 'Merseyside miracle'. From these three worlds we may draw out twelve key themes of a liberation theology as it has emerged in these chapters so far:

- Conscientization
- Praxis or orthopraxis
- Base communities
- Evangelization
- The New Humanity
- The New Society
- Non-violence
- Kingdom and Church
- Contradicting reality
- The suffering God
- Continuity with tradition
- The bias to the poor

These are the themes to which I will return in the final chapter of this book.

Notes

[1]See below, chaps. 6-7, especially on the prophets of Ancient Israel.

[2]Jeremy Seabrook, *Unemployment* (Quartet Books, London, 1982), p. xiv.

[3]Ibid., pp. 30-31; the place is Sunderland.

[4]Ibid., p. 68; the place is Balsall Heath.

[5]Ibid., p. 31.

[6]Ibid., p. 42.

[7]The Church of Scotland Minister W. Graham Monteith similarly speaks from the wheelchair in his challenging book *Disability: Faith and Acceptance* (The Saint Andrew Press, Edinburgh, 1987) with its thinking through of a Christian faith appropriate for disabled people.

[8]Peter Mayhew, *Justice in Industry* (SCM, London, 1980).

[9]Peter Mayhew, *Unemployment under the Judgement of God* (Churchman Publishing, Worthing, 1985), p. 140.

[10]Ibid., p. 146.

[11]Robert Laken, *More than a Friend* (Lion Publishing, Tring, 1984).

[12]Seabrook, *Unemployment*, p. 96.

[13]David Sheppard, *Bias to the Poor*, pp. 133-134.

[14]Ibid., p. 57.

[15]Ibid., p. 151.

[16]Ibid., p. 74.

[17]Ibid., p. 225.

[18]*Faith in the City—A Call for Action by Church and Nation* (Church House Publishing, London, 1985), p. xiv.

[19]Ibid., p. 176.

[20]Ibid., p. 232.

[21]Ibid., p. 273.

[22]Ibid., p. 273.

[23]Ibid., p. 351.

[24]Ibid., p. 295.

[25]Ibid., p. 336.

[26]*Faith in the Countryside* (Churchman Publishing, London, 1990), p. 191.

[27]Ibid., p. 125.

[28]Ibid., especially chap. 11 on 'Mission, Evangelism, and Community'.

[29]Trevor Hubbard was also my predecessor at Leamington Road Baptist Church, Blackburn.

[30]David Shepherd and Derek Worlock, *Better Together—Christian Partnership in a Hurt City* (Hodder & Stoughton, London, 1988), pp. 58-59.

[31]Ibid., p. 65.

[32]Ibid., p. 74.

[33]Ibid., p. 279.

[34]Douglas Hurd, speech to the General Synod of the Church of England, February 1988. Media release by the Conservative Party.

[35]Cited in José de Broucker, *Dom Helder Camara*, p. 148.

[36]The statistics come from information supplied by Interserve, an organization committed to cross-cultural evangelism.

[37]The phrase is cited from Bob Dylan's protest song of the 1960s, "The Times They Are A-Changin' " .

[38]George Appleton (ed.), *The Oxford Book of Prayer* (Oxford University Press, Oxford, 1985), p. 269.

[39]Justin Martyr, *First Apology for the Christians*, chaps. 8, 10, 13.

[40]C. S. Lewis, *Surprised by Joy* (Fontana, Collins, London, 1974), pp. 187-188.

[41]Augustine, *Confessions*, Book XIII.

[42]Quoted in David H. C. Read, 'Other People's Religion', *Expository Times* Vol. 98 (1986), p. 210.

[43]This witticism is by Graham Cray, a writer on Christianity and culture. American readers will need to know that 'Tesco' is a large national chain of shops in the UK.

PART II
'SHOW ME PLAIN SCRIPTURE'
The Biblical Roots of Liberation and Evangelization

Chapter 5
The New Testament

1. The Sacred Library

The Bible, the Old and New Testaments, has inspired God's people over many centuries. As the written word of God, witnessing to Jesus Christ *the Word* of God, the Bible is all about liberation. John Wesley once said in one of his many sermons to an antagonist who disagreed with him: 'I expect you to show me plain Scripture for your assertion—otherwise I dare not receive it, because I am not convinced that you are wiser than God'.[1] It is my conviction that the themes of liberation and evangelization, which are the subject of this guide, rest on plain Scripture and so pass Wesley's test.

In this, the second part of this study guide, we will therefore seek to obtain some insights from the pages of the New and Old Testaments on our subject. We shall survey every book in the Bible, not trying to cover the whole of their contents, but highlighting the theme of liberation at every level of society—the individual, whole communities, the nation, and the world. We shall constantly see the way this also opens up the theme of evangelization. This is a task we can only begin but never complete. In the words of the Early Church Father Chrysostom, 'It is a great thing this reading of the Scriptures! For it is not possible ever to exhaust the mind of the Scriptures. They are a well that has no bottom'.[2]

The nineteenth-century Christian poet Samuel Taylor Coleridge once called the Bible a 'sacred library'. So it is. The Bible is a library of sixty-six books and not just one or two. To read the whole of it, a book at a time, with a notebook at hand to record reflections and some of its contents immediately afterwards, is an important intellectual and spiritual discipline. How many otherwise 'well-read' people have never actually done this? The version used in what follows is the New International Version (NIV). This is a version that reads well publicly and privately and that was also blessed by stylistic editing at an early stage in its publication. The important thing, of course, for us all is to find a Bible whose translation we can respect and one that is also, as the computer idiom has it, user-friendly. Our personal copy of the Bible nearby then, we turn to the task at hand.

Is God really a God concerned for the liberation of individuals, communities, even whole nations? *Show me plain Scripture.* In the exercise that follows, readers of this book may follow one of two courses. Some readers might just skim the references and trust the accuracy of those I have given. But others might read the sections much more slowly than they had intended with an open Bible before them to check the case I am making for this broader understanding of evangelization. We begin with the Gospels.

2. Matthew

Matthew reminds us early in his Gospel account that Jesus was born into a land occupied by Roman soldiers and ruled by a tyrant, Herod the abuser and slayer of infants: 'A voice is heard in Ramah, weeping and great mourning, Rachel weeping for her children and refusing to be comforted, because they are no more' (2:18). We see how very soon the outcasts of Galilee and the surrounding regions gather to him and around him (4:23-25). The Sermon on the Mount inverts so many worldly values: the kingdom of heaven belongs rather to the poor in spirit, not to say the wealthy Sadducee; the meek will inherit the earth, not the Herods or Caiaphases or Pilates; those who hunger and thirst for righteousness will be filled; it is the peacemakers, not the Roman warmongerers, who truly belong to God (5:3-10). The people of the Kingdom are to be as salt that preserves and flavours, also as lights within the darkness of whole cities. Their good deeds will point others to God the Father in heaven (5:13-16). Love comes relatively easily among friends, but true Kingdom love must embrace enemies as well (5:43-47). Giving to the needy is expected of disciples, and is to be done unostentatiously (6:2-4). Mammon (or money) must not be allowed to usurp God's place of utter priority (6:24).

Elsewhere Jesus explains just how very hard it is for the rich truly to enter his Kingdom (19:23-4). The Good News is for all, and it brings liberation in its wake—even for those tormented by the grip of evil and sickness (8:14-17). Healing and a deliverance ministry for individuals are part of Jesus' message of liberation. He also came for those such as the prostitutes, the tax collectors and sinners, and for the spiritually sick such as the self-righteous Pharisees who failed to realise their need (9:9-13). The true people of God can expect to be persecuted by 'the powers that be' (10:16-20). Indeed, the Gospel may well divide families and whole communities. Not all will receive Christ (10:34-42). The Gospel was never meant to be proclaimed only to individuals; sadly it is we who have reduced it to this in our contemporary church practice. Jesus had whole communities in mind as he sent out his disciples. Korazin, Bethsaida, and Capernaum were strongly rebuked and warned by him (11:20-24). Later Jerusalem, the capital, was also both warned and lamented over (23:37-39).

Humankind is more important to God than rules and regulations. The religious leaders may have worked out more than 600 additions to and 'explanations' of the Torah (or Law), but to God it is the religion of the heart that counts: 'These people honour me with their lips, but their hearts are far from me. They worship me in vain; their teachings are but rules taught by men' (15:8-9). Forgiveness again and again of those who have sinned against us must characterize the followers of Jesus. After all, God has forgiven us so much (18:21-35). As for those who commercially exploit the taxation system of the House of God, turning it into a place of profit, bartering, and selling, the overturning of the tables was part of Jesus' praxis: 'My house shall be called a house of prayer, but you are making it a den of robbers' (21:13). The religious authorities are castigated in the woes of Matthew 23: 'They tie up heavy loads and put them on men's shoulders, but they themselves are not willing to lift a finger to move them'. 'The greatest among you will be your servant'. 'You blind guides! You strain out a gnat but swallow a camel'. 'You snakes! You brood of vipers! How will you escape being condemned to hell'? Whatever happened to 'gentle Jesus meek and mild'? Note, too, who is actually at the Messiah's banquet. There is a delightful mix of people 'good and bad' (22:10). Jesus had time and room for the good religious people also. The pious, homely, devout types—middle-class Baptists, Catholics, or Anglicans perhaps?

The Gospel is not just for the poor, the tax collectors, prostitutes, and sinners. Caesar is to be honoured with what is his by right. How much more so, however, is God (22:15-22). Love is the hallmark of the Kingdom, of his ministry, and of his message. It is the true currency of the Kingdom. All the Law and the prophets hang on it (22:37-40). The parable of the sheep and the goats strongly reminds us of the need for praxis—action that flows from, and is inspired by, faith and love. This will involve feeding the hungry, giving water to the thirsty, welcoming the stranger, clothing the naked, and visiting the sick and the prisoners. Hell, no less, awaits those who fail Christ here (25:31-36).

Before the people of his day, Jesus lived out the law of love and forgiveness right on to its inevitable conclusion. St. Matthew's Passion narrative is surely among the world's most moving literature. Before the Sanhedrin, Pilate and his wife; before the crowds and the soldiers, gathered to curse and view his shame; before these, the Suffering Servant faultlessly practised the way of love and forgiveness that he had preached. So he did, even as the lifeblood poured from him and the flies gathered round, even as tetanus and the excruciating agony of a crucifixion victim's struggle to breathe set in. Dead. Buried.

Then the Easter faith is affirmed for the first time in the ordering of our New Testament pages as we now have them. This is not the place to rehearse the doctrines of the cross and resurrection and the liberation and forgiveness achieved for humankind there.[3] Nor is this the place to marshall arguments for or against the resurrection or particular understandings of it. Suffice it here to speak personally and say that my own life was transformed as the realization dawned on me that the Jesus I had learned about over the years really was alive and that he offered me forgiveness. For me, the cross and resurrection of the Lord Christ are the foundation of my life, the source of my hope, and the force and power I seek to live by. 'He is not here; he has risen, just as he said' (28:6). Matthew's Gospel points us powerfully to the one and only source of all Christian liberation: the crucified and risen Messiah Jesus Christ. The risen Jesus' Great Commission makes it very clear that the emphases of his teaching and life must now find strong and clear expression in the emerging work of his Church:

> Therefore go and make disciples of all nations, baptizing them in the Name of the Father and of the Son and of the Holy Spirit and teaching them to obey everything I have commanded you. And surely I am with you always to the very end of the age. (28:18-20)

3. Mark

In considering the Gospels, I have concentrated on Matthew's account. Nevertheless, the Gospel of Mark is widely accepted to have been the first Gospel to be written, and it was one of Matthew's sources. Mark was also probably a source, directly and indirectly, for John and Luke as well. The treatment of these Gospels here will reflect this overlap of material and try not to repeat it.

We note in Mark how Jesus numbered several different kinds of people among his disciples (3:13-19). He drew together fishermen, a tax collector, and women (Mary and Martha, for example), as well as at least one political radical, Simon the Zealot, in the service of the Kingdom of God. Why should it be any different for us in contemporary evangelization? Surely Christ and his Kingdom, and love and respect for all his followers, should matter more to us than our political party preferences or gender prejudices. The Zealots were political radicals who longed to drive the occupying Roman authorities into the sea and to institute the rule of God in their own land. They were surely the forerunners of many a modern-day political radical. Jesus was prepared to use and work with militants and radicals such as these. He taught them other ways to view God's action and the needs of humankind, but the point remains that he worked with them. One of the sad things in some contemporary First World church life is the scornful and dismissive, even hateful, way that some Christians treat the political activists in their local communities. Little wonder there are so few of them at worship on a Sunday! This un-Christian attitude can even extend to active trade unionists in the local church. As always, we need to look to Jesus' own praxis for guidance here.

We also see in Mark how Jesus affirmed the presence and worth of children. They were, for him, never objects to be 'seen but not heard' but valued members of the Kingdom. They did not have to wait for their bar mitzvah celebrations before they were affirmed by him. Nor did they have to be boys only to receive his blessing and welcome! Rather all children were presented by Jesus, in their childlike trust and faith, as models of true discipleship. Humanity's treatment of children has so often been scandalous over the centuries: from slave labour to cannon fodder, from the point of the bayonet to abuse and incest. Jesus showed the correct model of adult-child relationship some 2,000 or so years ago, and we are still catching up. Liberation is for children too (10:13-16).

Let us note from Mark also how Jesus exposes the mentality underlying much secular authority. The Jewish people had known countless tyrants and overlords from the days when the northern kingdom of Israel fell to the Assyrians and later the southern kingdom of Judah to the sadistic Babylonians. The pattern of leadership and government they had come to expect, most recently from the occupying Romans, was one of overlordship, dominance, tributes, and exploitation. Consider, in that perspective then, the power of Jesus' words:

> You know that those who are regarded as rulers of the Gentiles lord it over them, and their high officials exercise authority over them. Not so with you. Instead . . . whoever wants to be first must be slave of all. For even the Son of Man did not come to be served but to serve, and to give his life as a ransom for many. (10:42-45)

4. John

We turn now to John's Gospel. Here we are given the secret at the very beginning even before the story is told. We are to read the story in the light of this disclosure, just as in a modern screenplay we may be shown the conclusion of a piece of drama first, and only then be led to trace the events through to their endings. Jesus is the Word of God made flesh: 'Through him all things were made; without him nothing was made that has been made'. He 'became flesh and made his dwelling among us'. His is the glory of the One and Only, who came from the Father, full of grace and truth' (1:1-14). Some familiar Marcan stories are retold in the light of this 'open secret', and some new ones are also introduced and lovingly handled.

We see how individuals are featured again and again. Jesus has time for people. One by one the disciples are called: Philip, Nathanael, Andrew, and Peter. Then there is Nicodemus. Jesus has time for the nobles and the professionally religious as well as the outcasts of society, especially when they are genuinely seeking the Kingdom. To Nicodemus the importance of the new birth by the Holy Spirit of God is explained (3:1-21), and here all fully Christian liberation begins. We read of the woman at the well to whom Jesus affirms that he is the Messiah and the one who alone can satisfy the spiritually thirsty (4:1-42); there are the official and his sick son, the man at the Pool of Bethesda and the woman caught in adultery. While the Lord challenges society, the individual always matters to him.

The 'I am' sayings spoken by Jesus—there are seven in the Gospel—give us further insights into his character and true nature. Consider the description of Jesus as the good shepherd who will protect the sheep from dangers such as the wolf or the thief. This is, as we have seen, the rôle that some priests and lay leaders had to play during the 1970s and 1980s in the base communities of Latin America or in the parishes of Poland. Shepherds, of course, are sometimes savaged by the wolves (10:1-21); so Jesus warns that hatred is to be expected by those who follow in the way of the new commandment to love (13:34-35). Meanwhile, the Holy Spirit of Jesus will continue to build his new community and gather into it new believers. The presence of unity among believers will be a sign of the love between the Father and Son and will always be directed towards evangelization (17:2-23). Finally this new commandment of love is lived out before Annas and Caiaphas (keeping religious and social privileges in the family is an-all-too-common practice), before Pilate, before a hostile band of soldiers, and before the crowds (19:1-6). Even from the cross, Jesus notices and cares for his mother and a disciple (19:25-27). After his resurrection, the risen Messiah breathes peace and forgiveness into his previously cowering disciples. Peace and forgiveness: these are two liberating gifts they will be able to communicate themselves and share with others (19:25-27). We are at the end of the beginning (20:31-41). 'Feed my sheep' and 'follow me': the Risen Lord's clarion call continues to sound down through history (21:15-19).

5. Luke and Acts

The books of Luke and Acts are designed to be read one after the other. Of his Gospel Luke writes: 'I myself have carefully investigated everything from the beginning, so as to write an orderly account for you, most excellent Theophilus' (Luke 1:3). Theophilus may have been a well-connected Roman official or else simply a 'lover of God', which is what the name actually means in Greek. In the prologue to Acts, the godly doctor Luke makes a similar point: 'In my former book, Theophilus, I wrote about all that Jesus began to do and to teach until the day he was taken up to heaven, after giving instructions through the Holy Spirit to the apostles he had chosen' (Acts 1:1).

Luke

Early in Luke's account, two songs celebrate God's liberation, past, present, and future (1:46-56, 67-79). The first of these, the 'Magnificat', includes the phrases:

> He has performed mighty deeds with his arm; he has scattered those who are proud in their inmost thoughts. He has brought down rulers from their thrones but has lifted up the humble. He has filled the hungry with good things but has sent the rich away empty.

Zechariah's song similarly celebrates the Messiah's coming and what it will mean for Israel thus: 'Salvation from our enemies and from the hand of all who hate us'. The Messiah is seen as 'the rising sun from heaven' that will 'shine on those living in darkness and in the shadow of death, to guide our feet into the path of peace'. In accord with these expectations, John the Baptist did not only preach about spiritual repentance. Repentance was to have practical social effects. Those with tunics or food to spare must share them. Tax collectors must collect what is required—no surcharges. Soldiers must not abuse their power by extortion or false accusations; nor are they to grumble about levels of pay. Enough is enough. The political tyrant Herod's evils and sins are likewise castigated (3:1-20).

Luke 4 has been termed a 'messianic manifesto', not least by John Howard Yoder in his book, *The Politics of Jesus* (1972).[4] Yoder claims that Jesus was announcing the Jubilee, that time when social and personal debts are to be annulled so that all of God's people may begin again at the same point.[5] Many of us today long for the moment when these Jubilee principles will free the developing countries in the Second and Third Worlds from the enormous burdens of their many foreign debts, usually so unwisely entered into. Only such Jubilees will allow these nations and their poor to live and breathe again. Only then can many governments begin to address the desperate plight of their starving, poor, and dispossessed who cry out to the God of liberation. There are those, and Christians prominent among them, who are arguing that the end of the millennium in A.D. 2000 and the beginning of a new century is an ideal time to practice the Jubilee and to release Second and Third World countries from their debts; not least as so much of the original capital has long since been repaid by them anyway.

So Jesus' words in Luke 4 must not be merely spiritualized, but must also be read literally. Fresh insights begin to emerge as we do so. Echoing words from Isaiah, Jesus describes his ministry thus:

> The Spirit of the Lord is on me, because he has anointed me to preach good news to the poor. He has sent me to proclaim freedom for the prisoners and recovery of sight for the blind, to release the oppressed, to proclaim the year of the Lord's favour. (4:18-19)

The Jubilee has arrived. His whole ministry is to be understood against the backdrop of these words. They were not popular then, especially when he made it clear that this was a message for other people as well and not just for the Jews (4:24-30). The ugly spirit of nationalism has long been around.

Once again in Luke, as in the Sermon on the Mount in Matthew, Jesus is seen turning worldly values upside down in his blessings and woes.

> Woe to you who are rich, for you have already received your comfort. Woe to you who are well fed now, for you will go hungry. Woe to you who laugh now, for you will mourn and weep. Woe to you when all men speak well of you, for that is how their fathers treated the false prophets. (6:24-26)

In line with these new values, Jesus breathes words of acceptance and forgiveness to a woman who has lived a sinful life, whereas others can only condemn (7:36-50). Luke, perhaps above all the Gospels, emphasizes the revolutionary attitude of Jesus towards women. He is, however, not alone in doing this. Jesus' revolutionary treatment of women is recorded by the Gospel writers and conceded by even the most reactionary Christians today. Consider, for example, how Jesus sat so lightly to all the taboos about menstruation and ritual uncleanness when he welcomed the touch of a woman who had been 'subject to bleeding for twelve years' (8:43-48).

The disciples, we should note, are sent out to preach a whole Gospel: 'to drive out all demons and to cure diseases . . . to preach the Kingdom of God and to heal the sick'. They are also sent out with a minimum of fuss or baggage (9:1-6). As for the parable of the Good Samaritan, this makes it crystal clear that Jesus is interested more in deeds of love and kindness than in impressive social or spiritual status or indeed in nationalistic or religious differences: 'Go and do likewise', we read (10:25-37). From Jesus' lips, too, issue the challenging words: 'From everyone who has been given much, much will be demanded; and from the one who has been entrusted with much, much more will be asked' (12:48). These words are surely not just a reference to spiritual responsibilities, especially when they are set against Jesus' teaching elsewhere in Luke on riches and money. It is in Luke that we see a lament for a capital city (13:34-35). The three parables of Luke 15 about what is 'lost' (a sheep, a coin, a son) again reveal God to be concerned deeply for the sinner, the rebel, and the outcast, not just the 'righteous'.

The story Jesus tells about the rich man and the beggar Lazarus makes it clear that the wealthy have a responsibility to the poor, and that the Living God who sees all has the power to reverse fortunes in the life of the age to come. The gulf between rich and poor is unbridgeable in heaven, it seems, for those who fail to bridge it on earth—but with surprising consequences:

> Abraham replied, 'Son, remember that in your lifetime you received your good things, while Lazarus received bad things, but now he is comforted here and you are in agony. And besides all this, between us and you a great chasm has been fixed'. (16:25-26)

Wealthy Zacchaeus does certainly find a place in the Saviour's heart, but following Jesus correctly has enormous personal implications in the redistribution of his wealth (19:1-10).

How easy it is to read the Gospels through the filter of our particular tradition, our familiar and comforting interpretations, and indeed our many prejudices, and so fail to see in them what is blindingly obvious. In Yoder's words:

> [Jesus is] not just a moralist whose teachings had some political implications . . . not primarily a teacher of spirituality whose public ministry was seen in a political light . . . not just a sacrificial lamb preparing for his immolation *or a* God-Man whose divine status calls us to disregard his humanity. . . . He is also the bearer of a new possibility of human, social, and therefore political relationships.[6]

The call of Jesus was to a new kind of community and to a radically new way of life. It was the way the Master trod. Should not the servants tread it too?

Acts

If the Tower of Babel in the book of Genesis stands for the dividing of human-kind, then the day of Pentecost in the book of Acts describes the re-uniting of humankind in the crucified and risen Messiah, Jesus Christ (Acts 2:5-11). The Good News henceforth belongs not only to Jerusalem and Judaea but to Samaria and to the ends of the earth (1:8); indeed, Luke skillfully weaves together his account so as to trace the spread of the Gospel from the banks of the River Jordan on to the very heart of the then known world—Rome itself. After repentance, conversion, and baptism, the new converts discover a new lifestyle together. The apostle's teaching, prayer, fellowship, and the breaking of bread are at the heart of a lifestyle where possessions are regarded differently from before: 'All the believers were together and had everything in common. Selling their possessions and goods, they gave to anyone as he had need' (2:42-47). Later we read: 'No one claimed that any of his possessions was his own, but they shared everything they had' (4:32).

Before the self-same religious authorities who a few months earlier had put Jesus to death, the apostles declared: 'Salvation is found in no-one else, for there is no other name under heaven given to men by which we must be saved' (4:12). The apostles also make it plain that loyalty and obedience to God take priority over all other claims and that they are prepared to pay the price for that conviction (4:18-21). The first Christian martyr, Stephen, was soon to pay the ultimate price here (4:18-21). This conviction of a higher loyalty to God was one increasingly heard throughout the South African liberation struggle, in Poland during the Solidarity years, and among the believers in the Latin Ameri-can base communities. For an earlier Christian generation it was also the theme of the confessing Church so brutally repressed in Hitler's Germany. There too some had to pay the ultimate price for their higher loyalty to God, the theologian Dietrich Bonhoeffer among them.

Descriptions of people finding wholeness and liberation, just as in Jesus' earthly ministry, are repeated by Luke here (5:14-16). The Good News remains fully practical. It includes the distribution of food to widows, albeit this is poorly organised at first (6:1). As the Church is persecuted, so it scatters and new communities of faith are born (8:1-4). The witnessing, the evangelism, the proclaiming of the risen Jesus go on and on. In Samaria, a sorcerer's grip on a whole people is released, and the sorcerer himself is converted and delivered (8:9-24). The African Church is born in a chariot on the desert road near Gaza (8:26-39). Saul comes to proclaim the faith he once tried to destroy (9:1-30). Gentiles (non-Jews) are saved and drawn into the embrace of the Good News. Famine relief becomes a priority for action: 'The disciples, each according to his ability, decided to provide help for the brothers living in Judea. This they did, sending their gift to the elders by Barnabas and Saul' (11:27-30). Would that such a vision would claim more First World Christians as they look to the needs of the Third World! A mission to new countries, towns, and communities is launched (13:1-3). As new non-Jewish converts are won to Christ, every effort is made—after due debate—to secure them in their new faith without undue burdens (15:28-29). In Athens an entire culture is challenged using its own terminology and religious belief systems (17:16-24). In Ephesus, a whole community is transformed as it turns its back on evil deeds and sorcery (19:18-20).

Before rulers petty and great, Saul, who is now Paul, proclaims Christ as the Risen Lord, and then declares the full message of new life in him. Indeed, Paul understands his rôle in terms similar to Jesus in the manifesto of Luke 4; God, he claims, has said to him:

> I am sending you to them to open their eyes and turn them from darkness to light and from the power of Satan to God, so that they may receive forgiveness of sins and a place among those who are sanctified by faith in me. (26:17-18)

Finally, we see Paul in Rome. Who could have known then that the Gospel he proclaimed there would survive and indeed one day conquer that great city? We read: 'Boldly and without hindrance he preached the Kingdom of God and taught about the Lord Jesus Christ' (28:31).

This book then records a call to repentance not only for private individuals, but also for rulers, whole cities, and countries. It narrates the coming of salvation as wholeness, showing new communities springing into being wherever the risen Jesus through his Holy Spirit leads. It shows a revolutionised people, transforming the known world. The 'Acts of the Holy Spirit'—which would be a more accurate description of this book—have continued to rebuke, challenge, and inspire Christians towards liberation since first they were scribed.

What though of the other New Testament writings? What relevance do they have to evangelization and liberation in the New Europe. Or to all Three Worlds and especially to the new Europe?

6. The New Testament Letters

Letters. What images does that particular word conjure up for us? The letter to or from home each week? Perhaps the telephone, the fax, and the e-mail long since killed that! Somehow letter writing was of a higher order in the New Testament age than we seem to manage in ours. It seems strange to consider that, under the providence of God, some twenty-one first-century A.D. letters should be preserved as part of our New Testament, and therefore as an integral part of the Bible. Yet what letters they are! Some of them were written from prison cells, from the homes of converts or in hiding places from the persecuting authorities. Some were written on the move, in the middle of demanding missionary journeys. They were dictated via a scribe or trusted co-worker, sent by sea or land to address not only individuals but whole communities and entire regions. Imagine receiving a letter containing Paul's poem about love (1 Cor 13), surely one of the high points of all world literature! Or, rather differently, imagine receiving a letter extolling the virtues of the mysterious Melchisedek (Heb 5:1-10). There were no photocopiers, circulars, or word processors for Paul and his fellow letter writers, just beautifully thought-out and painstakingly written originals that continue to inspire whole new generations. Some of the New Testament letters are really sermons in the guise of a letter; Colossians, for example, may well be a baptismal sermon put to scroll. Others, such as Romans, present a carefully constructed statement of doctrinal theology. With regard to our theme, however, we are not surprised to find that all the letters in the New Testament, of whatever kind they are, continue to witness to a God who is concerned for liberation.!

Paul's concern in his *Letter to the Romans* is 'the salvation of everyone who believes: first for the Jew, and then for the Gentile' (1:16). God sees the lifestyle and behaviour of the immoral and the violent. Sexploitation, as some First World tabloid newspapers have come to call it (and to profit from it), is no new phenomenon (1:24-27). There are those, he warns, 'filled with every kind of wickedness, evil, greed, and depravity . . . full of envy, murder, strife, deceit, and malice . . . senseless, faithless, heartless, and ruthless' (1:29-31). A day of judgement is coming—and indeed to some extent it is already taking place—when 'God will judge men's secrets through Jesus Christ as my Gospel declares' (2:16). In a tapestry of Old Testament quotations, Paul describes the sinfulness of the human condition when divorced from the life-giving God (3:10-18). All have sinned. But all are also—potentially—justified freely by his grace through the redemption that came by Christ Jesus (3:23-24). Peace, joy, and reconciliation are now freely offered. Christ died for the powerless and the ungodly—for all of us. 'Justification' (being 'in the right' in a new relationship and standing before God) is now available and can be received by faith. All this means personal liberation, as sin is no longer our master, but rather God (6:11-14).

Jesus is our deliverer from the torment of civil war within ourselves between the good we desire and the evil that comes all too readily (7:24-25). But this is not only liberation for the individual person. Creation itself benefits from what God has done for us in Christ: 'The creation itself will be liberated from its bondage to decay and brought into the glorious freedom of the children of God' (8:18-22). 'Save the Planet' is not just a twentieth-century refrain, although it is one that carries a sense of painful urgency as the next century will have to learn to cope with the untold damage we have done to Planet Earth over the course of this century. We are indeed leaving a sad legacy for our children and grandchildren. Paul also has a vision of wholeness for nations; by the time he comes to write his letter, it is clear that the Good News of Christ is for all races, but Paul argues that the Hebrew peoples, whether in Israel or scattered as the diaspora Jews are still precious to God and part of his plans and purposes (chaps. 9–11).

Christians must no longer conform to the pattern of this world—we find 'Sermon on the Mount'-type thinking again here—but must rather 'be transformed by the renewing of your mind' (12:2). The Christian faith must issue in deeds of love and kindness: serving, encouraging, contributing to the needs of others; cheerfully showing compassion and mercy, as well as in demonstrating the more obviously 'spiritual' gifts (12:6-8). The law of love must now work itself out in Rome (12:9-16; 13:8-14). Love for enemies is an important part of this (12:17-21). The authorities are to be respected, and appropriate dues given (13:1-7). Nevertheless, the book of Acts has already shown us, though, that there are times when obedience to God will need to take precedence over the State, especially if unjust decrees are passed by the authorities. Paul has a strong concern about caring for the 'weak', and we notice that this even extends to those who interpret the Gospel differently from us (chap. 14). The God who shows compassion to the weak expects similar compassion from those who are spiritually 'strong' or, perhaps more accurately, from those who like to *consider* themselves to be strong. Paul ends his letter, characteristically, by encouraging contributions 'for the poor among the saints' (15:26).

In his *First Letter to the Corinthians*, Paul emphasizes that the Christian faith, rooted in the rejected and crucified Christ, is for ordinary people. Indeed, it prides itself on attracting such followers, so as to 'shame the wise (and the) strong and to nullify the things that are' (1:26-31). This letter also portrays Christian leaders as 'fools for Christ'. Hungry, thirsty, in rags, brutally treated, homeless, cursed, persecuted, and slandered, they are 'the scum of the earth, the refuse of the world' (4:8-13). But Christ's they are, far more than the ones abusing or slandering them. We are bound to ask how the 'prosperity Gospel' thinking and the multi-dollar preaching that has prostituted at least some First World Church life in recent years fit in here. Sexual immorality is also to be confronted and changes in lifestyle demanded (chap. 5). Paul's example of personal witnessing and his passion for people to come newly to faith in Christ are to be owned by his readers, too: 'I have become all things to all men so that by all possible means I might save some' (9:19-27).

In this new life, class divisions are to be ruthlessly exposed and put down. Some enjoy humiliating those who have nothing, even at the Lord's Supper (11:17-22). How many 'haves' kneel or sit for the Eucharist in our First World churches alongside 'have nots' in the same church, and certainly in the same county or state, week by week in similar circumstances without even realising it? Then for Paul comes the way of love again. Like a theme in a Beethoven symphony, reaching its climax in the last movement, the major New Testament motif of love reaches its climax in the poetry of chapter 13 of this letter. Even giving to the poor, if it is out of cold duty and not out of love, is claimed here to be worthless (13:3). The liberation love brings is not, we should note, for this present age only (13:8). Paul's superb words on the resurrection, so often read at funeral services (15:50-57), remind us that God's ultimate liberation is designed to transcend even human death. As the early Anabaptists put it, we should 'learn to look not to but through death'. This indeed is Paul's claim (15:55). 'Do everything in love', he pleads as this letter reaches its close (16:14).

The Second Letter to the Corinthians describes Christians as being in a triumphal procession (2:14-17). They have an experience like the Victory in Europe (VE) day celebrations following Hitler's suicide and the liberation of the continent in the summer of 1945. But this procession is not an imperialistic one; as it goes on its way, through Christians, God is now choosing to spread far and wide the 'fragrance' of Christ. Christian communities are called moreover to experience a process of ongoing transformation. Just as Moses glowed and was transformed in his meeting with God, so too we should grow and mature as communities into the Spirit of the Lord. For 'where the Spirit of the Lord is, there is freedom. . . . and we, who with unveiled faces all reflect the Lord's glory, are being transformed into his likeness with ever-increasing glory, which comes from the Lord, who is Spirit' (3:17-18). We see again in this letter Paul's conviction that heaven is the ultimate liberation. The tragedy is that so often in history this truth has been abused to encourage compliance and acquiescence in an unjust status quo on earth. It remains, nonetheless, the worthy Christian hope: 'Our light and momentary troubles are achieving for us an eternal glory that far outweighs them all' (4:17). The day of salvation is now, and God has 'committed to us the message of reconciliation' (5:19). This must include generosity of giving, fair redistribution of wealth, and the over-coming of poverty by those with plenty (8:1-15). These qualities are encouraged just as clearly as our Lord encouraged them by his parables and teaching, as we have seen. His example must be ever before our eyes: 'For you know the grace of our Lord Jesus Christ, that though he was rich, yet for your sakes he became poor, so that you through his poverty might become rich' (8:9).

The Letter to the Galatians highlights the liberating new life to be found in Christ: 'I have been crucified with Christ and I no longer live, but Christ lives in me. The life I live in the body, I live by faith in the Son of God, who loved me and gave himself for me' (2:20). So 'for freedom Christ has set us free' (5:1). In Christ, human divisions lose their ultimate force and value, whether they be distinctions between Jew and Greek, male and female, slave or free. All are one in Christ Jesus (3:28). The tragedy is that it has taken us far longer to recognise the full equality of women as well as men in and before Christ than it ever did to free the Roman slaves. Woman is still, in John Lennon's deliberately scandalous phrase, 'the nigger of the world'.[7] Liberation in Christ is available to all, for the individual and the community. This echoes throughout Galatians. The symphony motif of love can be heard once again: 'The only thing that counts is faith expressing itself through love' (5:6). A new lifestyle must flow from the people of God in their Christian liberation: 'love, joy, peace, patience, kindness, goodness, faithfulness, gentleness, and self-control. Against such things there is no law' (5:22). Again, such love must be practical: 'Therefore, as we have opportunity, let us do good to all people, especially to those who belong to the family of believers' (6:10).

The Letter to the Ephesians delights in the grace by which we are saved (2:8-10). The graciousness of the Gospel undermines all our human-made divisions. It is not exaggerating to say that Ephesians anticipates the 'one world' movements of our day. Jew and Gentile (and biblically that is everybody!) are united and brought near to God through the blood of Jesus (2:11-22). We are to live as children of light. Worship and service together are designed to bind us to each other and to Christ (5:19-21). Liberation works itself out in a world where dark forces are at work and evil is real indeed (6:12). We can easily identify the 'powers of this present darkness' today in the torture cells of the political left and right, in the genocide of Pol Pot's Killing Fields in Cambodia or the ethnic strife of Bosnia, in the drug cartels that destroy present and future generations, in the homes of those who abuse and torment children, in the enormous debts of the Third World countries to First World banks whilst children quite literally starve, in the monies wasted on weapons of mass destruction while the world's poor suffer. 'Take your stand . . . against the powers of this dark world and against the spiritual forces of evil in the heavenly realms' (6:10-18). Evangelization faces *real* opposition.

In his *Letter to the Philippians*, Paul quotes what was probably a hymn of the early Church in order to encourage us to imitate the example of Christ who 'made himself nothing, taking the very nature of a servant . . . obedient to death

—even death on a cross' (2:5-11). The letter makes clear that Christian liberation in practice means both suffering and joy. Christians are those who hold fast to the word of life, and so they should 'shine like stars in the universe' (2:15). Their joy must be infectious: 'Rejoice in the Lord always, I will say it again: Rejoice' (4:4). But Paul also knew something of 'the fellowship of sharing in his sufferings, becoming like him in his death' (3:10).

The *Letter to the Colossians* strikes an immediate note of deliverance, reminding us that Christ has 'rescued us from the dominion of darkness and brought us into the Kingdom of the Son he loves, in whom we have redemption, the forgiveness of sins' (1:13-14). It celebrates the fact that in Christ 'are hidden all the treasures of wisdom and knowledge' (2:3), which is now a word for our First World culture and its values. Freedom in Christ also embraces freedom from human-made rules and regulations that oppress rather than liberate (2:20-23). God's people are to live the liberated life of Christ within them, 'the hope of glory' (1:27). Compassion, kindness, forgiving grievances, and worship are all to be part of this lifestyle: 'And over all these virtues put on love, which binds them all together in perfect unity' (3:12-17). Love and mutual respect must also characterise whole Christian households (3:18–4:1).

The two *Letters to the Thessalonians* anticipate the final liberation of creation and humankind in Christ, at the *parousia* or the 'appearing' of Jesus Christ in glory. This event will mean God's judgement on human life and human values (1 Thess 4:13-17; 2 Thess 1:5-10), but in the meantime there is a lifestyle to be lived, and there are values of love to be upheld (1 Thess 4:9-12; 5:1-11).

The *First and Second Letters to Timothy* are the writings of an older Christian minister to a younger one. They are full of care and advice for a young protegé, who is described as being like a son to the apostle Paul. Some scholars question whether these epistles (together with that to Titus) were really written by Paul, arguing that they show signs of early Church life several decades later, and suggesting that the writer is assuring his correspondent that he is to him 'like Timothy was to Paul'. It is surely in the end what God is saying through these letters that counts and not the human authors. Too many tempers have flared over such issues in this century! The Church has more important agendas than these, as the letters themselves make clear; riches and the use of religion for financial gain are clear dangers to avoid: 'Godliness with contentment is great gain' (1 Tim 6:3-10). We must assume by this time that some of the Gospels at least, and perhaps Paul's earlier letters as well, are already being seen as 'scripture' in addition to the familiar Old Testament. This is to be understood when we read that the Holy Scriptures are 'able to make you wise for salvation through faith in Christ Jesus'. Again, 'All Scripture is God-breathed and is useful for teaching, rebuking, correcting, and training in righteousness, so that the man of God may be thoroughly equipped for every good work' (2 Tim 3:15-17). Whatever their specific cultural context, the Timothy letters portray for us a community based on mutual respect between leaders and people, old and young, weak and strong, employers and employees. These qualities of mutual respect, too, are part of a mature Christian liberation vision and truly in accord with Scripture.

The *Letter to Titus* similarly sees Christ preparing his people to be his 'very own, eager to do what is good', people who will in every way 'make the teaching about God our Saviour attractive' (2:10-14). It includes the 'washing of rebirth and the renewal by the Holy Spirit' for transformed existence in this life, as well as 'the hope of eternal life' (3:4-7).

A much earlier letter appropriately included at this point, to *Philemon,* shows us the apostle Paul applying pressure to have a Christian slave reinstated without penalty and forgiven by his fellow-Christian master. The whole letter is itself a deed of kindness to one of Paul's converts, which emphasises (within the social constraints of the time) that, in the sight of God, all human beings are equal. Philemon is to be welcomed 'no longer as a slave, but better than a slave, as a dear brother' (1:16).

The Letter to the Hebrews is a skilful treatment of Old Testament texts, designed to encourage Jewish Christians especially to persist with their faithful following of Christ. Some say it was written by Barnabas 'the Encourager'.[8] Christ has liberated us from sin to 'serve the Living God' through his final and willing sacrifice on the cross. Regular corporate worship, fellowship, and good deeds (13:15-16) are to be part of our own sacrificial service to this living God. So liberation will be personally painful, even sacrificial. Discipline and growth in holiness are often related (12:1-13). The prisoners are to be remembered: 'Remember those in prison as if you were their fellow prisoners, and those who are mistreated as if you yourselves were suffering' (13:3). Amnesty International, our newspapers, our letters of Christian workers overseas whom we know—these may well be our contemporary sources for acting on such appeals.

James is a treasure of a book when it comes to the theme of liberation. 'Religion that God our Father accepts as pure and faultless is this: to look after orphans and widows in their distress and to keep oneself from being polluted by the world' (1:27). Faith and good deeds must go hand in hand like the body and the spirit. James points out that taming the tongue is a crucial part of liberation and a difficult one: 'Out of the same mouth come praise and cursing. My brothers, this should not be' (3:10). This surely applies to our own use of words in books, letters, reviews, and pamphlets. As for the rich who hoard wealth at the expense of their workers, who oppress the poor while living in self-indulgence and luxury, who have condemned and murdered innocent people, for such as these James has hard words indeed (5:1-6). They are called to 'weep and wail' in the face of God's justice and judgement. Passages such as this should cause us to reflect that one of the tragedies of our age is that people have lost contact with the Bible. As the churches have increasingly personalised religion, as the Bible has been hidden away in Shakespearian language or behind holy walls, so the 'uncomfortable words' of Scripture have not been heard.

In the ***First and Second Letters of Peter***, the writer exults that the greatest act of liberation of all, Jesus Christ's resurrection from the chains of death, gives hope to us all (1 Pet 1:21-25). As servants of God in Christ, we 'live as free men' (2:16), good news that must be shared with others (3:15). Knowing the security of the Father's love, we can 'cast all our anxieties on him' (2 Pet 1:5-7). This liberating experience can take years, indeed a lifetime, to practise, but spiritual growth like this must be ongoing. Maturity of character and growing personal spirituality can be both observed and measured (2 Pet 1:5-7).

A continuous 'walking in the light' and 'walking in love' are synonymous, as the three ***Letters of John*** especially make clear. In these letters love is characterized as practical and includes the redistributing of wealth: 'If anyone has material possessions and sees his brother in need but has no pity on him, how can the love of God be in him?' (1 John 3:17). Love to God is expressed by love to our fellow human beings (4:7-12). 'If anyone says, "I love God" yet hates his brother, he is a liar. For anyone who does not love his brother, whom he has seen, cannot love God, whom he has not seen' (4:20). We might well reflect what this means as we 'see' our neighbour on a Christian Aid video or pictured in a magazine, struggling to eat and to survive.

As the tailpiece of the New Testament collection of letters, ***Jude*** appeals for mercy for those who doubt, and appeals to Christians to 'keep yourselves in God's love as you wait for the mercy of our Lord Jesus Christ to bring you to eternal life' (vv. 21-22).

7. The Book of Revelation

Now here is a cosmic book long before the term 'New Age' was ever coined! A good commentary is the only way forward, and even then the reader will be bound to struggle. The first three chapters are relatively easy to understand, containing short letters to seven of the well-known churches of that period whose messages transpose quite readily to our own situation. They urge, for example, the need to keep Christ as our first love in the local church (2:4-5). They warn that Christ the ascended Lord 'searches hearts and minds, and will repay each one of you according to your deeds' (2:23). They urge the need to have more than just a reputation for being a live church but actually to be one

(3:1-3) and warn of the dangers of a lukewarm church (3:15). But then things get more difficult. On one level, Revelation goes on to describe the work of the Risen Christ during the whole century of the life of the Christian Church at that time. The language used is necessarily cryptic because it often includes veiled, and highly political, attacks on the increasingly corrupt Roman Empire towards the very end of the first century A.D. The particular emperor portrayed in coded language is probably Domitian, who unleashed terrible persecution on the Christian Church. Two images in particular are especially used by the Seer to communicate the dreadful, corrupt, and corrupting power of the then Roman Empire: the 'beast of the sea' and the 'great prostitute' or 'Babylon' (13:2-10; 17:1-6, 18). We may surely discern contemporary equivalents of 'Babylon' today in some First World multi-national corporations that grow ever richer on the destitution of Third and Second World communities. They do not, of course, always realize the misery they are contributing to, but the evidence is all around them, however painful it may be to have to face up to it.

On another level, Revelation concerns things that have not yet happened. It draws pictures of the beginning of the end of all things, pointing towards the Omega point of history and life on earth. This is heady stuff. But for our purposes in this study, we need to notice that, as well as a highly charged critique of contemporary politics and society, Revelation also makes clear to us once again that some idea of a 'new creation' needs to be included in any truly biblical theology of liberation (7:15-17; 21:4). In the heaven of God's presence lies the true destiny of the new humanity in Christ. God's judgements are painfully described. So are the new Jerusalem and the new heavens and the new earth. These are the stuff of nightmare, poetry, vision, and film. With regard to our theme, they remind us of the spiritual or heavenly dimensions to the New Testament and the consequent belief that liberation is truly cosmic in scale and not earthbound only. The process of liberation is part of the history of heaven as well as that of earth.

8. Summary

In closing this chapter, before going on to survey Old Testament material, let us remind ourselves of some findings to date. Luke 4 suggests a messianic manifesto that is highly practical, and indeed political, in its social implications. Jesus had much to say about the dangers of wealth and riches, about practical love not only for God but also for our 'neighbour' and fellow disciples. Love and forgiveness must even embrace enemies as well as the hungry, thirsty, the imprisoned, and the poor. Jesus lamented over whole communities and cities as well as a nation. He affirmed the vulnerable, the oppressed, and the marginalized, including radicals, women, and children. His criticisms and sayings, as well as his lifestyle, offended many of the leaders and authorities of his day. His call was for a transformation of secular or 'this-worldly' attitudes and values. He expected repentance from a nation and from whole communities as well as from individuals. If his message was rejected, he warned of God's judgement and shared the Good News elsewhere instead. His followers were encouraged to pass on this teaching to all who would listen and respond.

The 'base communities' of the early Church, as we see them in the pages of the New Testament, were also concerned with liberation for all who would listen. Conversions to Christ, healings, and 'deliverance ministry' were part of this. So were famine relief; voluntary redistribution of personal wealth; and care for the vulnerable, the prisoners, and the suffering. All of these were featured in the praxis of the early Christians, for they were not preoccupied with the Church and its insiders only. Theirs was a vision for God's Kingdom way beyond their homes or synagogues or other places of worship. Finally, 'heaven', or the life of the age to come, completes the liberation of God's people. Indeed we can only begin to appreciate the New Testament fully when we find throughout its pages a creative blend of the 'now' and the 'not yet', the present age and that of the age to come. The Kingdom of God has immediate practical and socio-political implications for a New Humanity and a New Society. It will not be consummated, however, until the end of all things. It is this denouement towards which Christ's resurrection points and ever beckons. Judgement and the open exercise of God's justice at the end time, at the *eschaton*, are the backdrop against which all of this teaching is given by Jesus and his followers.

These are not words meant only for a group of first-century believers. They did not cease being relevant after they were first read to their intended congregations or communities. The Christian Church's claim is that God, by his Holy Spirit, intended that these writings should be preserved so that they might continue to speak to earth's people over all succeeding generations. The New Testament continues to be God's active Word pointing to Christ the living Word for all with ears to hear and eyes to see. Its importance is literally eternal. Through it God the Liberator made known in Jesus Christ still speaks.

Notes

[1] John Wesley, *Forty-Two Sermons* (Epworth Press, London, 1967), Sermon XII, p. 144.

[2] Source unknown.

[3] For a stimulating introduction to these issues, read John Stott, *The Cross of Christ* (IVP, London, 1986) in conjunction with Paul Fiddes, *Past Event and Present Salvation*

(Darton, Longman, and Todd, London, 1989). Frank Morrison's beautifully written book, *Who Moved the Stone?* (Faber, London, 1930) remains a challenging treatment of the Gospel resurrection narratives and their implications. The studies by Jürgen Moltmann, *Theology of Hope* and *The Crucified God. The Cross of Christ as the Foundation and Criticism of Christian Theology* (SCM, London, 1974), explore the resurrection and the cross of Jesus and were heavily drawn upon by many of the theologians of liberation we have been considering.

[4]John Howard Yoder, *The Politics of Jesus* (Eerdmans, Grand Rapids, 1972), pp. 62-63.

[5]See, for example, Leviticus 25.

[6]Yoder, *The Politics of Jesus*, pp. 62-63.

[7]Song by John Lennon and Yoko Ono, Onomusic/ATV Music, © 1972.

[8]See Acts 11:2-4.

Chapter 6
The Old Testament
Writings, Law, and History

In Jewish tradition the Hebrew Bible, or the Christian Old Testament, is divided into three main sections: the Law, the Prophets (Former and Latter), and the Writings. My own practice in reading the Old Testament, and in encouraging others to do so, has been to begin with the Writings, which are probably the most accessible point of entry into the world of the Old Testament. Our concern here is to enquire whether the Old Testament also reveals to us, as the New Testament has, a God committed to liberation. Moreover, 'liberation' means the deliverance from oppression not only of individuals, but also of communities, the people of God, whole nations, and the natural creation itself. Put another way, is the God of the Old Testament committed to the overthrow of tyrants, the better government of nations, and the changing of religious and political structures in the better interests of humankind, especially the poor and oppressed? Is God concerned and active in history and in society in ways that transcend the confines of religious groups and their rituals?

That is the question. What follows can in no way claim to be a complete study and so a complete answer. Inevitably, there will be some passages given undue emphasis and others neglected. The Bible is a big book in more ways than one! 'We may drink what we need from the living water of the Scriptures but never imagine that we have drained that water dry' (Ephrem the Syrian). My aim, as a pastor in a local church, is to test a growing conviction that our churches are often failing to hear God's call in our time to participate in holistic evangelization and, therefore, in liberation. To test this conviction in the wisest way possible, I have gone back again to the written source of our faith and belief as Christian people: the Scriptures of Old and New Testaments. These I have sought to read afresh from the perspective of some of the claims of the theologians of liberation, letting the Scriptures speak for themselves and using scholarship only as a 'handmaiden'[1], serving the text. I have also ventured from time to time to indicate how I believe these ancient texts speak anew in our age. Again, as in the New Testament chapter, the reader may choose to pass over the references quickly or to follow up the passages quoted at leisure.

1. The Writings

The Psalms

Often called the 'Songs of Praise' of ancient Israel, the Psalms contain far more than praise, including songs of lamentation, petition, and confession. There are 150 songs in all, divided for reasons no longer readily apparent into five sections clearly marked in our Psalters.[2] Throughout this variety, the theme of liberation persists, as the following examples should make clear. Psalm 2, for example, reminds us that our God is the God of all the nations and that to him their rulers answer: 'Therefore, you kings, be wise; be warned, you rulers of the earth. Serve the Lord with fear and rejoice with trembling'. Psalm 7 portrays God as the judge of the peoples, as a 'righteous God who searches minds and hearts'. His concern is to 'bring to an end the violence of the wicked'. Psalm 9 warns of the grave that awaits those who forget God, 'But the needy will not always be forgotten, nor the hope of the afflicted ever perish'. Psalm 10 similarly is a psalm for an oppressed community. The lifestyle of the wicked man who hunts down the weak is powerfully evoked: 'The victim commits himself to you', we read, 'you are the helper of the fatherless. Break the arm of the wicked and evil man; call him to account for his wickedness that would not be found out'. Psalm 10 ends with these words:

> You hear, O Lord, the desire of the afflicted. You encourage them, and you listen to their cry defending the fatherless and the oppressed in order that man, who is of the earth, may terrify no more.

The theme of God's care for the needy and desperate recurs throughout the book of Psalms (e.g., 72:12-14; 82:2-4; 102:19-20). To God again and again the psalmists turn for personal and community liberation (e.g., 18:16-19; 40:1-3; 68:19-20). In words that Christians have long associated with Christ's death at Calvary, Psalm 22 describes the lament of someone undergoing deep personal distress and suffering. To God he looks for deliverance: 'But you, O Lord, be not far off; O, my strength, come quickly to help me. Deliver my life from the sword, my precious life from the power of the dogs'. Psalm 44 is a similar cry for help, this time for and from an entire community: 'Yet for your sake we face death all day long; we are considered as sheep to be slaughtered'. As we have seen, in the first part of this guide, this experience remains a sadly contemporary one in Third World nations and elsewhere. Jesus was to teach disparagingly of wealth and riches. So do the Psalms. Riches are cheaply valued. Consider Psalm 49, which warns that wealth can be misunderstood; it is not necessarily a sign of God's favour, and, in fact, it can be the reverse: 'A man who has riches without understanding is like the beasts that perish.' God is repeatedly seen in the Psalms as the restorer of fortunes, the one to look to for an upturn in circumstances and for liberation from distress, as in Psalm 53: 'Oh that salvation for Israel would come out of Zion! When God restores the fortunes of his people, let Jacob rejoice and Israel be glad'. Concern for the powerless and weak can be clearly seen in, for example, Psalm 68:

His name is the Lord—and rejoice before him. A father to the fatherless, a defender of widows, is God in his holy dwelling. God sets the lonely in families, he leads forth the prisoners with singing; but the rebellious live in a sun-scorched land.

Creation, too, is to praise the Lord and experience God's liberation (e.g., 96:10-13; 98; 136). The plight of a man of peace among people of violence is powerfully described in Psalm 120: 'Too long have I lived among those who hate peace. I am a man of peace; but when I speak, they are for war'. Such was the voice of Christians and others in the Cold War as the superpowers stockpiled, in both First and Second Worlds, many weapons of mass destruction with all their terrifying annihilative potential. These weapons may or may not be necessary evils; the *necessary* has long been the subject of debate, but the *evils* are surely not. What is unacceptable to a 'person of peace' is to have such weapons regarded as a positive good.

Psalm 126 is another prayer, this time of anticipatory thanksgiving for the liberation of a whole community languishing under cruel oppressors in exile:

Our mouths were filled with laughter, our tongues with songs of joy. . . . The Lord has done great things for us and we are filled with joy. Restore our fortunes O Lord like streams in the Negev. Those who sow in tears will reap with songs of joy. He who goes out weeping, carrying seed to sow will return with songs of joy, carrying sheaves with him.

Psalm 137 similarly looks to God for deliverance, but also has a disturbing note of revenge for injustices done. It is an explanation, if not an excuse, to say that it is written in the bitter tears of slavery. The psalmists' desperation so often derives from social and economic weakness. Either they are the victims and playthings of their rich and powerful conquerors, or they find that even their neighbours, people they had counted their friends, now shun them or actively take advantage of their vulnerability. The book of Psalms is clearly central to our theme, full of concerns about liberation, deliverance, and justice for the poor and needy, as well as containing warnings about the misuse of wealth and about the consequences of violence.

Proverbs

Proverbs contains collections of homely, amusing, and powerful aphorisms; it preserves both words of 'The Wise' and popular sayings. Several quotations will be helpful in confirming our theme.

When a wicked man dies, his hope perishes; all he expected from his power comes to nothing. (11:7)

He who oppresses the poor shows contempt for their Maker, but whoever is kind to the needy honours God. (14:31)

He who mocks the poor shows contempt for their Maker. (17:5)

If a man shuts his ears to the cry of the poor, he too will cry out and not be answered. (21:13)

He who oppresses the poor to increase his wealth and he who gives gifts to the rich—both come to poverty. (22:16)

If your enemy is hungry, give him food to eat; if he is thirsty, give him water to drink. In doing this you will heap burning coals on his head, and the Lord will reward you. (25:21-22)

When the wicked rise to power, people go into hiding, but when the wicked perish, the righteous thrive. (28:28)

The righteous care about justice for the poor, but the wicked have no such concern. (29:7)

Two things I ask of you, O Lord; do not refuse me before I die: Keep false-hood and lies far from me; give me neither poverty nor riches, but give me only my daily bread. Otherwise, I may have too much and disown you and say, 'Who is the Lord'? Or I may become poor and steal, and so dishonour the name of my God. (30:7-9)

Speak up for those who cannot speak for themselves, for the rights of all who are destitute. Speak up and judge fairly; defend the rights of the poor and needy. (31:8-9)

This last quotation is attributed to the Arabian ruler Lemuel and was taught him, we are told, by the queen mother (31:31). The saying is instructive in at least two ways. First, we note how God was prepared to bring to the attention of the Israelite compiler words of wisdom from another culture (and probably an alternative religious faith); this is characteristic of the whole 'wisdom move-ment' in Ancient Israel that had international horizons, which knew that God's truth and wisdom were not only to be found in Israel. This material has left its mark on 'Holy Scripture'. Second, the content of these words of Lemuel might well be very useful ones for those who preach on the Sunday before election days in those countries privileged to have genuinely democratic elections. These verses provide a worthy perspective from which to decide how to vote locally and nationally. While Christians will differ in practice as to which party-political preference these verses indicate, they will surely ask whether a candidate and party do have the courage to 'speak up for those who cannot speak for themselves'. In my view, Christians might well vote differently on different occasions because of thinking seriously about the differing issues involved here and about the character and record of the particular candidates who wish to represent them at whatever level of government.

Ecclesiastes

Ecclesiastes is one of the finest works of religious apologetics ever written. If any book is designed to set a person thinking about life's deeper meanings, this one is. The Teacher laments the success of evil and injustice:

> And I saw something else under the sun: in the place of judgment—wickedness was there, in the place of justice—wickedness was there. I thought in my heart, God will bring to judgement both the righteous and the wicked, for there will be a time for every activity, a time for every deed. (3:16-17)

The wisdom writer could look out on the world, as we can through our televisions and newspapers and our own eyes, and notice: 'all the oppression . . . taking place under the sun. . . . I saw the tears of the oppressed—and they have no comforter; power was on the side of their oppressors—and they have no comforter' (4:1-2). Who has not in our day also spoken, or at least mentally voiced, those words?

Job

On one level, the magnificent poem about Job is the narrative of the fall and eventual rise of a now wiser, righteous man. On another level, it is as profound a treatise on the mystery of human suffering and a radical questioning of the fairness of God as you will find anywhere. Job is another example, along with Proverbs and Ecclesiastes, of the genre of Old Testament literature that the scholars call 'Wisdom Literature'. For our purposes we simply note that a major concern of these writers is to remind us of life's injustices and divisions:

> One man dies in full vigour, completely secure and at ease, his body well nourished, his bones rich with marrow. Another man dies in bitterness of soul, never having enjoyed anything good. (21:23-25)

There is no hope of eternal life, as in the New Testament, to offer comfort: 'Side by side they lie in the dust, and worms cover them both'. The violent, the people of evil, are also acutely observed. Rebels against the light they are:

> When daylight is gone, the murderer rises up and kills the poor and needy; in the night he steals forth like a thief. . . . deep darkness is their morning; they make friends with the terrors of darkness. (24:14-17)

Even the mighty, however, must be finally subject to the Lord:

> They die in an instant, in the middle of the night; the people are shaken and they pass away; the mighty are removed without human hand.

History demonstrates that God often uses night-time to bring a political tyrant to face his judgement. At the pinnacle of power they go to sleep and awake naked before the awesome God of the poor, with blood on their hands:

> Without enquiry he shatters the mighty and sets up others in their place. (34:20-24)

Human history confirms the truth of this statement. But Job's complaint and his perplexity, of course, are that sometimes "it's a mighty long time a comin'."

Ruth and Esther

Ruth and Esther are aptly included within the Writings of the Hebrew canon of Scripture. The charming story of Ruth reveals God's care for the alien or stranger, and we shall also presently see this concern emphasized in the Law (Torah). This book was probably, in part, originally an attempt to soften the harshness and exclusivism of some of the post-exilic Jews. Some were not accepting mixed marriages, even when the same faith was shared, across national cultures. Ruth makes the simple but profound point that even the great king David was descended from 'a foreigner' (4:22). In our day, when an understandable patriotism and an unforgivable racism sometimes go hand in hand, Ruth is a book we would do well to study closely. It is another example of the treasures of Scripture too often missed by our secular culture.

The story also demonstrates Ruth's willingness to be integrated. The acceptance and adaptation are two-way: 'Where you go I will go, and where you stay I will stay. Your people will be my people and your God my God' (1:16). At first Ruth is only given the gleanings left over at harvest. Eventually she comes to share her body and life with the owner of the farm in marriage. This woman of noble character from Moab (modern Jordan) marries the Israelite Boaz, kinsman to her mother-in-law Naomi. God's hand has been in all this, as we see from Naomi's lovely words: 'The Lord . . . has not stopped showing his kindness to the living and to the dead' (2:20). The importance of welcoming those who come to our land and of accepting and assisting their integration is a clear theme of Ruth. It is a theme with relevance for the nations of our world in these days of refugees, of the mass dislocation of peoples and the sensitivities of government involving immigration policies. I write, as I have already explained, as the son of a refugee who escaped slavery in Stalin's Gulag, and who fled to Britain from the traumas of Eastern Europe during World War II to build a new future and a family here.

The book of Esther also concerns liberation. 'For such a time as this', God —who is never explicitly mentioned in this book but is still implicitly at work just as in so much of history—raises up Esther to be queen of the land (4:14). Using her position of influence, Mordecai is able to deliver the Jews from a planned series of massacres or pogroms. Would that world history had known more Mordecais! Would that Germany in the 1930s had known a Mordecai! However, we also notice in this story the pre-Christian 'eye for eye and tooth for tooth' revenge mentality to be found in much of the Old Testament. Delivered themselves, the Jews—initially only in self defence let it be said—killed and destroyed (8:11). But then, in a chilling phrase, we read that they 'did what they pleased to those who hated them' (9:5). This complex story thus reveals a tendency in human nature that in our time has been fully exemplified in the horrors of revenge, multiple rape, and mass murder in the former Yugoslavia. *Kyrie eleison.* Lord have mercy. There is a terrible danger that even the experience of liberation can be turned into the oppression of others.

Song of Songs

As for the Song of Songs, it seems clear that the bridegroom and his bride have quite other priorities. We note, however, that this love poem refuses to compartmentalize life into two insulated parts: sacred and secular. Too many religious believers still seek to 'put asunder what God has joined together'. The Hebrew vision of the body and soul, like its vision of human history, is fully unitive. How good it is to find fulfilment through human sexuality affirmed, and love poetry included, in the Bible.

Daniel

Most modern scholars suggest Daniel was written in the Maccabean period (second century B.C.) with a particular goal in mind: to encourage God's people to remain loyal to the Lord their God and to their faith in him in the midst of the harsh and deadly persecution of those times. Daniel is, thus, a piece of skilful storytelling, drawing on surviving folk narrative and traditions with powerful contemporary implications; in this, of course, it is much like some of the parables of Jesus. Other scholars propose that we leave the book in the period where Daniel himself is placed—in the Babylonian exile, written then and for then. In the late twentieth century what matters now is what God might be saying to us through the book. He surely has much to say about loyalty and faithfulness in time of persecution, distress, or hardship. For the purposes of our study, let us note the 'dazzling statue' that comes to represent the transience of earthly kingdoms while the 'God of gods and the Lord of kings' survives and judges them all (chap. 2). The story also demonstrates the humbling of a tyrant for a period until his lessons were learned (4:28-37). We see in Daniel that people are to look to God for deliverance and for a better earthly future (9:17-19). Finally, chapter 9 offers a splendid example of an intercessory prayer. How feeble by comparison are the range and scope of what pass for intercessions in too many of our churches, where the vision is only for God's Church and all too rarely for God's Kingdom way beyond its walls and people.

It should be made clear at this point that there are other Old Testament books traditionally included with the 'Writings', namely, 1 and 2 Chronicles, Ezra and Nehemiah, and Lamentations. These will be considered elsewhere for reasons that should then become clear. Some of the experiences that have, in our day and age, given rise to new ways of being the Church can be found in those books we call the Writings. So too can the concerns and activities of God the Liberator. What can be said, however, of the Old Testament books that are the key texts in the eyes of many—the Law, or Torah?

2. Law

The five books from Genesis to Deuteronomy consist, at least in part, of the Law of ancient and modern Israel. These books, so significant in world and religious history, are often misunderstood. A large part of them is in fact narrative rather than lengthy descriptions of regulations and compilations of law codes we might initially expect. They do contain the code of the Covenant; the Holiness Code; food regulations; guidance on human sexuality; and legislation to protect the weak, the outcast, and the underprivileged. But they also give us stories about the origins of the universe and humankind, the lives of the patriarchs, Joseph in Egypt, the years of bondage in Egypt and the exodus from it, the wandering in the wilderness, and Moses the overburdened leader leading God's people right up to the verge of Jordan. Together with some songs of praise to God, all these elements constitute the Torah, or Law. They are far more than ancient legal text books.

Genesis

In Genesis we see the creative, liberating, magnificent Creator God at work forming the universe, causing life's emergence on earth and the ascendancy of humankind (1–2:4). While some Christians accept the Genesis accounts quite literally, others interpret them in the light of the scientific theories of the big bang and of evolution.[3] Many Christians rarely think about these matters at all but just get on with the task of living in the presence of this Creator God and serving humankind today, regardless of how we actually got here. We notice that it is not just the ancestors of the Israelites such as righteous Noah or faithful Abraham who are loved by the God of Israel. An Egyptian slave girl and her child matter greatly to this Creator God as well. He sees and notices her distress and misery: 'You are the God who sees me, . . . I have now seen the One who sees me', confesses Hagar (16:13). Jacob felt the same as he and his family fled from their economic bondage to a hard taskmaster, Laban: 'God has seen my hardship and the toil of my hands' (31:38-42). Some modern-day workers, even if not technically 'slaves', are similarly trapped by ties of blood and family into cheap labour for very low wages. And this is true of children as well as adults. Nor was the Jacob experience unique; Joseph, too, knew what it was to work as a slave and to be unjustly imprisoned.[4] The God of liberation was able, nonetheless, to use creatively his sufferings to rescue a whole people. World history is filled with similar testimony. Nelson Mandela is one modern-day example of a human being's suffering that has come to inspire and unite a whole people.[5]

Exodus

It is easy to see why Exodus has long been a popular book with the theologians of liberation. It describes a people in all the agonies of bondage, oppression, and slavery:

During that long period, the king of Egypt died. The Israelites groaned in their slavery and cried out and their cry for help because of their slavery went up to God. God heard their groaning and he remembered his covenant with Abraham, with Isaac and with Jacob. So God looked on the Israelites and was concerned about them (2:23-25).

How often over history that experience has been repeated—from the Roman galleys to the American cotton plantations, and from the migrant workers of Europe to the child prostitutes of Thailand. Sometimes, of course, speaking about and drawing attention to injustice and complaining make matters worse, at least at first: 'Ever since I went to Pharaoh to speak in your name', complains Moses, 'he has brought trouble upon this people, and you have not rescued your people at all' (5:23). God replies convincingly; liberation is imminent. The plagues are soon over, the tyrant is outwitted and defeated, the Sea of Reeds is crossed. *Now* God the Liberator is judged worthy of praise:

The Lord is my strength and my song; he has become my salvation. He is my God, and I will praise him, my father's God, and I will extol him. . . . Who is like you—majestic in holiness, awesome in glory, working wonders? . . . In your unfailing love you will lead the people you have redeemed. In your strength you will guide them to your holy dwelling. The nations will hear and tremble. (15:1-2, 11, 13-14)

This picture of Israel, developed in Exodus, as the 'special people' of God, is incontrovertibly present throughout the pages of the Old Testament. As we will see, that concept, however, needs to be—and is—balanced by other emphases and insights in the Old Testament Scriptures.

The Ten Commandments are also surely to be seen as part of God's plan for human liberation (20:1-21). For example, the principle of one day of rest every seven is seen as a clear creation ordinance. Not even 'the alien within your gates' is to be *made* to work without a break. How many foreign workers in Europe's cities today might that apply to? How many self-employed people obsessed with work and the income it generates also need to hear these words? Many work to the detriment of health, family life, and peace of mind. Some have no choice; others are too preoccupied to enjoy or even notice the sacred gifts of human life. Again, respect and honour for father and mother are valuable counters to the prevailing attitudes of our day and age that sees countless thousands of old people languishing in residential homes for the elderly 'so as not to be a burden' to family. That many elderly people choose such places and prefer them is not in question. That many such homes are compassionate and caring places of refuge again is beyond question, though it is correct to say many but not all. The stories of elderly people bled dry of their money and cruelly neglected in some such places are still far too many. And how many live in residential homes who would be happier and more secure if the old principles of the extended family still applied, except for all the agony of choice this can be for their sons and daughters?

Communities such as Blackburn, where I ministered for five years, include many Asian families where the principles of the extended family can still be seen very much at work. The Asian communities in the United Kingdom have much to teach and remind the rest of us about care of and respect for elderly people. For the Muslims among them, the Ten Commandments are part of their faith, too. The Commandments remind us that love for neighbour is essentially practical. If you love God and respect your neighbour, you will neither destroy nor violate the harmony of another's marriage bed. Nor will you kill, steal, falsely accuse, or covet what is his or hers. With regard to the last command, it seems to me that some of the party-political tirades against the rich we hear today are really covetousness disguised, or the 'jealous face of Socialism'. The Bible goes much deeper in its warnings about riches and its urging of a voluntary redistribution of wealth. We notice also how the Exodus laws insist on care for the stranger and the poor neighbour (22:21; 22:25-27; 23:9). God the Liberator from slavery in Egypt now lives among them and sets high standards accordingly (29:45-46).

Leviticus

When did you last preach or hear a sermon preached from Leviticus? Here too concern for the weak members in a community may be discerned. Respect for the elderly is encouraged: 'Rise in the presence of the aged, show respect for the elderly and revere your God. I am the Lord' (19:32). The ill treatment of an alien is forbidden with this reminder: 'Love him as yourself, for you were aliens in Egypt. I am the Lord your God' (19:34). As we saw implemented earlier in the story of Ruth, the poor are also to be considered at harvest time (23:23). The principle of the debt-freeing year of Jubilee that we referred to in Luke 4 also deserves consideration here. Every fifty years liberty is to be proclaimed and practised throughout all the land to all its inhabitants: 'Do not take advantage of each other, but fear your God. I am the Lord your God' (25:17). The prohibition on charging interest strikes modern readers as strange, of course (25:35-38). It is interesting to state the obvious here: we have built a whole Capitalist economic system on ignoring it! Given human nature, *that* is probably inevitable. This realistic observation should not be used, however, to excuse the need to examine critically the use made of interest by the rich and advantaged. Often it is used to consolidate their own strength and wealth and position, sometimes at the cost of great pain and suffering to the poor and disadvantaged. The various problems of Third and Second World debt are the most pressing examples of the misery that interest rates and the practice of usury can cause.

Consider, also, the First World here. All too familiar to us are the unemployed or underpaid struggling to keep their homes and therefore to pay their mortgages; the couple desperate to have a baby but unable to afford to stop working; the many driven further and further into debt by their folly in taking advantage of easy credit, whether by credit cards, store cards, or low interest or 'pay later' offers. Many in our world pay a heavy price for our economic system, built as it is upon usury. The principle of the Jubilee release, it is said, goes against human nature and is both naive and unworkable. Perhaps. But the suffering from ignoring it goes on month in and month out, all over the Three Worlds. That human nature is unworthy of Jubilee does not render it any the less challenging or worthy a concept. Leviticus too then is an Old Testament book highly relevant to our theme. The God we find there is mindful of the poor. He is in the business of breaking the bars of the yoke and of enabling his people to walk with heads held high (26:13).

Numbers

Numbers is perhaps best known to most Christians because of its containing the most delightful of the Old Testament blessings, the Aaronic blessing of Numbers 6:24-26: 'The Lord bless you and keep you; the Lord make his face shine upon you and be gracious to you; the Lord turn his face towards you and give you peace'. The book as a whole contains stories about the forty years of wilderness wanderings that followed the exodus of the Israelite people from Egypt. Numbers also presents census details, teaching on the role and functions of the priestly Levites, and instructions about the tabernacle and its worship. In this context, Numbers contains a most illuminating passage about the sharing of the burdens and responsibilities of spiritual leadership with others (11:10-30). Moses expresses the desire that God's work be undertaken by *all* of his people: 'But Moses replied, "Are you jealous for my sake? I wish that all the Lord's people were prophets and that the Lord would put his Spirit on them" ' (11:29).

Far too few church leaders over the centuries have challenged or encouraged the members of their congregations with the liberation from sacral roles contained in this particular passage. But the 'lay co-ordinators' in the Latin American base communities and the 'lay pastors' in churches of the Baptist World Alliance in many countries have entered into this Mosaic heritage.

Numbers also describes the chequered career of Balaam and his prophecy of the reign of a coming ruler in Israel's future, almost certainly intended by the writer to refer to the great King David (24:17-19); he will 'help Israel to grow strong'. Concern for the wholeness of both nation and individual marks the witness of the book of Numbers.

Deuteronomy

Deuteronomy, the fifth book of the Law, envisages a situation of relative wealth for some as the people stand on the borders of their new land, and it gives teaching on the correct attitude to maintain in these circumstances:

> You may say to yourself, 'My power and the strength of my hands have produced this wealth for me'. But remember the Lord your God, for it is he who gives you the ability to produce wealth, and so confirms his covenant, which he swore to your forefathers even as it is today. (8:17-18)

We heard much during the 1980s about the importance of wealth creation in Europe or North America. We needed this reminder, for it remains true that unless wealth is created from a healthy industrial base and a balance of trade, there will be little wealth to redistribute, whether through taxation or personal voluntary giving. But what we have not heard so much of is the need for wealth to be used in ways that both remember and please the Lord. In this context, we note that it is 'fear of the Lord' that gives rise to care for the widow, the alien, and the fatherless (10:12-22).

In chapter 15, Deuteronomy faces up to the further economic reality that 'there will always be poor people in the land'. Therefore, says God, 'I command you to be open-handed towards your brothers and towards the poor and needy in your land'. The ideal of course by which we shall be judged, beyond the reality, is that 'there should be no poor among you, for in the land your God is giving you to possess as your inheritance, he will richly bless you' (15:4). In the 1980s, we did not hear much about such redistributing of all the wealth that was being created. The evidence about what was happening seems—to many observers—incontrovertible: some already wealthy sections of society benefitted disproportionately from such wealth creation as there was, to the detriment of many other far needier peoples in all of the Three Worlds. Any credible First World theology of liberation needs to address itself to this issue.

Deuteronomy goes on to condemn the accepting of bribes by judges as anathema: 'Follow justice and justice alone, so that you may live and possess the land the Lord your God is giving you' (16:19-20). A cloak forfeited by someone as a pledge of security must be returned for the night-time 'so that he may sleep in it' (24:13). The people of Israel must remember that they were once themselves refugees, fathered (as it were) by a wandering Aramaean (26:5). In Egypt they languished:

> But the Egyptians mistreated us and made us suffer, putting us to hard labour. Then we cried out to the Lord, the God of our fathers, and the Lord heard our voice and saw our misery, toil, and oppression. So the Lord brought us out. (26:5-10)

Towards the end of Deuteronomy there are, in fact, anticipations that the people will again suffer conquest and exile from their own land, returning once more to a new kind of 'Egyptian bondage' (28:30-37, 64-68). Some scholars therefore suggest that Deuteronomy was edited and completed in the period after the exile in Babylon and that its contents reflect these exilic experiences in part, just as a sermon today may draw on contemporary observations to enforce a point. Others view them, rather, as prophetic warnings long ahead of their fulfillment.

We discover, then, that there is far more material about liberation and 'holistic salvation' in the books of the Law, the Torah, than just the few choice passages from Exodus that are often quoted. The Bible, it seems, is a dangerous book when we really listen to it.

3. History

The history books of ancient Israel are sadly neglected by many preachers and teachers. How much we miss in our selectivity! Preachers have their own canon of favourites: Samuel listening for God's voice at night, David's victory over Goliath and (perhaps) his adultery with Bathsheba, some Elijah and Elisha stories, godly Josiah's reforms and a passage or two on praise from Chronicles, Nehemiah's exhortation to joy. The rest is often uncharted territory for those of us who are pulpit-dwellers. The history books of Israel, which in the Hebrew canon were called 'The Former Prophets', deserve better than that. Again let us seek to mine them from the perspective of our biblical theme of liberation in its roundedness.

Joshua and Judges

Joshua and Judges are fascinating books, not least because they concern the use of violence, bloodshed, and fighting to obtain liberation and to secure new government for a nation. It seems that outright conquest, an attractive popular uprising among the people of the land, *and* a process of the peaceful assimilation of supportive peoples, all combined to create the emergence of the Israelites as the dominant rulers in the Canaan of that time. A few liberation theologians (but not all), as we have seen, have at times advocated a similar course of action in the Latin American struggle for liberation from oppression. They speak of the need to employ a *second violence* so as to overcome the *first violence* employed by a state and its army and secret police networks, though they usually stress that violence is to be employed when all else has failed. Peaceful popular uprisings and the support of people of goodwill everywhere are encouraged, but occasionally violence is also condoned if never explicitly invited. Let us note from Joshua and Judges, however, the high price paid by the vanquished, the enormous loss of life involved, and the ongoing struggles of the new rulers to survive even after initial victories and conquest. With war, skirmishes, and major battles breaking out subsequently, these books read like many accounts of coups, revolutions, and their aftermath in our century.

At times the killing and bloodshed is both bitter and extreme.

> When Israel had finished killing all the men of Ai in the fields and in the desert where they had chased them, and when every one of them had been put to the sword, all the Israelites returned to Ai and killed those who were in it. Twelve thousand men and women fell that day—all the people of Ai. (Josh 8:24-25)

Can God ever sanction, or indeed encourage, the use of force and violence to achieve his purposes? The Old Testament writers clearly believed the answer to be 'yes'. But were they, in fact, correct in this assumption? In such a case as the massacre of Ai, I believe this to be an instance of the Bible's human authors projecting some of their own very human emotions onto the God they believed in, the One who *had* helped their nation, though not always in the ways they suggested. The seminal figure in popular culture, Bob Dylan, dealt with this issue in his caustic protest song of the 1960s entitled 'With God on Our Side'. In Joshua do we hear just an earlier playing of a recurring mistake in human history—the identifying of God with *our* cause? To take a modern example, I believe that the Allied forces could claim with some justification that God was on their side in the fight against the demonic evil exhibited by Hitler and against the results of Japanese militarism in the Europe and Asia of the Second World War. But can that *ever* excuse a Dresden or a Hiroshima or a Nagasaki? It is still far too easy for humans to attach God to our causes with strings of our own making. At judgement we will each of us find out how the Lord God really feels about that.

Again, how are we to interpret a passage such as Joshua 11 about the destruction of the northern kings before 'the land had rest from war'? To our minds it seems an offensive piece of narration. Does the coming of Christ and the corrective teaching he gave about God suggest that Joshua and his contemporaries had it completely wrong? Had they simply misread God? In a violent age did they only do what otherwise would have been done to them? These are key questions, not just for reading the Old Testament, but also for knowing how to act in our world today—for example, in Latin America in the 1970s or in Romania during Christmas 1989. It is easy enough for those of us living in a relatively stable and reasonably democratic country to sit and debate whether a Christian or a resistance movement fighter can ever use violence. How very different it must all seem when friends have felt the lash of the whip, the injustice of prison, or the relentlessness of physical torture. How very different for those whose loved ones languish in ghettos in abject and institutionalised poverty within sight of the palaces and mansions of the wealthy. Does the God revealed in Jesus Christ sometimes encourage, or at least sanction, the use of violence in our Christian era? What of the wartime resistance movements of France or the conspiracies against Hitler in Germany, or the uprising in Poland's Warsaw ghetto? Can the path of violence be—sometimes at least—the better of two evils in bringing liberation to a country or continent? Christian people will differ in answering these questions, and I venture to express my own conviction below. But we cannot escape facing the key issues as we read Joshua and Judges. Nor let us miss the compassion and justice behind the principle of cities of refuge, for those who had 'unintentionally and without malice aforethought' killed another (20:3-6).

The violence of a Gideon or a Samson raises similar questions as Joshua. That lasting peace sometimes comes only after violent struggle is a sad truth of human history. It was certainly true in those days; consider Ehud and his campaign against Moab (3:12-20). The Nazirite vow likewise implicitly includes the assumption of violence that will lead to 'the deliverance of Israel from the hands of the Philistines' (13:5). Is the way of the Gospel always that of peaceful non-violent protest? Pope John Paul II has made his position clear: 'Violence is always an offence, an insult to man, both to the one who perpetrates it and to the one who suffers it'.[6] Leo Tolstoy similarly was convinced that 'a good proportion of the evils that afflict humankind is due to the erroneous belief that life can be made secure by violence'.[7] In the days of Joshua and Judges, by contrast, it was destroy or be destroyed. Is this still the only way humankind understands some three millennia on? In Voltaire's words: 'Is this history which I have just finished the history of serpents and tigers? No, it is the history of mankind; tigers and serpents would never treat their fellows so'.[8] I have already noted that Christians will differ on this issue. My own position is that the way of non-violence is always preferable and superior, but that violence and war, in a cause agreed to be good by common international consensus, can be *a necessary evil* that sometimes results in a greater good.

1 and 2 Samuel

The two books of Samuel trace the emergence of kingship in Northern Israel and later in the southern kingdom of Judah. We note that Saul became the popular choice by his successful campaigns against the marauding Philistines (1 Sam 11). David too came to prominence as the slayer of the giant Goliath (1 Sam 17). He also quite literally fought for his life against Saul and eventually succeeded to the throne and stayed there by the fierce use of violence combined with astute political skill. The moving of his capital to Jerusalem was a brilliant stroke—a geographically neutral centre acceptable to both the north and south he was to rule over. Second Samuel sees God promising David 'rest from all your enemies' and an enduring dynasty, with the intention that the whole nation should be freed from oppression:

> I will provide a place for my people Israel and will plant them so that they can have a home of their own and no longer be disturbed. Wicked people will not oppress them anymore as they did at the beginning and have done ever since the time I appointed leaders [judges] over my people Israel. I will also give you rest from all your enemies. (2 Sam 7:10-11)

There is liberation for individuals, too. The physically handicapped Mephibosheth is recognized and affirmed (2 Sam 9). The principle that kings too are answerable to God and that true men and women of God have the right to challenge and tackle even leaders and rulers is clearly evidenced by Nathan after David's sin with Bathsheba and the murder of her husband (2 Sam 12:1-14). The song of David in 2 Samuel 22:47-50 is also surely the epitome of liberation, although it still shows some of the ambiguities of violent actions and nationalism we have already reflected upon:

> The Lord lives! Praise be to my Rock! Exalted be God, the Rock, my Saviour! He is the God who avenges me, who puts the nations under me, who sets me free from my enemies. You exalted me above my foes; from violent men you rescued me. Therefore I will praise you, O Lord, among the nations.

1 and 2 Kings

Even as the new temple is completed and a new era in their worship is instituted during the reign of Solomon, Israel is reminded that it is God's people,
'brought out of that iron-smelting furnace' of slavery in Egypt (1 Kgs 8:51).
After Solomon, tyrants appear increasingly on the stage in the books of Kings,
and they always forfeit God's support. This time, though, they are ruling Israel,
not conquering it. The dictator Rehoboam promises to scourge the people with
scorpions as his father once scourged them with whips (1 Kgs 12:11). Schism
is the price he pays for his tyranny—and for poor political advice—as the people of the north split David's once great united kingdom into two nations: north
(Israel) and south (Judah). This schism is relatively bloodless as far as we can
see. The principle of God's people refusing to accept a tyrant's rule, as here, is
surely relevant to the theme of contemporary liberation. The Elijah stories
remind us that time and time again in the history of the people of God the Lord
has raised up men and women to speak his prophetic word of rebuke and to
issue a call to repentance to kings and other rulers. Witness Elijah scourging his
king and queen with words for their foul treatment of Naboth (1 Kgs 21:20-29,
72); Ahab and Jezebel liked this no more than today's presidents, prime
ministers, and party leaders do. We may recall the outcry from government
politicians when *Faith in the City* was published in Britain, for example.[9] We
observe the cost to Elijah; his championing of the people's cause against a
despot meant that he had to flee from official persecution and live in hiding, or
else face certain death.

Time and time again, in the second book of Kings whole careers are judged
by one standard: was this king, or was he not, faithful to the Jerusalem temple
and the worship of God it offered? Jeroboam II, for example, is judged negatively, even though it is quite clear that his was a good reign for Israel in other
respects, as God intended: 'The Lord had seen how bitterly everyone in Israel,
whether slave or free, was suffering; there was no one to help them. . . . He
saved them by the hand of Jeroboam son of Jehoash' (2 Kgs 14:24-31). The
Assyrian ruler Sennacherib is also to discover that he is fighting against the
Living God and not just against Hezekiah of Judah and his dispirited people
(19:21-28).

Josiah's reforms remind us of the importance of God's people setting their
own house in order (23:1-30). We gather from all this that 'liberation' also
means the renewal of God's people after a heartfelt return to him and his ways.
Even in the exile of the people of Judah to Babylon with which these books
end, and after all the horrors of invasion and conquest, God's secret hand can
still be discerned at work (25:27-30).

1 and 2 Chronicles

Although, strictly speaking, the Chronicles, along with Ezra and Nehemiah, belong to 'the Writings' in the Hebrew arrangement of the canon, it seems sensible to include them here among the Old Testament history books. Although narrative, they emphasize the importance of music to the worship of God, the value of sacred singing, and of worship well conducted. The liberation of the people of God may well be first experienced in their celebration and worship. The 'spirituals' of the black American slaves in the last century and the vibrant worship of the Latin American base communities in this century are examples of this truth. The books of Chronicles are really a retelling of the story of David, Solomon, and subsequent kings from the perspective of worship and especially of their attitude to the primacy of the Jerusalem temple. These are the glasses through which this writer, or perhaps a group of writers, views God's dealings with his people. God is portrayed as being behind David and those victories that first set Israel free to enjoy peace and prosperity; so free in fact that the Jerusalem temple could at last be built by Solomon (1 Chron 18:1-13).

It is interesting to see in these books that a whole nation can be called to repentance:

> If my people, who are called by my name, will humble themselves and pray and seek my face and turn from their wicked ways, then will I hear from heaven and will forgive their sin and will heal their land. (2 Chron 7:14)

There true revival of national life begins. We can learn also something from the story of Oded who prevented further slaughter of Judaean prisoners at a time of war between Israel and Judah by a firm rebuke to the then victorious king and by an appeal for mercy (2 Chron 28:9-15). After victory, God has often in history raised up men and, more usually, women to remind the victors of the need for compassion to the vanquished. Their voices have not always been welcomed or heeded. Chronicles finishes—almost—with the sorry tale of the murderous, terrifying Babylonian destruction of Jerusalem, the slaughter of its inhabitants, and the desecrating of its temple. The exile has begun (2 Chron 36:15-21).

Ezra and Nehemiah

The Chronicler, as the scholars call him, may well be responsible for Ezra and Nehemiah as well as for Chronicles. Certainly their tale is closely linked with that just described. The edict of King Cyrus in 538 B.C. means a hint of liberation at last for Jerusalem and for at least some of the exiles in Babylon (Ezra 1:1-4). Some can now return and seek to rebuild their once glorious capital: 'So our God gives light to our eyes and a little relief in our bondage' (Ezra 9:8). There is opposition, and the task of re-building a destroyed city is never easy. Yet God raises up Nehemiah for the task, helped by the condescension of his Persian master. In our century the people of Poland had this to do in Warsaw, Gdansk, and many other places after the hell of the Nazi occupation. They were far more successful in this, as it turned out, than Nehemiah.

The poor still need protection, it seems, from their fellow-citizens, even after the experience of exile in a foreign land. In the re-building process, some have become better off already and are accumulating the lands and houses of their fellow Jews and even enslaving their children. 'What you are doing is not right', Nehemiah fumes, 'Shouldn't you walk in the fear of our God to avoid the reproach of our Gentile enemies? . . . Give back to them immediately their fields, vineyards, olive groves, and houses, and also the usury you are charging them' (Neh 5:1-13). Although they have returned home, the Jewish people remain vassals, of course, slaves to a foreign over-lord in their own land; their plight is poignantly described: 'They rule over our bodies and our cattle as they please. We are in great distress' (Neh 9:36-37). God is with them, however, and is still at work. They can experience his joy as their strength even in slavery and hardship. At the dedication of the walls of Jerusalem, we read that 'they offered great sacrifices, rejoicing because God had given them great joy. The women and children also rejoiced. The sound of rejoicing in Jerusalem could be heard far away' (Neh 12:43).

Where the God of liberation is at work, joy is never far away. In the next chapter we will conclude our survey of the Old Testament by considering its collection of prophetic writings and sayings.

Notes

[1] I owe this metaphor to John Morgan-Wynne, New Testament tutor at Regent's Park College, Oxford, when I was preparing for ministry.

[2] The sections are: Psalms 1–41, Psalms 42–72, Psalms 73–89, Psalms 90–106, Psalms 107–150.

[3] For a lucid account of these issues see John D. Weaver, *In the Beginning God* (Regent's Park College/Smyth & Helwys Publishing, Oxford, and Macon GA, 1994).

[4] The Joseph cycle of stories can be found in Genesis 37–50. See especially 45:7 and 50:20.

[5] See Nelson Mandela, *Long Walk to Freedom* (Little, Brown, & Co., London, 1994).

[6] As cited in Anthony Lane, *The Hodder Book of Christian Quotations* (Hodder & Stoughton, London, 1982), p. 249.

[7]Ibid., p. 249.
[8]F. Voltaire, *L'Ingénu* (1767), ch. 10.
[9]For details, see chapter 4 above.

Chapter 7
The Old Testament
The Prophets

1. The Major Prophets

The Old Testament prophetic writings are usually divided into 'Major' and 'Minor' Prophets. This is really a reflection on the number of their chapters more than their spiritual status! Amos or Micah are Major Prophets by any standards, as we shall come to see. Within the narratives of the historians of Israel and Judah, the voices of the prophets were often heard. Long after the reigns of David and Solomon were but fond memories, those we now know as the Old Testament 'writing' prophets appeared on the scene. Elijah and Elisha had paved the way, but the schools of the prophets had been there even before them (see 1 Sam 10:9-13). The Prophets are particularly concerned with God's word to his people in times of invasion and of exile. They also speak about the torments of exile itself and later about the scenario of return and rebuilding that follows it. Again let me commend the practice of reading these books one at a time as part of God's sacred library. How powerfully they read. How moving they so often are. How readily applicable to societies where similar injustices and inequalities, divisions and hurts remain. How relevant to a modern society whose false gods may not be made of wood or stone but who place many equally inferior objects in the place of the Living and True God and of the service of humankind. These 'Latter Prophets', as they are called in the Jewish tradition, also have a great deal to teach us about the biblical foundations of liberation and evangelization.

Isaiah

Immediately one faces a contentious question when considering Isaiah. Much ink, and one suspects nearly blood, has been spilled over the years between those who consider Isaiah a unified book and those who do not. Some Christian readers see the book of Isaiah as the work of one prophet who, miraculously, was given to see political and social realities and events several hundred years ahead of their actually happening. He then described them, they say, in specific detail right down to the name of a then unknown future ruler, Cyrus. Other Christians, however, see Isaiah as in fact a compilation of at least three different prophets' work that echo each other, like some modern-day trilogy. The conclusion of many of us who have carefully studied the evidence is that this book as we now have it reflects the work of three different prophets, probably members over several generations of the same prophetic tradition or 'school'. Isaiah 1–39 contain the prophecies, warnings, and encouragements of a prophet living in Jerusalem and concerned with the life of Judah, shortly after the fall of the northern kingdom of Israel to Assyria and before the horrors of the Babylonian exile had yet taken place. Isaiah 40–55, which includes the superb 'Servant Songs', take us on a century and a half to the time when the people of God had been in exile in Babylon for several decades and were beginning to sniff the wind of liberation and the 'new thing' God was about to do for his defeated, much abused, and long-suffering people. Isaiah 55–65 finally takes us on still further in time to the conditions obtaining when some exiles were actually back in Jerusalem and were actively involved in the process of reconstruction and rebuilding.

Is this a miraculous anticipatory prophecy, or is it God using several of his human servants over several hundred years to speak his living word to people who need to hear it? Each reader must decide from his or her own study, but let us remember that it is what God as the final author continues to say through these chapters that is paramount, not the identity of the human author or authors.

Isaiah 1–39. Isaiah never fails to rebuke and expose the sins of the people of God who 'persist in rebellion' (1:5). God is not impressed by their outward piety. He sees the heart and what is going on in society: 'Your hands are full of blood; wash and make yourselves clean. Take your evil deeds out of my sight! Stop doing wrong, learn to do right! Seek justice, encourage the oppressed. Defend the cause of the fatherless, plead the cause of the widow' (1:15-17). God's concern was for peace and an end to the threats of invasion and of wars between the peoples of the world: 'He will judge between the nations and will settle disputes for many peoples. They will beat their swords into ploughshares and their spears into pruning hooks. Nation will not take up sword against nation, nor will they train for war anymore' (2:4). Those who are 'grinding the faces of the poor' will have to answer to God (3:14-15). The vineyard of Israel is full of bad vines. In it God looked 'for justice but saw bloodshed; for righteousness, but heard cries of distress' (5:7). The land acquirers and property developers who 'add house to house and join field to field until everyone else is displaced' need to beware. So do the alcoholics and those obsessed with drink, who revel while Judah perishes from within (5:8-15). Those who are 'heroes at drinking wine and champions at mixing drinks' but 'who acquit the guilty for a bribe, but deny justice to the innocent' will have to confront God's fierce anger (5:22-23).

The destruction of their nation is imminent, and their sins contribute to its weakness in the face of the ruthless Assyrian invader. Something of the anger and judgement of God will be experienced in the process. The messianic hope has its roots here. As the earthly line of King David was failing spectacularly, dreams of a future new ruler in the Davidic dynasty grew and grew. This messianic hope was to deepen through the exile and through the disappointments of the post-exilic period. It was to grow in fervency throughout what is termed the inter-testamental period right up to the time of Jesus Christ. Christians believe that these aspirations were perfectly and fully answered in him. The Jews continue, of course, to await the Messiah. The familiar Isaiah Advent readings are among the finest expressions in Scripture of these messianic hopes (9:1-7; 11:1-9).

Not only Israel stands condemned by God, however. So does cruel Assyria who has already conquered northern Israel and now threatens southern Judah; later Babylon too will stand under the same judgement. The day will come, the prophet promises, when 'the Lord gives you relief from suffering and turmoil and cruel bondage' (14:3-23). God's judgement on Assyria, the Philistines, Moab, Damascus, Cush, Tyre, and Egypt, as well as Jerusalem can be found between chapters 13 and 25 of this book. The Old Testament never lost its perspective of God as the Lord of all the nations on earth; nor should we. As for liberation, this will come for the people of God:

> He will swallow up death forever. The Sovereign Lord will wipe away the tears from all faces; he will remove the disgrace of his people from all the earth. The Lord has spoken. In that day they will say, 'Surely this is our God; we trusted in him, and he saved us. This is the Lord, we trusted in him; let us rejoice and be glad in his salvation'. (25:8-9)

As for the beautiful words of Isaiah 35, these can be seen either as an inspired prophecy of the later return from exile or as a promise relevant to any period of the joys of a people restored to right relationship with the Lord and so free from all threat of exile or invasion. There is evidently still hope in Isaiah 1–39 that catastrophe can be avoided if God's people will repent and turn back to him. This, Isaiah insists, *is* still possible (30:18). The story of the defeat of the Assyrian King Sennacherib and Hezekiah's deliverance, with which these chapters end, are also intended to make this clear. This liberation was, however, to prove only too temporary. Our study of the history books of Israel and Judah have already made it very clear that the Babylonian invasion happened and with ferocious cruelty. Isaiah's message went, we must assume, largely unheeded. It would seem that not even God could hold off foreign invaders for long from a people who were bent on destroying themselves by failing to repent, act justly, or really trust in him.

Isaiah 40–55. Here are some of the most inspiring pages of the whole Bible—poetic, full of drama, and with a power to move the reader. These chapters include the haunting Servant Songs that apply at one level to the suffering Israel of the time and also, Christians believe, at a deeper level to Christ himself. God the Liberator breathes through all of these poems (e.g., 40:28-31; 42:1-9; 43:1-18). God has forgiven his people and now intends to liberate them: 'I have swept away your offences like a cloud, your sins like the morning mist. Return to me, for I have redeemed you' (44:22). What is more, God is quite capable of using secular rulers to achieve his purposes, even a Persian star on the ascendant, 'Cyrus: He is my shepherd and will accomplish all that I please; he will say of Jerusalem, "Let it be rebuilt", and of the temple, "let its foundations be laid". . . . I have called you by name, . . . though you do not acknowledge me' (44:28; 45:4). The impact of Cyrus would have been similar to that of the former Soviet leader Mikhail Gorbachev in Eastern Europe, and it may not be going too far to see him as a late twentieth-century Cyrus raised up by God for the liberation of whole nations. The remarkable scenes the world witnessed in the autumn of 1989 as the Iron Curtain melted and as whole nations celebrated their newfound freedoms give some credence to this comparison.

Babylon itself will now know defeat and judgement. The country has gone too far (47:6-7). Israel, God's people, has now been refined and 'tested in the furnace of affliction' (48:10). God's love for his/her people is a deep and tender mother-love, suggesting that God is also female or, better, is beyond masculinity or femininity (49:15). There comes an echo of Isaiah 35, now perhaps more fully understood: 'Free yourself from the chains on your neck for the time of liberation is at hand' (52:2). Knowing God's timing, not making human guesses about it, is always critical in the liberation struggle. God is with and for them: 'The Lord will lay bare his holy arm in the sight of all the nations, and all the ends of the earth will see the salvation of our God' (52:10).

With this announcement we must take off our shoes, for in the sequence of the poems we are now near holy ground, that walked by the Suffering Servant who was 'despised and rejected by all men'. Israel's torments during the exile foreshadowed other torments and especially, Christians believe, those of Christ; he indeed was the suffering Messiah 'pierced for our transgressions, crushed for our iniquities' (52:13–53:12). Many Christians, myself among them, believe that God inspired this passage not only as a portrayal of exilic sufferings under the Babylonians, but also to point us to the events of a Calvary still to come. God can use even the suffering of his servants to achieve liberation for others. Such liberation is imminent for God's people in exile, and creation is also to be involved in singing its praises:

You will go out in joy and be led forth in peace; the mountains and the hills will burst into song before you, and all the trees of the field will clap their hands. (55:12)

Isaiah 56–66. The reality of life in the post-exilic period for God's people was not easy, as we have seen in the chronicles of Nehemiah and Ezra. Liberation never comes easily. God's people must fully co-operate with him *after* deliverance as well before, to secure liberation in all its wholeness. Consider Isaiah 58:6-7, for example, with its description of true fasting:

Is not this the kind of fasting I have chosen: to loose the chains of injustice and untie the cords of the yoke, to set the oppressed free and break every yoke? Is it not to share your food with the hungry and to provide the poor wanderer with shelter—when you see the naked to clothe him, and not to turn away from your own flesh and blood?

Similarly, the words of Isaiah 61:1-3 were quoted to great effect as his manifesto by Jesus in Luke 4, as we have already seen. In accord with this concern for wholeness in society is the vision of the new Zion where Jerusalem shall be the praise of the earth and be renamed 'Sought After, The City No Longer Deserted' (62:12). Jerusalem will become a delight and its people, a joy, and 'the sound of weeping and of crying will be heard in it no more' (65:17-19). Certainly by the time of Christ, Jerusalem, although still under foreign occupation, had become, as Isaiah prophesied, a major international centre for religion with proselytes and the Jewish Diaspora (i.e., spread across the nations) coming to her from all over the world. It needed Christ, however, Christians believe, to live out and fully declare the liberation of God for his people and for all the nations that had been initially prophesied by the Isaiah of chapter 55. The liberation of God's people also needed a far more radical tackling of the problems of sinfulness in human nature. This is what Jeremiah recognized all too well.

Jeremiah

How strangely reassuring the Bible is at times. Sulky, self-pitying, complaining, deeply human Jeremiah proves to be one of God's bravest, wisest, and most creative servants. To Jeremiah, living in the last days of Judah before its exile, God gives the task of speaking to a people who are convinced that their religious rituals will protect them. In particular, they are relying on the presence of the Jerusalem temple in their midst, like an enormous brick talisman, to keep them safe from invasion and harm. The big bad Babylonian wolf may huff and puff as much as he likes, but their house was built of stone. No, says Jeremiah in effect, it is only straw! The temple is no security as long as they 'oppress the alien, the fatherless, or the widow' and run after other gods (7:1-7). He proceeds to expose relentlessly the sins, the superficiality, and the spiritual poverty of a people capable of such thinking. He lampoons the paid priests and prophets who merely pronounce platitudes as they mouth 'peace, peace, when there is no peace' (6:14). The situation is grim: 'The prophets prophesy lies, the priests rule by their own authority, and my people love it this way. But what will you do in the end?' (5:30-31). False religion is worthless; true religion and care for the weak go hand in hand. If only God's people would put their trust again in the Lord and amend their ways and deeds, then there would be some hope at least (7:5-15).

Why, nevertheless, does the way of the wicked prosper? When Jeremiah asks God about this, part of God's anguished reply is that 'there is no one who cares' (12:10-11). For evil to triumph, it is necessary only for the good to do nothing. This is as true now as it was then and has been stressed by modern theologians of liberation. Still, the righteous suffer as Jeremiah is not slow to point out—especially about himself (15:15-18; 20:17-18). Consider too the message that Jeremiah was ordered to present to Jehoahaz, the king of Judah at that time: 'Do what is just and right. Rescue from the hand of his oppressor the one who has been robbed. Do no wrong or violence to the alien, the fatherless, or the widow, and do not shed innocent blood in this place' (22:3).

In the end, however, Jeremiah is reduced to foretelling only *future* liberation for God's people. They have now long missed what little chance they had of any escape. First must come the nightmares of exile during seventy long, hard years. Then and only then will there be any prospects of restoration and hope. Liberation at that future time is painted in glowing terms (29:10-14). Jeremiah's thinking about all that has happened goes deeper still, however. He comes to see even more clearly the deep intractable sinfulness of the human heart and that only a deep spiritual inner work of God can change this:

'This is the covenant that I will make with the house of Israel after that time,' declares the Lord. 'I will put my law in their minds and write it on their hearts. I will be their God, and they will be my people. No longer will a man teach his neighbour, or a man his brother, saying, "Know the Lord," because they will all know me, from the least of them to the greatest,' declares the Lord. 'For I will forgive their wickedness and will remember their sins no more'. (31:33-34)

Christians see these words more completely fulfilled, not in the conditions obtaining in post-exilic Israel, but through the making of a new covenant in the New Testament events of Calvary, Easter, and Pentecost.

We see again in Jeremiah the insistence that all the nations are judged according to their deeds in the sight of the Living God (not just because they are Israel's enemies!)—Egypt, Philistia, Moab, and Ammon among them (chaps. 46–49). As for Babylon, it will face invasion from the north (50:9-10). God will one day restore his people's fortunes and have compassion on them again, but in the meantime, Jeremiah's message is—to use the stirring words of the Revd. Jesse Jackson from the 1988 USA presidential election campaign —'Keep hope alive; keep hope alive'. Significantly, this book also ends, as does 2 Kings, on a note of hope with Jehoiachin honoured in exile (52:31-34).

Lamentations

Lamentations is the bleakest work in the Bible and one of the saddest in world literature. I include it as this point, rather than with the 'Writings' to which it belongs, because it follows on so clearly from the scenario just painted by Jeremiah. In its five agony-filled chapters the full horror of what has happened to Judah, Jerusalem, and the temple dawns (e.g., 1:7-13; 2:13-14; 5:11-16; 5:21-22). The nation of Judah has become the scum and refuse of the world. Lamentations is a theological reflection on sheer tragedy and urges us never to become accustomed to suffering. Perhaps 5:11-18 best communicates the horrors of all this. These were days of sheer terror coupled with the desolation of what appeared to be rejection by God. Here is a book for an Auschwitz or a Beirut, or for an overcrowded and filthy refugee camp where not even the prayers seem to get through, never mind the deliverers (3:44). Poland as the death camp of Europe during the war years was one such 'time of Lamentations' in modern history. The former Yugoslavian 'safe zones' after their capture by the Serbs in the summer of 1995 were another.

Ezekiel

Speculation about whether or not Ezekiel saw a flying saucer (1:4-28) and a song about 'dem dry bones' (37:1-14) are perhaps the nearest secular woman or man comes to deliberating on this Old Testament prophet of doom. There is far more to his book than such things. His prophetic ministry straddled both the remains of Israel in the north and Judah in the south and occupied many of the early years of the exile in Babylon. For a time, he seems to have been with his fellow-countrymen and women who had been deported into exile—though whether present in spirit or body is not clear. On other occasions, he appears to have stayed behind in Jerusalem. Both, of course, may well have been true at differing times. To a 'rebellious house' Ezekiel is called to speak. Detestable

things are going on among the people left in Jerusalem. Violence stalks the land
(8:7-18). The glory of God has departed from the temple where once his honour
and presence dwelt. The false prophets, as Jeremiah also complained, are too
busy peddling false comforts to be of use. They are whitewashing flimsy walls
just before a hurricane! There is a reluctance to face up to the situation of defeat
(13:10-12).

How many Christian ministers and church leaders have similarly propped
up corrupt governments and even dictatorships with weasel words over the centuries, failing to notice the coming judgement of God? I venture to mention, for
example, the church in nineteenth-century Russia, in the China or the Germany
of the 1930s, in the Nicaragua of the 1970s, or the El Salvador of the 1980s.
Ezekiel insists that the judgement of God is now inescapable. Indeed, Ezekiel
describes a new pattern of individual responsibility before God for sin, each
person fully accountable. The principle of community responsibility for sin,
atoned through communal Jerusalem sacrifices, will soon no longer be feasible.
With no temple, a new system of atonement will be needed. The righteous
person will 'give his food to the hungry and clothing for the naked'. He will
avoid usury and will judge fairly. He will follow God's decrees and keep his
laws. 'That man is righteous; he will surely live, declares the Sovereign Lord'.
By contrast, the son of that same man will face judgement if he is himself
unrighteous (18:1-13, 33). We notice, however, that individual responsibility
is tested by the individual's responsible actions *for* the community.

Strangely enough, although Ezekiel is very much a prophet of doom (see
the bitter and crude allegory of chapter 16, for example), his book is full of
hope and of the promised joy of restoration:

> This is what the Sovereign Lord says: I will gather you from the nations and
> bring you back from the countries where you have been scattered, and I will
> give you back the land of Israel again. . . . I will give them an undivided heart
> and put a new spirit in them; I will remove from them their heart of stone and
> give them a heart of flesh. Then they will follow my decrees and be careful to
> keep my laws. They will be my people, and I will be their God. (11:17-21)

God will be as the Good Shepherd gathering in his flock and caring especially
for the weak, sick, injured, straying, and lost. A chastened, repentant, and spiritually refined Israel *will* return to the land (36:24-32). The dry bones of the
nation can live again. 'I will gather them to their own land, not leaving any
behind. I will no longer hide my face from them, for I will pour out my Spirit
on the house of Israel, declares the Sovereign Lord' (39:25-29). God's glory
will return to his new temple. The boundaries of the land will be restored, and

healing waters will flow from Jerusalem's new temple far and wide (47:1-12). Ezekiel ends with these words of liberation, hope, and promise: 'THE LORD IS THERE' (48:35).

These prophecies were never fulfilled in post-exilic Israel of course. The post-exilic period was hardly glorious for Israel by any stretch of the imagination. After the Babylonian exile, many Jews who had been scattered throughout the then known world did return to their former homeland, but not all and far from in triumph. More significantly, for our century, the Jews returned to Palestine/Israel in 1948, the nightmare of Hitler's 'final solution' over, fulfilling many ancient hopes. The book of Revelation in the New Testament further reworks Ezekiel's prophecies (such as the new temple and the river of life passages) into its description of the dimensions of heaven, the new creation, and the glories of the age to come. Dietrich Bonhoeffer once wrote: 'It may be that the day of judgment will dawn tomorrow; in that case we shall gladly stop working for a better future. But not before'. Ezekiel lived his life and served his God like that. His is an example of a prophet realistically assessing the present situation, the status quo, and helping God's people to come to terms with it. At the same time he points God's people on to a better hope and a better future. He encourages them to look beyond the present and to work for the new future God is leading them on towards. Another German theologian, Jürgen Moltmann, spoke of this as a call to participate in God's contradiction of reality.

2. The Minor Prophets

Our survey of the New and Old Testaments from the perspective of seeing God as a God of liberation is nearly complete. We have explored this theme through the Gospels and Epistles; Acts and Revelation; the Writings, Law, and History of Israel; and now through the Prophets. The last twelve books of the Old Testament—Daniel we have already considered among the Writings—are often known as the Minor Prophets. God the Liberator is clearly to be discerned at work in and through them too.

Hosea

God used Hosea's experience of a painful marriage and his treatment by a promiscuous wife to bring home to the prophet, and through him to Israel, the enormity of the crime of spiritual adultery (1:2-5). That, too, after all God had done for his human partner (11:1-4):

There is only cursing, lying, and murder, stealing and adultery; they break all bounds, and bloodshed follows bloodshed. Because of this the land mourns, and all who live in it waste away; the beasts of the field and the birds of the air and the fish of the sea are dying. (4:2-3)

This all reads like many a First World tabloid newspaper or *Greenpeace* report. However, God's forgiving love is alive and ready to welcome his people back if they will return to him (2:23). History reveals that these warnings and pleas went unheeded and that Hosea was speaking his prophecy in the last period of the northern kingdom of Israel, before its fall to the Assyrian invader.

Hosea's times offer an instructive comparison with the New Europe, a continent where the majority of the people are now unchurched save for the Christian festival or special family occasions, if even then. There are surely modern forms of 'spiritual adultery' among us, new 'lovers' and contemporary idols. I mean undisciplined sexual expression, the luxurious holiday abroad, the god of garden or leisure, the obsessive hobby, the bank balance, the lottery, the concentration on the family to the exclusion of all other relationships in society, and the escape to fantasy worlds, including those provided by the computer. We need Hoseas today, prophets with the ability to address whole nations to bring them to live more closely to the Living God. The message of scripture needs to be read and acted on; in the words of the South African Christian leader Desmond Tutu: 'I love the Bible because it is subversive of all injustice'.

Joel

Joel is a charismatic prophet in more ways than one. His message is similar to Hosea's: return to God. 'Return to the Lord your God, for he is gracious and compassionate, slow to anger and abounding in love, and he relents from sending calamity. Who knows? He may turn and have pity' (2:13-14). Then the foreign army from the north need not be feared. Israel's liberation will be full and complete (2:18-32).

Amos

Living shortly before the time of Hosea, Amos paints a picture of a corrupt and yet pseudo-religious society. The inequalities portrayed between different members of society have often been compared by preachers with similar conditions today. The rich have their mansions and the poor their hovels, some sleeping on beds inlaid with ivory (6:4) and others on the streets. Bribes and injustices are everywhere. The heads of the needy and helpless are ground into the dust, and the poor are sold into slavery for the price of a pair of shoes (2:6-7). Truth is in short commodity, and sexual degradation is commonplace (2:6-8). In short, the times are evil (5:10-13). Judgement and the justice of God are on its way, however. What should Israel do? The repeated refrain of chapter 4 makes plain what they have not done: 'Yet you have not returned to me', declares the Lord. Against this social and political background Amos cries out in immortal words: 'Let justice roll on like a river, righteousness like a never-failing stream' (5:23-24). Is not this also the continuing and heartfelt cry of all those living and working among the poor of three worlds?

Obadiah, Jonah

Obadiah's short tract speaks to all of us who are troubled by the enormous forces of evil we see in the world around us. It awakens echoes in all who are troubled by the pain of injustice and by human failure to act to change things for the better. The Edomites had mocked Judah on the day of its disaster from the Babylonian invader and had failed to help the country in its misery. It is understandable, in human terms, that Obadiah reacts as he does: 'As you have done, it will be done to you; your deeds will return upon your own head' (v. 15). But the book of Jonah, which follows immediately in the canon, provides us with an important, if unpopular, lesson here. No one is beyond repentance or a return to the Lord, not even bloody tyrants and their minions (3:6–4).

In the summer of 1995, we witnessed painful attempts by some Japanese leaders to apologize for their crimes during the Second World War, and equally painful attempts by some of their former victims and prisoners to accept this apology. Faced with the enemy city of Nineveh, Jonah struggles with such issues as well. He anticipates our Lord's praxis of love for enemies and insistence on the inclusiveness of the Kingdom of God. God welcomes and forgives all who repent, even those who have deeply hurt us (4:2-11). This is the hard lesson Jonah had to learn about those who did not belong to his own nation.

Micah

There is surely a faith for our day to be found in Micah, with its several themes of liberation and evangelization. In a truly integrated way, Micah blends a concern for the individual, for the people of God, and for the community, nation, and world. So must any credible modern biblical preaching and effective local church. Those who covet and steal other's land and houses repel the Lord (1:1-3); they are around today in their flashy cars and power-dressing suits, speaking poison-sweet words to trick old people in their own homes, or threatening words to harassed tenants. Also still around today are the priests and preachers who serve money, not the Lord (3:5-7). Better the way of peace, not war, Micah pleads. As for the individual, how shall he or she best serve God? 'He has showed you . . . what is good. And what does the Lord require of you? To act justly and to love mercy and to walk humbly with your God' (6:8). The dishonest shopkeepers must beware. So must those who are rich and violent (6:10-12). In a return to the Living God and to his ways alone there is hope:

> Who is a God like you, who pardons sin and forgives the transgression of the remnant of his inheritance? You do not stay angry for ever but delight to show mercy. You will again have compassion on us; you will tread our sins underfoot, and hurl all our iniquities into the depths of the sea. (7:18-19)

Nahum, Habbakuk, Zephaniah

Nahum prophesies for tyrant Assyria the same miseries it has caused Israel. The desire for revenge is never far from human nature. It may lie dormant for decades, as it did under Tito in the former Yugoslavia, but when it awakens, misery results. Nahum's clear pleasure in the downfall of his nation's enemy is a warning to us all. Habbakuk, by contrast, shows a very positive way to confront calamity (3:17-19). In accord with the theme of our present study, however, we note only his vision and his prayer: 'For the earth will be filled with the knowledge of the glory of the Lord, as the waters cover the sea', and 'Lord, I have heard of your fame; I stand in awe of your deeds, O Lord. Renew them in our day, in our time make them known; in wrath remember mercy' (2:14; 3:2). This is a prayer for our world as a new millennium dawns. Graham Kendrick, the contemporary Christian songwriter, uses this prayer superbly in his modern hymn: 'O Lord the Clouds Are Gathering'. The book of the prophet Zephaniah ends similarly with a delightful passage about God the Liberator restoring his people after disaster: 'He will quiet you with his love' (3:14-20).

Haggai

At the time of the rebuilding of the Jerusalem temple following the return from exile, Haggai is concerned to secure for this place of worship a rightful place in the giving and affections of God's people. That he was unsuccessful tells its own all-too-familiar story. God's people, of all ages, are often too busy feathering their own nests to be able to give worthily to God and his work (1:2-4). If God's people were all giving even one tenth of their income each month for the work of the local church, for evangelism and mission, and for relief agencies in the Second and Third World, how very different parts of our world could be. The principle of the tithe does not have to be religious; it could also be taken up, where it is not already, by the many humanists and atheists in our country and the proceeds given to charities and to the oppressed. Who was it that said, 'When it comes to money, we are all of the same religion'?

Zechariah and Malachi

Zechariah envisages the deliverance and new freedoms of the people of God in language that should now be familiar to readers who have been following the many Bible references we have considered in this part of the study guide. Restoration after a time of bleakness and hardship is his theme (1:17; 2:7-13; 8:1-8; 14:9-11). Today we are beginning to see something, at least, of this—for all their new problems—in Poland or Romania or Hungary as the dangerous years of Stalin and the dull years of the Communist Party have been left behind and the search for a new and wiser future has begun. In Malachi the meanness of God's people in failing to give from their substance is again castigated and still needs to be today. We sometimes give to God what we would never dream of passing off to someone of only human importance. Here, too, are by now very familiar words:

> 'So I will come near to you for judgement. I will be quick to testify against sorcerers, adulterers, and perjurers, against those who defraud labourers of their wages, who oppress the widows and the fatherless, and deprive aliens of justice, but do not fear me', says the Lord Almighty. (3:5)

3. Summary

We are now in a position to state some conclusions to be drawn from the Old Testament, just as we did from the New Testament. We have discerned, throughout its pages, the picture of a God who is seen by his people, again and again, as their Liberator; a God concerned for the oppressed, the victim, the alien, the widow, the orphan, the poor; a God who expects social justice and integrity, be it in accurate scales or the refusal of bribes; and a God to whom all nations are accountable, and not just Israel and Judah. The God of the Bible has been seen humbling tyrants and overthrowing and rejecting unjust 'dictator' kings. He has encouraged liberation even through a Gentile ruler.

We have also, sadly, found a triumphalism in many places of the text as God's people have enjoyed their own liberation at the bloody expense—and pain—of others. We have seen how the recurring Old Testament concept of

Israel as the especially chosen people of God has needed to be balanced by the similarly recurring theme of Old Testament missionary concern and by a picture of God alive and active a long way beyond the boundaries of the temple, the children of Israel, and the Promised Land.

We have seen the beginnings of the law of love and of concern for neighbour and stranger, not least in Leviticus. We have also seen how a growing this-worldly disillusionment and disappointment in priests and rulers and people led to a burgeoning messianic tradition. That is, the expectation grew of someone worthy and able to fulfill the promises of the Davidic dynasty, as the Liberator supreme. Problems of the sinfulness of the human heart and of the hypocrisy of the people of God have also been exposed in our study. It is no good just honouring God with rituals and lips when a heart or lifestyle is far from him. God desires a 'new covenant' written on the heart, an inner conversion to his laws and ways. In all of this we have discerned God to be a God of liberation concerned indeed for the planet and the world, whole nations and communities, as well as for families and individuals. The Old Testament God is concerned and active, not just among those who claim to be his own people but in the other nations as well. God's compassion is seen to stretch to the vulnerable foreigner as well as to the high priest. Christian liberation and evangelization must reflect and express the breadth of this biblical vision and concern. Ours truly *is* a missionary God.

I have—I believe—showed you plain Scripture.

PART III
PRAXIS

Chapter 8
Issues Facing the New Europe

1. Welcome to the European Union

The richest club in the world—such is the European Union (EU) as we must now come to call what was the European Community (EC) and even earlier the European Economic Community (EEC), which was popularly known as 'The Common Market'. Prior to November 1993, the European Union was called the European Community. The EC itself was composed of what originally were three separate organizations: the European Coal and Steel Community (ECSC) created in 1951, the European Economic Community (EEC), and the European Atomic Energy Community (Euratom). The latter two were both set up in 1957. Welcome to the world of Eurospeak! For those unfamiliar with Eurospeak, I apologize at the outset for all the abbreviations that soon become necessary in any analysis of the European Union.

The EU is a European supra-national organization dedicated to increasing economic integration and strengthening cooperation among its member states. It was established on November 1, 1993, when the Treaty on European Union, popularly known as the Maastricht Treaty, was ratified by the then twelve members of the EC: Belgium, Denmark, France, Germany, Britain, Greece, Ireland, Italy, Luxemburg, the Netherlands, Portugal, and Spain. Upon ratification of the treaty, the countries of the EC became members of the new EU. Under its terms, European citizenship was granted to citizens of each member state. Customs and immigration agreements were facilitated to allow European citizens greater freedom to live, work, qualify, or study in any of the other EU member states. Also some border controls were relaxed. A goal of establishing a common European currency was also set, initially, for 1997.

With the ratifying of the Maastricht Treaty, a European Union now officially exists. The 'club' has traveled far since the days of the aftermath of World War II when several of the key antagonists of that war determined to rebuild a different Europe, one free of the nationalism and violence that had characterized the continent in the 1930s and 1940s. The founder members recognized that a willingness to share some sovereignty and decision making was in their own best interests as well as those of Western Europe as a whole. Initially Belgium, France, Western Germany, Holland, Italy, and Luxemburg formed the European Economic Community (EEC). In 1973 the EEC was enlarged as Britain, Ireland, and Denmark joined. In 1981 Greece also became a member. In 1986 Spain and Portugal were added. Most recently, in 1995, Austria, Sweden, and Finland further enlarged what is now the Union.

Does the future for the New Europe in the twenty-first century lie in a kind of 'United States of Europe' with growing economic, political, and defence partnerships? Or is it to be sought in a much looser partnership of national governments co-operating in some areas but not in others? The 1990s will clearly play a large part in determining the answer to this fundamental issue. This on-going debate in the Union's history—the one between supra-nationalism and inter-governmentalism—is currently being replayed in the Europe of the 1990s. As we shall see as we tell the story, it can be clearly traced through the many EU changes, debates, and decisions of the past four decades.

2. The Path to the New Europe
A Brief History

1945–1957

Several factors contributed to the birth of the EEC, the forerunner of the EU. As early as 1946, the British wartime leader Winston Churchill had called for a 'United States of Europe'. The United States Marshall Plan, or European Recovery Program, with its concern to reintegrate Germany into mainstream Europe, was another precipitating factor, as was the Schuman Declaration, an appeal for a supra-national coal and steel community. The founding father of what was to become the EU, alongside Robert Schuman, however, was the Frenchman Jean Monnet. Schuman was a foreign minister, and Monnet a civil servant. 'People only accept change when they are faced with necessity and only recognize necessity when a crisis is upon them', Monnet wrote in his memoirs.[1] The 'crisis' was a dual one of postwar Capitalist reconstruction in general and of ascendant Communism in particular. Capitalism had been com-promised, in the eyes of many, both by the depression of the 1930s and by the war itself. The 1950s saw, then, significant progress towards European eco-nomic co-operation. Sharing sovereignty politically or for defence purposes was, at that time, not a feasible prospect. In the Treaty of Paris in 1951, West Germany, France, Belgium, Italy, Luxemburg, and the Netherlands formed the ECSC. The signing of the Treaty of Rome in March 1957, however, marked the actual birth of the EEC. One participant wrote of this in glowing terms:

> I do not believe that it is exaggerating to say that this . . . represents one of the greatest moments of Europe's history. Who would have thought during the 1930s, and even during the ten years that followed the war, that European

States which had been tearing one another apart for so many centuries . . . would form a common market intended eventually to become an economic area that could be linked to one dynamic market?[2]

1958–1969

In January 1958 the first meeting of what was to become the European Parliament was held. There were nine portfolios: administration, external relations, economic and financial affairs, the internal market, competition, social affairs, agriculture, transport, and overseas countries and territories. In 1960, anxious about the initial success of the EEC, several countries, Austria, Denmark, Britain, Norway, Portugal, and Sweden, with Finland and Iceland joining them later, formed a rival economic association: the European Free Trade Association (EFTA). The French President, Charles de Gaulle, was the indisputably dominant figure of this period of the Union's history. His 'Non' to Britain's application to join remains one of my own earliest political memories. Speaking at a press conference in January 1963, de Gaulle explained his reasons:

> Thus far, the entry negotiations have given little assurance that Britain can place herself inside a tariff that is genuinely common . . . renounce all Commonwealth preferences . . . cease any pretence that her agriculture be privileged . . . and treat her engagement with other countries as null and void.[3]

De Gaulle was particularly unhappy about the so-called 'special relationship' between Britain and the United States of America. Observers of the British political scene in the 1990s will see the continuing force of some of his arguments here. Britain then and now is not alone in the EU in wanting to both have and eat any European cake offered unless it can find a better bakery elsewhere! It was to be nearly a decade before the issue of Britain's membership of the EEC would be finally resolved. As well as restoring French dignity in the post-war world, de Gaulle undoubtedly helped to give to Europe a sense of its own destiny and importance at a time when the Cold War between the superpowers was a chilling reality. He must stand out as one of the great figures of the twentieth century accordingly. In July 1967 the EEC, ECSC, and Euratom combined to create the European Community with its headquarters in Brussels, Belgium.

1969–1979

The 1970s were marked by vacillations in the relationships between the two superpowers, the Soviet Union and the United States of America. Domestic difficulties in the USA, not least Vietnam and President Nixon's threatened impeachment after Watergate, undermined something of American international effectiveness and credibility. Western Germany emerged during this period as probably the key player in the EC and certainly as the most economically adept. Exchange rate problems and quite varied economic performances in other EC countries also characterized the western Europe of this period. In Paris in 1972 the seeds of the Maastricht Treaty were sown. The concluding communiqué of the Paris summit included this affirmation: 'The member states of the Community, the driving force of European construction, affirm their intention before the end of the present decade to transform the whole complex of their relations into a European Union'.[4] Right idea; wrong time scale!

In 1974 the decision to move towards direct elections to the European Parliament was taken with effect from 1978. It was also agreed to hold three yearly European Councils. A key report, also premature as it turned out, on the possibilities for the future was published in 1976. This 'Tindemans Report' focused on the need to reform existing Community institutions and to strengthen European integration. Interestingly, it also raised the possibility of a two-speed Europe with differing rates of integration in the Community depending on the will and ability of each member state to participate.

1979–1988

The 1980s began in crisis for the EC and ended in triumph. Early in the decade five prominent professors in EC countries shared a joint conviction:

> Western Europe is drifting, and the existence of the European Community is under serious threat. If nothing is done we are faced with the disintegration of the most important European achievement since World War II.[5]

Among the problems to be confronted were a paralyzed EC decision-making process; a Common Agricultural Policy (CAP) abused by some and held in contempt by others; a series of French economic advancement policies that stretched EC solidarity; and a belligerent new British prime minister, Mrs. Thatcher, determined in negotiations that were to last five years to secure a budget rebate from the EC for Britain. She, perhaps above all, brought home to the EC member states the need to control over-expenditure and to reform the

CAP. Her early advocacy of a single market also paved the way for its eventual acceptance in the 1990s. As early as June 1984, at the Fontainebleau summit, Mrs. Thatcher argued for the EC to tackle mutual problems of growth, outdated industrial structures, and unemployment with a 'genuine common market in goods and services (which is envisaged in the Treaty of Rome) and which will be crucial to our ability to meet the US and Japanese technological challenge'.[6] A draft treaty for such a market was agreed on in the same year. Its aim was to replace existing treaties with a single one, formally establishing a European Union.

By 1985 the EC's new Commission President, Jacques Delors, full of drive and vision, was in confident mood: 'All the family quarrels have been sorted out. The family is now going to grow, and we can think of the future', he affirmed.[7] Certainly the British budgetary issue had by now been resolved, some institutional reform was underway, new members were wanting to join, and the momentum towards a single market was developing apace. A report to the Brussels summit of 1985 identified several priority areas: creating a homogeneous internal market area; moves towards majority instead of unanimity voting in the determinative Council of Ministers meetings; an increased legislative rôle for the European Parliament; and greater powers for the EC's executive, the European Commission. The July 1987 Single European Act confirmed these initiatives and also moved the EC closer towards common policies on such issues as taxation, employment, health, and the environment. December 31, 1992, was agreed as the date by which the single economic market was to be achieved. A flurry of mergers, improved trans-national networks, and business rationalizations resulted as European entrepreneurs and businesspeople began to prepare for a different Europe in the 1990s. Just how different it would be, no one could then have anticipated.

1989–1994

The collapse of Communism in the Eastern part of Europe changed the world for the new millennium. The collapse resulted, with almost Leninist historical inevitability, from the Soviet Union Leader Gorbachev's policies of *perestroika* and *glasnost* (reconstruction and openness). We have already traced something of this story in the Poland of the 1980s. In a quite remarkable autumn in 1989 the New Europe was born. Poland held almost free elections in June 1989. Within six months, most of the Stalinist and neo-Stalinist regimes of Eastern Europe were overthrown. In Poland and Hungary this happened relatively peacefully in the end. In East Germany, Czechoslovakia, and Bulgaria, as well as the Baltic republics, the process was more painful. In Romania, it was both painful and violent. After liberation, these Second World nations began to discard central economic planning and to embrace both market reforms and liberal democratic processes enthusiastically.

Most significantly for the EC, the re-unification of Germany was speedily, some say hastily, concluded. The resulting shock waves were considerable. How does a Union such as the EC absorb and integrate an entire Second World economy and political system? In many ways, what Germany experienced in the early 1990s could be said to anticipate a possible future for the New Europe a decade or so later in the twenty-first century. There were other related issues as well, for example, how to deal with the suspicion of a re-unified Germany and all the concomitant memories of the emergence of national Socialism in the 1930s and the Nazi war machine of the early 1940s. The new Germany now accounted for 27 percent of the EU's income overall Gross Domestic Product (GDP) and 25 percent of its total population! The German novelist Thomas Mann had called in 1953 'not for a German Europe but for a European Germany'. His vision was now being realized. An emergency EC summit held in April 1990 confirmed the incorporation, through Western Germany, of the former East Germany into the European Community.

John Major's election as the new Prime Minister of Britain coincided with the later stages of what was to become the Maastricht Union treaty and caused him many problems, not least within his own Conservative political party! Among Maastricht's many provisions is the goal of a unified European currency system by the end of the century. Despite his stated caution, John Major's own advocacy when he was Chancellor of the Exchequer of an evolutionary process whereby European Currency Units ('ecus') might become the dominant currency of Europe over time may still have its day. During the 1997 General Election he still refused to rule out the possibility of Britain's joining a common currency 'when the conditions are right', though he remained opposed to its being imposed by some administrative *fiat* from Brussels. Further, Britain's initial opting out of the Social Chapter policy provisions of Maastricht, as well as the ferocity of the debate over ratifying Maastricht in some EU member countries, indicates that the idea of a two-speed Europe may also be one whose day is still to come.

There is also likely to be further enlargement of the EU before the twenty-first century. Turkey applied for membership in 1987; Austria in 1989; Cyprus and Malta in 1990; Sweden in 1991; and Switzerland, Finland, and Norway in 1992. Several Second World countries—Poland, Hungary, and the Czech Republic, for example—are also expected to apply for membership again after initial rejections early in the 1990s. Switzerland later withdrew its membership application to avoid violating its history of neutrality; and Norway in 1994, as it had done previously in 1972, decided not to join after a referendum. By contrast, in June 1994, Austrian voters overwhelmingly affirmed a referendum on EU membership and prepared to join in 1995 as did Sweden and Finland.

In 1991 the then EC and the European Free Trade Association completed an agreement to establish the European Economic Area, which would provide a single market for goods, services, and capital. The European Economic Area, which came into being on January 1, 1994, eliminated trade barriers between the EU and EFTA, each of which is the other's largest trading partner.

In setting something of the context of Europe in the late twentieth century, we should note finally that decision making in the EU is divided between several supra-national European institutions and the governments of the member states. The European Commission and the European Parliament are administered by the EU, and the Council of Ministers is composed of ministers from each of the member governments. The Court of Justice serves as the final arbiter in legal matters or disputes among EU institutions or between EU institutions and member states.

3. Issues Facing the New Europe

Integrating East and West

Almost all the nation-states of Europe now share broadly similar goals, whether in West or East. These are to create free market economies similar to those in First World Western Europe, to privatize much of state industry, and to move in the direction of becoming more genuinely liberal democracies. The pace and levels of conviction vary enormously here however. The attractions to First and Second World companies and businesspeople of an expanded New Europe are obvious. The EU's population is an estimated 325 million. Russia's 148 million and the 160 million people of the remainder of Eastern Europe together almost equal that. The whole area forms quite a market, especially if significant progress *is* made in Second World countries to improve their GDP levels as the twenty-first century approaches.

- In Poland, by the end of 1993, considerable progress had been made towards privatization. Many subsidies to state industries had been removed as had many of the restrictions on private firms; 1.7 million private firms accounted for nearly 45 percent of the country's Gross Domestic Product (GDP).

- The Czech economy is already estimated to be stronger than that of EU member Greece. Tourism income is a major factor in this as is the considerable foreign capital invested there since the 'velvet revolution'.

- Romania suffered severely under the form of Communism endorsed by President Ceausescu, but now, under new laws, foreign investors are allowed to own up to 100 percent of firms, property, and land and are given tax incentives to invest. Between 1990 and 1993, 30,000 foreign companies set up in the country with capital investment totaling £600 million.

The possibilities for full political integration are perhaps best demonstrated by the unification of Western and Eastern Germany in the early 1990s. Other Second World countries hope to become EU members as soon as is practicable. The Warsaw Pact (the now obsolete Eastern European mutual defence treaty) has disappeared, and there are possibilities at least of Poland, Hungary, Bulgaria, and the Czech Republic joining the North Atlantic Treaty Organization (NATO) by the end of the century. A new organization, unthinkable before 1990, called the 'Conference on Security and Co-operation in Europe', has also been formed to try and develop military and political co-operation across Europe.

Such early signs of integration between the First World and the Second World should not be taken to guarantee the eventual outcome, however. There are serious problems and clear signs of disillusionment with the New Europe in both East and West. Here are some examples.

The new democracies are vulnerable. One commentator observes that 'almost everywhere, the new democracies seem fragile. Semi-authoritarian regimes masquerade as democracies. . . . Instead of consolidation there is fragmentation. . . . At the extreme it is possible to argue that democracy is only an outer crust. Necessary institutions are missing. . . . Where they exist they do so without public support or understanding'.[8]

Capitalism is creating poverty as well as wealth. Another commentator warns: 'Now that Communism has been discredited, Capitalism especially must be its own sternest critic. . . . When we see it exported to the old Socialist countries of Western Europe it is revealed to be good for some but obviously not for the many'.[9] We have, of course, seen similar processes in the recent history of Latin America.

Some First World companies experience considerable frustration and leave. A journalist reports: 'Firms seeking to set up in Poland find themselves battling with a lethargic and incompetent bureaucracy, outdated and obstructive laws, and inexperienced or greedy officials. While many struggle on and succeed, others give up or go elsewhere'.[10]

The showpiece of integration, unification in Germany, has already revealed many problems. Eastern Germany has been rapidly de-industrialized and is experiencing high levels of unemployment. Differing policies on social issues such as abortion, free nursery education, public transport, and subsidies for housing rents have caused considerable friction. Crime, prostitution, racist behaviour, and drug use levels, as elsewhere in the Second World, have been rising. Western Germany has been experiencing unprecedented recession as a direct consequence of unification. The country is still effectively divided into those who see themselves as *Wessis* and *Ossis*. One young German executive put something of this dramatically: 'If they had to buy some underdeveloped country, why couldn't they have chosen a smaller, cheaper one'?[11]

The key decisions on future integration are presently being made, beginning with the EU Intergovernmental Conference (IGC) held in March 1996. A likely scenario for these latter years of the 1990s is a long, drawn-out confrontation between those who want a more tightly integrated Europe and those who want a looser partnership. At the same time, there will be a difference of opinion (not necessarily corresponding to the former two groups) between those who believe that integrating the former Second World countries into the EU will lead to a more stable Europe for the twenty-first century and those who believe that the economic and social costs of this expansion for member states are too high. The potential for enlargement is considerable and could conceivably mean a EU of some twenty-six states. There would be even more if the former Yugoslavia reaches equilibrium and—at last—peace. Potential members by the twenty-first century are Estonia, Latvia, Lithuania, Poland, the Czech Republic, Slovakia, Hungary, Romania, and Bulgaria, as well as Cyprus and Malta.

Problems over Maastricht

As we have just seen, events in Eastern Europe have overtaken the Maastricht treaty. Major developments have happened that could not have been envisaged in the initial stages of what was to become the Treaty on European Union. The growing desire of the Second World nation-states of Europe to join the EU have rendered almost obsolete the desire to integrate only twelve, or now fifteen, West European countries. But other problems can also be identified.

A single European currency by the end of the decade seems less and less likely. The convergence criteria of the treaty, the essential prerequisites for economic integration, can only be achieved by economic policies with high social costs, not least unemployment. The 1993 Exchange Rate Mechanism problems have also demonstrated how naive the plans for full economic integration are in practice. At the time of this writing, the likelihood is increasing of significant delay, perhaps lasting on into the next century, to the plans for full EU economic integration.

Nationalism remains stubbornly alive. France, Britain, and Denmark all demonstrated serious misgivings over Maastricht in the internal debates of 1993–1994. They were not alone. Many in all the EU countries still prefer national government to the pan-European kind. Given a choice, they would jettison Brussels altogether. One indication of the continuing power of nationalism is the widespread resistance to the loss of internal national currency units among electors across the EU.

The European Union is losing credibility and appeal in parts of Western Europe. The Britain-based Henley Centre conducted research recently that suggests this strongly. The EU is widely seen as offering only pointless institutional change at best and, at worse, economically destabilizing policies. In Spain, only 48% of those polled affirmed that economic prosperity depends on a United Europe, compared to 73% in 1991. Apparently only 1 in 4 British people see the EU as the way to increased prosperity. In Germany, as well as in Spain and Britain, some 40% of people on low incomes believe that European integration has been responsible for increasing unemployment in their countries. Only a third of Germans support the moves towards a single currency. As the Centre comments:

> It seems plain that the EU can no longer depend on the normal lightening of the public mood that would usually follow a period of sustained growth in Europe. A generation of economically vulnerable electors seems in no frame of mind to endorse a deepening Europe. Their concerns are localized on jobs and personal security.[12]

International failures only compound the problems. The continuing failure of the EU to resolve the conflicts in Northern Ireland and the former Yugoslavia have also undermined the credibility of the EU at a crucial juncture in its history. Many ask, 'What does Maastricht mean in practice if such conflicts can be allowed to happen inside our continent'? A powerless EU is an unappealing sight.

The EU seems to have lost momentum and drive. Many of the above factors have contributed to this, of course. It also seems clear that all the political manoeuvring over the successor to the impressive Jacques Delors has had its effect on the EU in practice. Jacques Santer, whatever his merits, has probably been no match for the energetic Frenchman who presided over the EU's moves towards a New Europe. One commentator gives this verdict:

> The vacuum means that there is no representation for the many millions of (mainly younger) Europeans who are more likely to speak another language and to have traveled, worked, or studied in another European country but who are instinctively sceptical of big, top-down, self-serving institutions. For them, Jacques Delors' replacement by Jacques Santer has simply replaced an over-zealous leadership with no leadership at all.[13]

To integrate Second World nations and manage the aftermath of Maastricht are the largest issues facing the New Europe. There are others we will touch on below. For a fuller treatment of these issues, readers are encouraged to read Graham Drake's excellent textbook on this subject, *Issues in the New Europe,*[14] which I am happy to acknowledge as the source of many of the facts in this chapter.

The Need for Agricultural Reform

The EU 'Common Agricultural Policy' (CAP) aims to aid farmers across the Union by

- ensuring that the prices farmers receive for their products do not fall beneath a certain level
- controlling imports of cheap foods from countries outside the European Union
- financing projects that improve agricultural efficiency when farm productivity and yields are low

The CAP takes up a major part of the EU's total budget. During the 1980s, the CAP accounted for about two-thirds of the annual EC expenditures. The CAP encouraged the production of large surpluses of some commodities that the EC was committed to buy (in popular imagination, the 'wine lake' and the 'butter mountain'), resulting in subsidies to some countries at the expense of others. At an emergency summit meeting in 1988, EC leaders agreed on mechanisms to limit these payments; under the 1989 budget, agricultural subsidies comprised less than 60 percent of total EC spending for the first time since the 1960s. Nonetheless, the average EU farmer would still receive about half of his or her income in CAP subsidies. In 1991 the cost of the CAP was £80 billion, or £250 per EU citizen. Such huge sums to support only about 7% of the total

EU workforce, or in Britain only 3%, surely cannot be justified much longer. Estimates of the surpluses that result from these anachronistic policies vary. However, 17 million tons of grain, 1.5 million tons of butter, more than 1 million tons of milk powder, and 15 million hectolitres of wine are probably near the mark.[15] Fraudulent claims for CAP subsidies also occur on a large scale and lead to the loss of millions of pounds, a problem exacerbated by inadequate EU policing. Meanwhile, a world starves.

A Christian Aid publication, *Trade for Change*, draws attention to the effects of some of these CAP policies on the Third World. A cow in the EU receives twice as much in subsidy as the average income of a Third World farmer! All over the world people are affected by the over-production of the EU. Billions of pounds in subsidies encourage EU farmers to over-produce, and further billions are then used to sell these same surpluses on the world market. In northern Burkina Faso, for example, nomadic herders rely on cattle-rearing for their livelihood. They used to be able to sell beef to neighbouring countries, but now the EU has taken away that possibility by supplying frozen beef to West African markets that is 35-50% cheaper than local beef. 'Since the international dumping started, we are no longer able to sell our animals. To stop it, all we can do is rely on making foreign opinion more aware of what this is doing to us', says farmer Jean-Marie Kabor.[16] The CAP undoubtedly hurts the Third World in many ways, affirms Christian Aid:

- Surplus EU products compete with local food production.
- Surplus EU products pull down Third World prices so that Third World producers do not get a good price for their exports.
- The CAP erects trade barriers against Third World goods.
- The CAP protects EU farmers from price instability by passing it on to Third World farmers.
- Cheap EU exports create a demand for expensive and inappropriate foreign foods such as wheat.
- The CAP distorts the EU budget, leaving less money for international aid or environmental spending.

Similar EU protection policies are also seriously affecting the attempts of Second World European nations to improve their overall economic performances. There can be no ethical justification for such practices. Nor can there be a just future for the European Union in the twenty-first century until these anomalies and injustices are tackled and further progress is made towards significant reform of the Common Agricultural Policy.

Environmental Concerns

Europe's current environmental problems have their roots in all the 'Capitalist'-type of expansions that have taken place since the 1950s. This is even, curiously, true of Eastern Europe, whose policies have been fueled by an understanding of economics a hundred years old, relying on the analyses made by Marx and Engels of some European industry in the nineteenth century. With all the force of totalitarian dogma, Communist governments tried to manage whole economies on such anachronistic theories. In practice, they were blind to the environmental effects of all of this, including pollution, waste, and limited resources. Here are some examples of this negative legacy from the Communist era.

* In the Czech Republic, North Bohemia, open-cast coal mining has badly disfigured the landscape. Unacceptably high levels of sulphur dioxide are emitted. Coniferous forests have died; pollution masks are routinely issued in schools; and there are abnormally high levels of birth defects, miscarriages, and multiple sclerosis in the area.

* In Hungary, at Copsa Mica, a metal factory and a car tyre factory produce appalling levels of pollution, blackening an area with a radius of some 30km. A permanent covering of black soot results. An estimated 30,000 tons of pollutants including lead, cadmium, and sulphur dioxide have been emitted. Many local children have been found to have lead poison in their blood, a condition that affects the central nervous system. Local milk and dairy products have been declared unfit for human consumption.

* In Slovakia, a coal-fired power station relied on coal with a high arsenic content. This was being deposited on the surrounding countryside. Various cancers and partial deafness have been among the side effects.

* In Russia and the Ukraine almost one-sixth of the total land area is unfit for human habitation because of toxic or nuclear waste. Just under 3 million people are living in areas affected by the 1986 Chernobyl nuclear accident. Some 1.3 million people have registered with related illnesses and medical conditions from this one incident. All the main Russian rivers, including the Volga and Don, have been polluted; and 84 Russian cities and towns, including Moscow, have rates of pollution at least ten times higher than acceptable levels.

Most East European governments feel they have no choice but to continue with nuclear energy. They have few alternatives, particularly given the disruption of oil, gas, and coal supplies from the former Soviet Union. More than half the nuclear reactors in the world are in the Second World. In the mid-1990s thirty-six new ones were being built in Russia and the Ukraine. That was despite a government enquiry that concluded that half of the country's existing nuclear reactors should be closed because of inadequate safety standards. Chernobyl may not be the last major incident involving nuclear fall out from collapsed or damaged reactors. In 1991 in Bulgaria a nuclear power station was declared to have serious design flaws by the International Atomic Energy Authority. In 1992 two of the newer, *safer*, Bulgarian reactors were destroyed by fire.

These environmental problems are not limited to the Second World in Europe. Acid rain is a continuing problem across the whole of Europe, damaging lakes, rivers, and aquatic ecosystems. Forests have been severely damaged and rendered more vulnerable to pests and diseases. Stonework in buildings has been damaged, including that of priceless historic buildings. Soils are experiencing leaching, a process whereby toxic metals such as aluminium are released into lakes and rivers killing fish and other species. Much of this particular environmental problem results from the continued practice of burning coal in power stations.

Global warming will have a devastating effect in parts of Europe, not least of which is the Mediterranean. Coastal wetlands will be destroyed by salt water infiltration or flooding. Salt water may well infiltrate drinking water supplies; whole tourist beaches could vanish; and harbour and sea walls could become redundant or be destroyed as the rate of coastal erosion is likely to increase rapidly. The types of crops that can be grown in affected regions will also change. Cultivated land levels will decline by as much as 25% and soil productivity will also decline. Forest fires are another likely side effect.

Road building and the increased use of cars have led to many anxieties about damage to the environment:

• Plans to improve road links, with EU help, between Spain and France in the Aspe valley of the Pyrenees have led to local opinion being bitterly divided. Some see the road as the key to the area's regeneration, whereas others consider it as an unacceptable disruption of a peaceful mountain environment. The issue is complicated by the effects of the road building programme on the only remaining brown bears in the Pyrenees. Local militia has clashed with militant environmentalists on several occasions. Even riot police have not been able to prevent serious disruptions to the road building.

- Twyford Down, England, has been the scene of similar divisions and protests. Plans to complete the M3 between Winchester and Southampton have been resisted locally in arguments that have a twenty-five-year-old history already. Friends of the Earth and more militant groups such as 'Earth First!' and the 'Dongas Tribe' have clashed repeatedly with developers and the authorities concerned. This issue was complicated by a U-turn on a decision by the European Commission. Protesters argued that the changed ruling was part of a high-level trade off for Britain's acceptance of the Maastricht Treaty.

- Athens, Greece, is probably the European capital most seriously affected by traffic pollution. A combination of high car ownership, a hot sunny climate, and a large number of older cars with poor emission standards have caused a frequent photochemical smog, the *nefos*.

- Urban decay can also be discovered across Europe. Whole districts of Turin, for example, are languishing from rampant theft, drug addiction, and poverty. In the words of a parish priest, Don Andrea, 'Those who can do so send their children to school elsewhere. The schools here are closing. . . . And every day young people are taking the bus and going off in search of work. . . . Not a single cinema, only bars and amusement arcades which regularly get closed down for a few days because of drug dealing'.[17]

Examples such as these could be multiplied across both Second and First World Europe.

Nationalism and Racism

The collapse of Communism has led inexorably to an increase in both nationalism and racism. The former Soviet Union has fragmented. The Baltic States of Estonia, Latvia, and Lithuania were the first to break away and achieve independence between 1989 and 1991. Each state has its own language and history. Each state also has a significant proportion of Russians living in them who are unhappy with these New Europe changes, feeling that they have become, in effect, second-class citizens. In Latvia, only 40 percent of Russians, Ukrainians, and Jews have been granted Latvian citizenship and, therefore, the right to vote, even though some have lived there for nearly two decades. Belarus, Moldova, and Ukraine also emerged from the ashes of Gorbachev's Soviet Union. In addition, further east in Asia and the Caucasus, other nation states have been reborn such as Georgia, Armenia, and Azerbaijan. Attempts by Gorbachev's successor, Boris Yeltsin, to hold these nation states together in a loose confederation of independent states—the Commonwealth of Independent States (CIS) —have met with mixed success. This was designed to ensure much needed co-operation on defence and economic matters, but the omens are worrying.

There are other examples of racism and nationalism facing the new Europe. These include the continuing 'troubles' of Northern Ireland where, since 1969, hundreds of lives have been lost. For all the early encouragements of the 1994–1995 Northern Ireland peace process and the impetus towards a lasting peace of American President Bill Clinton's historic visit there in the autumn of 1995, most of the underlying problems there remain unresolved as the twenty-first century approaches. As of 1996, the IRA cancellation of its cease-fire and the consequent failure to achieve full participation in the 'all-party talks' deepens fears of a volatile future. In my view, they will remain until some kind of international commission, perhaps EU-led, is allowed into 'Britain's backyard' to suggest new and creative ways forward. Until then, Nationalist and Loyalist hostilities, exacerbated by religious differences, will continue to plague Britain's economic, political, and domestic life. Though nowhere near as acutely, similar nationalistic and racist tensions are also to be found in Wales and Scotland where there are significant devolution movements.

The cause of Basque separatism in Spain, which has also led to hundreds of maimings and deaths over the past twenty-five years, is another example of the persistence of tribalism in the late twentieth century. So are the nationalistic Neo-Nazi attacks against foreign workers and their families in the New Germany. These have been accompanied by violence, the use of swastikas, verbal abuse, and, on occasion, deaths. It is, however, the continuing civil war in what we once knew of as Yugoslavia that best demonstrates the continuing power of nationalism and racism in contemporary Europe.

The conflict and pain of the former Yugoslavia—Europe's El Salvador— have been well documented, not least by the world's media. In 1991 a civil war erupted in Croatia that continued with horrifying levels of violence for more than four years until an American-brokered peace treaty was signed towards the end of 1995. Atrocities became almost commonplace throughout this civil war. Young women were singled out for gang rape. Mass slaughter resulted in fields knee deep in the blood of those summarily executed. Death pits, common under the Nazis, reappeared in continental Europe. Literally millions became refugees in the largest movements of peoples in continental Europe since World War II.

Who could have anticipated it? Slovenia in the north of the former country achieved independence in 1991 with little pain, helped by the fact that some 95 percent of its population was already Slovene. Macedonia also declared its independence in 1991 and achieved this in the eyes of the United Nations (UN) in 1993. Croatia's attempts to declare independence in 1991, however, led to the outbreak of civil war between Serbs and Croats. The Serb army sought to create autonomous Serbian areas within the new Croatia by using superior ex-Yugoslav army weaponry and a policy the world has come to know as ethnic cleansing. Decades of resentments, grievances, and anger surfaced as a result. It was like the opening of some demonic Pandora's box.

In 1992 the first United Nations peace-keeping troops entered the disputed areas. That same year, the conflict was extended when the area of Bosnia declared itself to be an independent nation. Serbs fought against both Bosnian Muslims and Bosnian Croats to help preserve a Greater Serbia, which stretched through Croatia and Bosnia. In 1993 a non-aggression treaty between the Croats and Muslims broke down as the Croats also sought to create autonomous Croat areas within Bosnia. By 1995 the Croatians had built up considerable weaponry and fighting personnel of their own and so were able to reverse some of the defeats from earlier in the civil war. Until that point of the civil war, the emergence of a Greater Serbia seemed inevitable. Some of the worst atrocities had happened in Bosnia, and the vulnerability of the Bosnian Muslims, despite a renewed partnership with the Croats in fighting against the Serbs over the summer of 1995, remained a concern, even after the signing of the 1995 peace treaty. Without strong and determined international protection, they continue to face an uncertain future. Bernard Henri-Levy, one of France's leading intellectuals, drew out some of the implications of this conflict for the New Europe in these words:

> I believe the time has come to count the cost of . . . non-intervention, in other words of acquiescence by the West. . . . This cost we know only too well. It amounts to the destruction of a country, two million refugees in camps or in exile, the collapse of our system of collective security, the discrediting of the UN, the establishment of the principle that might is right, and the risk of establishing in the heart of Europe a Muslim State which the Bosnia Muslims themselves did not want.[18]

The breakup of former Yugoslavia, and within that the division of Bosnia into Muslim and Serbian states, is now irreversible. Only tiny Montenegro, for example, has actually chosen to stay within Serbia. The possible outcomes and longer-term territorial permutations remain unpredictable at the time of this writing. A mentality of vengeance, the language of militarism, and disregard for peace have characterized so much of this civil war. It has been a devastating testimony to the potent forces of nationalism, xenophobia, and ingrained racism in late twentieth-century Europe.

4. A Re-Evangelization of Europe?

Evangelization in the New Europe takes place in the overall context we have examined in the larger part of this chapter. The context is a Europe that must decide between an enlargement that embraces both First and Second World nations or one that perpetuates the existing economic and social inequalities of the Old Europe. It is a Europe that must decide between the advantages for a new century of supra-nationalism or of a looser inter-governmentalism. The framework is a European Union that needs to examine critically the defects and injustices of its Common Agricultural Policy or lose much ethical credibility. The setting is a Europe that could still conceivably be destroyed from without by decades of environmental abuse or from within by the demons of nationalism and racism. As the English Cardinal Basil Hume summed it up,

> Europe needs to be given a new soul and a new self-awareness. That is the magnitude of our task. In many ways, the evangelization of Europe must be started all over again as if it had never before taken place.[19]

My own conviction is that the European Union is one significant vehicle that God can use for good. Like Cyrus in the story of Israel, it is an agency outside the Church through which more of the goal of liberation for all *can* be reached (Isa 44:28).[20] One of the aims of this study guide, then, is to dispel some ignorance about the workings and policies of the European Union, where this ignorance exists, and to remind more Christians of its importance. Christian leaders need to pay far greater attention to the signs of the times emerging from Brussels and their own parliaments, and less from their own narrow inter-church networks or church meetings. God is concerned for the whole of Europe, not just for one small local church or even a diocese or association within one of its many nations!

I believe there are clues to be found within the theologies of liberation that have developed within all three worlds we have been exploring, pointers as to how this task of holistic evangelization and liberation in the New Europe might be implemented as the new millennium begins.

Lessons from the Third World

What we can learn from the Third World here is helpfully summarized in the four essentials for effective evangelization highlighted by José Comblin. As we saw earlier in this guide, they draw upon his ministry in Brazil.

(1) *Praxis is a wiser first step than mere words.* Christianity is better communicated through deeds, actions, changed attitudes, and lifestyles than through sermons or religious language. In the final chapter of this book I will suggest some specific ideas for this.

(2) *Dialogue is necessary.* Genuine dialogue means both proclaiming *and* listening to those of other faiths or none. Our dialogue partners in the New Europe include the politicians and the social scientists as well as the political analysts from whom, as Christians, we can learn a great deal.

(3) *The supremacy of Christ and his teachings must still be affirmed.* Whether it is by affirming the integrity of creation or castigating the ethical failures of the CAP; whether it is pleading for a vision of one integrated Europe or resisting racism and destructive nationalism; in all these areas Christian voices *must* be heard in the debates about the destiny of Europe in the late 1990s. Our Scriptures compel us to do exactly this.

(4) *We always need the Holy Spirit's help in evangelization.* This is part of the distinctiveness of Christian witness. We are those who are explicitly co-operating with the Spirit of the Risen Christ, and so we must help all who are concerned for true liberation to co-operate with Christ's spirit too, however dimly they may discern his presence in the liberation struggle.

Lessons from the Second World

From the 'Second World' we can surely learn much from the concept of Solidarity popularized by Polish Christians in the 1980s. As we saw from their story, God's work of liberation was achieved by differing groups of people in partnership, in solidarity, with God and each other. It was not the Church, or party reformers, or even dissident intellectuals who took the lead there. All were to play a part later, but the lead was taken by trade unionists and other working class leaders: 'Workers of all enterprises unite'. Then Pope John Paul II, Father Jankowski, Jerzy Popielusko, and, in all the delicacies of his position, Cardinal Glemp were some of the high-profile Christian leaders who committed themselves to this Solidarity. Alongside them in the liberation struggle were literally millions of Polish Christians together in mutual solidarity, in prayer and committed action. Let us hear again some of the words of Jerzy Popieluszko in this context:[21]

> Let us have the courage to acknowledge Christ in public, to profess our loyalty to the Church, our faith in everything that makes up the glory of our nation; the courage to speak about it openly in the school, in the university, in the workshop, as well as in the office.

We stand here with a hope in our hearts that a rightful place will be found for God in our schools, offices, and factories, that truth, justice, and charity will become the uppermost values in the life of the State and nation.

Some may accuse me of involving myself in politics, but in a country where politics endeavour to penetrate, unhampered, all walks of life, then there is an additional reason why we should examine some matters from a moral point of view.[22]

Solidarity between people of goodwill committed to justice and co-operating with the God of liberation can change the face of a nation and of a continent. Christians are not alone in the commitment to build a new society. As we have seen before in our study guide, God's Kingdom is bigger than God's Church.

Lessons from the First World

As for the First World, it may be that at least some of our answers in the areas of effective evangelization are to be found in the commitment to the values and work of God's wider Kingdom, which are outlined in the Church of England reports, *Faith in the City* and *Faith in the Countryside,* considered earlier in this guide. The meaning of this commitment is also to be glimpsed in the ecumenical vision of the so-called 'Mersey Miracle' described in the book, *Better Together.*[23] Other ways forward, consistent with this commitment to the Kingdom, may be to draw on the Celtic revival emerging in many parts of the First World. Britain and much of Europe were first evangelized by Celtic missionaries whose challenge was to communicate Christianity within many different cultures and to a Europe, then as now, of many religions. As Ian Bradley suggests:

It is not I think being unduly pessimistic to suggest that we are entering another Dark Age. The threat now comes not from savage tribes like the Vandals, Goths, and Huns but from the brutalising pressures of advertising and the mass media, the crudeness and violence of much popular music and entertainment, and the inexorable rise of the consumer society with its rampant acquisitiveness and selfishness.[24]

We can only sketch some of the possibilities here. The principal response of Celtic Christianity was, as in parts of Latin America today, to build both communities and community. In contemporary Christian language they were church planters, and in this activity they learned to view contemporary cultures positively and built bridges to them creatively. They integrated Word and Spirit,

Scripture and Spirituality. Their worship was holistic with liturgy drawing on nature, the arts, and human experience. Creation was respected but never worshiped. The Creator was seen in creation but was never fully identified with it. Women played a creative rôle as both leaders of community and as missioners. The Celtic missionaries were wanderers, fully dependent on the Holy Spirit, who were prepared to travel in flimsy boats or to walk hundreds of miles on pilgrimage to spread the Good News of Jesus Christ. The First World Church in Europe desperately needs to rediscover such qualities in its own evangelization.

5. Baptist Solidarity

The significant rôle being played in liberation praxis in Europe by one group of Christian churches, the European Baptist Federation (EBF), deserves far higher prominence, especially among Baptists in all the three 'worlds' we have been exploring. Since 1949, the EBF has nurtured Christian co-operation among its member Unions, bringing people and resources together for the good of all. Though not numerically as large in Europe as some other Christian denominations (with 48 Baptist Unions, some 10,300 churches, and 770,000 baptized church members), Baptist churches are more widely distributed in the countries and regions of Europe than any other Christian denomination. This reflects the global scope of the Baptist World Alliance, whose member Unions are present in more countries of the world than any other Christian communion.[25] Baptist Christians are very well-placed to demonstrate the interconnectedness of Christianity in the three worlds within the 'global village' of the new century.

This chapter therefore closes with three examples of solidarity between Baptists in the New Europe that may well prove to be pointers to the kind of solidarity, the new internationalism, that will be needed again and again in all the challenges of the twenty-first century.

Children of Chernobyl

In Belorussia the nation continues to live with the aftermath of the Chernobyl nuclear disaster and the concomitant widespread radiation poisoning. The areas around Minsk and Brest, as well as the areas around Gomel and Mogilev, are all 'officially' contaminated areas. The European Baptist Federation's Children of Chernobyl project has been particularly appreciated by the Belorussian Baptists. Beginning in 1992, many groups of children from Chernobyl-affected areas (including some from the Ukraine) have been brought to countries in the

'First World' of Europe for a holiday lasting three to four weeks in the homes of Baptist church members. There is good evidence that the change in climate has brought about a general improvement in health and outlook and even some strengthening of their immune systems. Host churches have included those in the Czech Republic, Denmark, Germany, Italy, the Netherlands, Slovakia, Spain, Sweden, and the United Kingdom.

Religious Liberty in Bulgaria

In Bulgaria in 1995 the Baptist Union of Bulgaria found itself at the centre of a fight to keep Baptist property in the Bulgarian capital, Sofia. In Advent 1993, the Baptist Union had received permission to build a church centre including a school and orphanage on newly purchased property. The city council had since determined to get the property back, fueled by violent anti-Baptist propaganda. 'Baptists eat babies for breakfast' was one headline in a national newspaper! The Council denied permission on the grounds of the bad influence that 'Baptists might have on people and especially on children'. Dr. Denton Lotz of the Baptist World Alliance (BWA) spearheaded the counter-attack and mobilized Baptists in positions of influence throughout the world to write in support of the life and work of Bulgarian Baptists. The sheer volume of letters and international protests received by the city council in Sofia had the desired effect. Among those writing were the Southern Baptist Association of the Baptist Union of Great Britain, whose churches have been developing twinning links with Bulgaria for many years now. In July of that year, the council agreed to allow the work to proceed, though with some restrictions. Theo Angelov, the Bulgarian and European Baptist Federation leader, expressed deep gratitude for 'the prayers and support of our brothers and sisters in the Baptist world. Without the international pressure brought by these people, this would have been impossible'. He warned, however, that it is 'possible that there will still be difficulties ahead'. The underlying difficulties with the Bulgarian State, exacerbated by harassment from sections of the Orthodox Church of Bulgaria, are still largely unresolved.

Theological Education in Poland

Visiting Poland, on several occasions during the 1990s, it has been my privilege to see the emergence of the splendid new Baptist seminary at Radosc to the southeast of Warsaw. This seminary is a typical example of the new confidence among East European Baptists in the New Europe. Such seminaries have sprung up all over the Baptist Second World since 1990. In September 1994 the new centre was officially opened. This was a decade after the then Communist régime leased the land to the Baptists on a 99-year lease. 'We decided it was logical to have several activities on the property', explained the then Baptist Union President Konstanty Wiazowski. 'It is ours for 99 years, and that is clear. After that, whoever is around at that time will have to worry what to do'. The project has been made possible because of generous support from the Polish Baptists, the skilled labour of Moldovan Baptists among others, and some significant practical and financial support from First World Baptists, not least in America, Sweden, Germany, and Britain.

The theologians of liberation were the first to remind us of the potential of the social and political sciences to establish the context for evangelization. This chapter has sought to use that methodology as a preparation for praxis—the integration of Christian theology and action. It has ended with some possible ways forward drawn from the theologies of all three worlds. We have been painting, then, the backdrop for Christian evangelization in the New Europe. To this theme we will return in the final chapter of this book.

Notes

[1]Quoted in Desmond Dinan, *Ever Closer Union* (Macmillan Press, Basingstoke, 1994), p. 14.

[2]Robert Marjolin, quoted in Dinan, op. cit. p. 34.

[3]Quoted in Dinan, op. cit., p. 54.

[4]Quoted in Dinan, op. cit., p. 81.

[5]Quoted in Dinan, op. cit., p. 99.

[6]Quoted in Dinan, op. cit., p. 118.

[7]Quoted in Dinan, op. cit., p. 135.

[8]Article, 'Order Disguised as Chaos', *The Economist*, 13 March 1993.

[9]Charles Handy, *The Empty Raincoat* (Hutchinson, London, 1994), p. 130.

[10]Patricia Clough, writing in *The Independent*, 20 April 1992.

[11]Quoted by Charles Handy, *The Empty Raincoat*, p. 143.

[12]Victor Smart, 'European Union loses its appeal', *The European*, 9 August 1995.

[13]Geoffrey Mulgan, 'A Vacuum at the heart of Europe', *The Independent*, 15 August 1995.

[14]Graham Drake, *Issues in the New Europe* (Hodder & Stoughton, London, 1994).

[15]Figures quoted by Graham Drake in *Issues in the New Europe*, p. 99.

[16]Quoted in *Trade for Change* (1995) available from Christian Aid, PO Box 100, London SE1 7RT.

[17]Article, 'In fear and loathing', *The Guardian*, 16 April 1993.

[18]Bernard Henri-Levy, 'The spirit of Europe lives or dies at Sarajevo', *The Independent,* 31 July 1995.

[19]Basil Hume, *Remaking Europe* (SPCK, London, 1994), p. 4.

[20]For the place of Cyrus in the biblical tradition, see above p. 132.

[21]These quotations are all from sermons that are recorded in Jerzy Popieluszko, *The Price of Love* (1985).

[22]Cardinal Basil Hume develops the theological theme of solidarity in his book *Remaking Europe*; see esp. chap. 2, 'Solidarity and Morals', and ch. 3, 'Solidarity and Freedom'.

[23]For details, see above pp. 75-81.

[24]Ian Bradley, *The Celtic Way* (Darton, Longman, & Todd, London, 1993), p. 119.

[25]Statistics for 1996 show 153,310 local churches in 113 nations. For more details, see below, pp. 198-199.

Chapter 9
Liberation and Evangelization
for the New Europe

In the concluding chapter of this book we will explore what the relation between liberation and evangelization might mean in praxis in the New Europe. The theologies we have considered and, especially, the twelve key themes that emerged in the course of Part I are drawn upon to provide us with the ingredients of a theology for evangelization in the contemporary world. This chapter focuses on the situation of a contemporary First World local church and advocates unashamedly a particular model for such a church, whether it be large or small, rural or urban. It seeks to portray a model of a local church in a translocal fellowship of churches committed to a thoroughly biblical evangelism and to a mission praxis.

I believe that our local churches need to be turned inside out to reproduce something of the breadth of the Bible's commitment to liberation. Only such churches deserve, in fact, to win back at least some of the world's unchurched in the decade that some have dared to call one of evangelization. To seek to illustrate something at least of what such local church praxis might mean, and with some diffidence, this chapter is interspersed with a brief record of some of the author's experiences as a local church pastor in three different parts of Britain.

1. First Case Study
John Bunyan Baptist Church, Cowley, 1980–1987

For ten years my wife and I lived and ministered in and around Oxford. Three years of ministerial training at Regent's Park College in the setting of the University were followed by seven years as a minister in Oxford's principal industrial suburb, Cowley. Since the early years of the twentieth century, when the Morris Motor Company began to build its factories there, Cowley and the car industry had become closely identified. The Baptist church in Cowley was founded at the beginning of World War II, a church-plant by the central Baptist Church in Oxford. During an early ministry there, the new church building, dubbed 'the Coventry Cathedral of Cowley', had been built, and by 1965 the church's membership had peaked at 130 members. By the time of our call there in 1980, the membership statistics were down to the 60s, the church was largely white, and the number of children and young people associated with us was around 50. By the time we left in 1987, the membership had returned to 130 members, but now the congregation was multi-racial with black and Asian families in membership, and more than fifty people had been baptized in the church's large grey baptistery.

Our evangelism took many forms. A 'crusade' in the area by a charismatic evangelist in 1983 had resulted in many people placing faith in Christ; I had taken responsibility for follow-up to the mission in East Oxford and was inundated with more than thirty contacts to visit in just a few days. A baptismal service followed, and, as was often the case for us in those days, one baptismal service led to another. During Billy Graham's Mission England visit in 1984, we traveled, with several unchurched people, to two of the football stadia and saw conversions to Christ. Later we followed this up by a video-linked partnership mission with several other churches in what we called 'Mission Oxford East'. With others in the Cowley Council of Churches, we took part in a door-to-door visitation programme, leaving an ecumenical invitation to our churches behind as we left each home.

A relationship developed with some of the leaders of one of the many house groups of a thriving city centre Anglican church (St. Aldates) that met in Cowley. Together we undertook a community survey and built a mission week around the responses. Five events were planned: 'Cowley Past and Present' with slides and testimonies; a focus on nuclear disarmament issues; an 'Any Questions?' evening for whole families; a pensioner's lunch with several testimonies; and, finally, an evangelistic presentation evening to seal the week that we called 'Faith for the Future'. We publicized these events in a number of ways, including leaflet distribution and a Christian literature table in the Cowley Centre. All of this, coupled with the far more important 'routine' evangelism through friendships, pastoral care, and personal witness, led to the church growth outlined above.

Our commitment to mission was multi-faceted. In the course of those years, for example, I found myself liaising between the police and one of our black Christian families whose son had been wrongly imprisoned for a time after an early-morning police raid. I was kept busy with providing basic redundancy counselling in all the vagaries of the employment scene at the car factory. The church was encouraging letters of support for the Soviet prisoner of conscience, Dmitri Minayakov, organizing Third World hunger lunches and protesting against the bed and breakfast crisis in 1980s Oxford—a social issue that came alive for us when one of our own Sunday School families had to live for a while in such a 'home'. As a church we supported the 'Helen House' children's hospice project locally. The protests formulated by our Church Meeting against the closure of local hospital wards received significant media coverage in both the local and Baptist press. We played a key rôle locally in the successful campaign in 1986 (though later reversed by legislation) to prevent changes in Sunday trading legislation, arguing from several perspectives and not just 'churchy' ones. Newspaper cuttings saved from the period capture something of our church's praxis at that time:

'Church willing to pay more tax to help NHS'
'Churchgoers protest at health cuts'
'Church's worries over Centre'
'Church man ticks off top Tories'
'Hands off Sunday call to traders'

The church became best known in that period, however, through the activities of the Oxfordshire Pensioners' Action Group, which I led as chairman from 1983–1987; I should add that I was then a youngish man in my thirties! Appearances on Radio Oxford and letters and articles in the Oxford papers were all part of a deliberate policy of consciousness-raising by our group. We had, quite literally, a county-wide vision. In 1984, the *Oxford Mail* published a full-page spread on our group and on the kinds of pensioners' issues we had been raising consistently in the local media: 'Scrimping, Saving—the Twilight Years', it was headed. We lobbied over those years for a more equitable concessionary transport fares policy across the county. We drew on comparative material provided for us by the Labour politician Barbara Castle to help the 1984 European Community elections come alive for pensioners. We involved key people in the local political scene, such as Steven Norris and Andrew Smith—who won the Oxford East national parliamentary seat in 1983 and 1987 respectively—the community physician, local funeral directors, and city and county councillors. We protested against post office closures. We traveled to Parliament to lobby our own MPs and others. We drew attention to the low pension levels obtaining in Britain, especially when compared to those elsewhere in the then EC. We prepared a combined lobby of the county and city council on a wide range of issues. We lobbied funeral directors locally for a funeral policy at prices the bereaved could afford. We played our part in various hypothermia campaigns. Just before our leaving Cowley, the Oxford *Community Care* magazine published a two-page article on our group that said: 'The Oxford group may or may not be typical of what is happening throughout the country, but it is a clear pointer to the future'. Again newspaper cuttings capture something of those years well:

'Pensioners are neglected'
'Pensioners' fares—rap for MPs'
'Fare deal for all'
'Supporting the NHS adequately'

'Group slams health cuts plan'
'When the old and cold get all het up'
'Fowler paper attacked as step backwards'
'A safety code for pensioners'
'OAPs in death grant fight'
'Old folk seek a better bus deal'
'Give us more, demand old folk'

More than a decade later the Oxfordshire Pensioners' Action Group continues to meet, lobby, protest, and raise awareness.

2. Conscientization

It is essential that the local church be involved in the process of conscientization, the raising of social and political awareness. Here are three examples of what this insight from the Latin American experience of liberation might mean in our First World scene.

Poverty

First World local churches need to become much more aware of the poverty that results in human misery, desperation, and a struggle to survive for many in their own communities and millions in their continent and world. The policies of national and local governments need to be judged by the effects they have, not on the newspaper leader-writers and the comfortable, the powerful and the influence makers, but on the poor, the vulnerable, and the inarticulate. If we have interpreted the Scriptures correctly, then it is by these standards that the God revealed in Jesus Christ will judge each one of us. Dom Helder Camara urges us:

> What God does not want is a world torn between an excess of money and mortal hunger, between loveless pleasures and appalling suffering, between soaring palaces and tumble-down shacks, between those who give orders and those who bend the knee.[1]

Materialism

Conscientization in our local churches will mean exposing the evils of the empty materialism all around us. The experiences many of us have increasingly in the shopping centres of our towns and cities bring this home forcibly. The easy use of credit cards is encouraged everywhere, greed and acquisition are written over people's faces including our own, and we are surrounded by an over-abundance of consumer desirables but not necessities. Such naked materialism distracts us from the real problems of humanity and of planet earth as the twenty-first century approaches. The future of the vast majority of earth's inhabitants who struggle to eat at all, to drink clean water, to breathe pure air, and to remain human is, in part, in our own hands under God. The money we give to the Third World agency or missionary society may well be the most significant item of expenditure in our local church or personal budget.

Ecology

Conscientization must also involve pleading for our battered and bruised planet, groaning from the pains of deforestation, the exploitation of its scarce resources, and the environmental equivalents of multi-national death squads— the international polluters. A reformed Christian network of local churches has a key rôle to play in developing a social conscience about the state of the natural world. This is one of the major tasks of contemporary Christian evangelization. The Living God made known in Jesus Christ demands it. So does our common humanity under him. Our now bleeding planet was God's other precious gift to humankind long before he gave us Jesus.

3. Orthopraxis

The local church must renew its commitment both to right doctrine (orthodoxy) and to right practice (orthopraxis). The theologians of liberation have made an irrefutable case for orthopraxis as a biblical priority. Contemporary Christians must be committed, insofar as we are able, to a lifestyle of solidarity with the weak, the poor, the marginalized, and to action not just *for* them but *with* them as they struggle for their own liberation. The public face and the actions of our national, regional, and local churches are the visual aids that most clearly communicate our true values and belief patterns. So often throughout church history Christians have failed the Gospel miserably here, despite tomes of theology, detailed creeds, expensive architecture, and empire building by local and national churches. Again and again, it has been a case of a magnificent tree and yet pathetic fruit. Where we are not so involved—and each of us makes our particular compromises with conscience—the Gospel of Christ will judge us. We cannot say we did not know; our Bibles are full of warnings to us. We shall be as those saved, 'but only as those escaping through the flames' (1 Cor 3:15).

Orthopraxis may well mean for some of us:

- supporting the necessary changes that come to our local churches and communities
- the firm but polite letter to Parliament
- the involving of a local councillor in a project or mediating with a local council department
- a refusal to condone racist remarks or to leave them unchallenged
- a protest against the closing of a hospital ward provided by the National Health Service or by other public means of funding
- signing a protest petition for an international prisoner of conscience
- a gift to a development agency or to the children's charity
- sharing in a prayer vigil for El Salvador or the former Yugoslavia
- the unheralded Good Samaritan deed
- adapting a building so that its 'Welcome' to disabled people is meaningful
- a personally-costly conscience vote against the party-line in Parliament or Church Meeting
- the re-affirmation of sexual dignity in a culture obsessed with sex
- lobbying for new legislation or policies that are informed by a genuine concern for the 'other' part of our country that we are less familiar with
- supporting an environmental action group

The list is almost endless. Such acts of solidarity and protest by local churches are all part of contemporary evangelization. They are orthopraxis—right living, Christ-inspired, God-pleasing living. Many of us could do much more in and with the local communities where God has set us to work. Many Christians hide behind local church walls, singing hymns, on spiritual highs, massaging our spiritual egos and re-tuning our guitars. Our only friends are fellow church-goers. We hardly meet the unchurched except briefly in the supermarket or on the children's playground. The local church that has become pre-occupied with its own doctrinal purity or obsessed with its own structures and maintenance while a world starves is being called to repent. The issues that really concern God's heart are not the songs we sing, the organ or roof we may well need to restore, or the version of the prayer book we prefer, but the plight of the home-less, the pensioner, the overworked and the underpaid, and those desperately in need of conversion and so of Christ: 'Faith by itself, if it is not accompanied by action, is dead' (Jas 2: 17).

4. Base Communities

The theologians of liberation have helped the contemporary Church to recognize again the value of communities in human society and in the life of the Christian Church. In his well-argued and well-researched patristic study, *The Memory of the Christian People*, Eduardo Hoornaert reminds us that this alternative model of the Church was the essential model operated by the Church in the first two centuries or so of its existence.[2] The Latin American base communities provide a model for local church activity. They are holistic in their lifestyle. Community action and worship, campaigns for human rights, and catechesis go hand in hand. The Bible is studied and applied to personal and corporate spirituality and to issues such as the right to land, the workers' associations, problems of water supply, education for children, community health needs, literacy classes, and sanitation problems. Is this not the direction for the local church to move in as the new millennium approaches?

Dom Helder Camara affirmed such communities and saw them springing up all over the world. Such groups, he said, 'have as a common denominator the same hunger and thirst for a world that is freer, more than just more brotherly. When I see the vitality of these groups, I have enormous confidence in the future'.[3] European local churches are called to be part of this worldwide movement, too. In October 1994, the Conference of European Churches (CEC) organized an All-European Consultation on *Diakonia* (service) in Bratislava, Slovakia. Representatives from twenty-six European countries were present. Introducing the book that resulted from the Consultation, Jean Fischer, CEC's General Secretary at that time, wrote:

> In our contemporary world, the challenge to *diaconia* is to develop new forms of action which will continue to meet the needs of individuals, families, and the wider community, while at the same time promoting social justice on local, national, regional, and global levels.[4]

There are many examples of Christian community action groups in its pages.

- The Albanian Orthodox Church with a programme of clinics, day-care centres, and agricultural projects
- The Evangelical Lutheran Church's *Alternativa* project in Petrzalka, Slovakia, offering friendship and hope to young people caught up in the drug scene, vandalism, and sheer boredom of their city
- A Baptist church in Pozzouli, Italy, involved in a literacy programme

- The Russian Orthodox Church with sisterhoods and brotherhoods working in local hospitals often in the most difficult departments set aside for the unwanted: criminals, drug addicts, and alcoholics
- Church of England workers in Salford, Manchester, wrestling with the problems of a local housing estate, creating a people's bank, and credit union
- An ecumenical agency in Romania—*AID-Rom*—supported by CEC and the World Council of Churches (WCC) holding literacy classes and providing health and emergency medical care, counselling, and overnight shelters
- Christian women from the Dutch Reformed Church in the Netherlands protesting forcefully against the trafficking in women from the Second World for the purposes of prostitution
- The Reformed Church in Hungary working with disabled people
- Finnish Christians working to set up a safety net for some of the victims of recession
- The Ecumenical Employment Initiative in Germany and its Open House project for unemployed people
- The Ecumenical Humanitarian Service (EHS) in Novi Sad in the former Yugoslavia caring for refugees and providing meals and medicine for some of the victims of the civil war

Robin Gurney draws the following lesson from the Consultation: 'In the diversity of the new Europe, *diaconia* takes its form around the variety of human needs. In view of the multicultural situation, *diaconia* should seek the maximum possible partnership with other movements and organizations . . . learning to work with rather than for people, aiming for empowerment and transformation'.[5]

Many First World local churches have rediscovered house fellowships and small Bible study groups in recent years. Would that more First World local churches had also discovered the vision for their local communities that the 'base communities' in Latin America have! In fact, groups with such a concern are all around us in 'secular' society. There are, for example, tenants' associations, community health councils, pensioners' voice branches, Age Concern and Oxfam shops, Save the Children Fund committees, third world agency campaign groups, trade union meetings, neighbourhood advice centres, parent-teacher associations, women's refuges, environmental action groups, caregivers support groups, Alcoholics Anonymous. . . . The list of such groups in Britain alone is enormous, and similar examples could be reproduced all over Europe and North America. Whether or not any Christians are present in such self-help groups, God certainly is. Might they not be seen as forming, at the local level, something in Europe comparable to the base communities in Latin America? Perhaps, however, the Church should also be creating groups closer to the Latin American model, involving a wide range of people both inside and outside the Church and reflecting on Scripture with reference to their particular context and community concern, so working towards liberation in various spheres of life. We surely need to create such empowered and empowering groups, serving the community, served by Christians and inspired by Scripture and worship. It has taken more than two decades of liberation theology to make clear to the World Church just how important base communities are in God's plans and purposes for the twenty-first century. We should never doubt that a small group of thoughtful, committed people can help to change the world. Indeed, it can be argued that they are the only thing that ever has.

5. Second Case Study
Leamington Road Baptist Church, Blackburn, 1987–1992

In 1987 we were called as a young family to a pastorate in the north of England. It was in Blackburn, a nineteenth-century industrial town set near the heart of Lancashire's spectacular hills and countryside. The church began at a historic moment in the life of the Baptist Union, founded in 1895 as part of the Union's visionary fund for strengthening church life in the twentieth century. Built in quality red Accrington brick, the church had been transformed in the 1970s by visionary leaders who had also overseen the refurbishing of the sanctuary. The area where the church is set is a multi-racial one with Christians, Muslims, Hindus, and unchurched whites living side by side as neighbours.

The beginning of a new pastorate was an ideal time to key into the Baptist Union's fine audit programme: Action in Mission (AIM). This incorporated a survey of both church and community. We agreed on an area of streets immediately around our church and began knocking on doors. Somehow it is easier to do this in the north than in the south, especially in the closely-built terraced housing community all around. Local people, we found, were both pleased and displeased with our area. They liked the accessibility of the various amenities such as the park, the shops, and schools. They did not like the litter, the state of the roads and pavements, and the various traffic and parking problems. Interestingly, in harmony with similar surveys all over the country, more than 75% of those we surveyed said that God was important to them. Making allowances for the usual courtesies in such surveys, our church also came out quite well as 'a good and friendly place'. Clearly there was potential for outreach and service here.

We supported the Billy Graham 'Livelink' mission in Preston. We held training seminars in personal evangelism and witnessing that drew in people from other parts of East Lancashire. We launched an ambitious three-year family holiday club programme for the autumn. This was to be a holiday club aimed not just at young children, but one that had a programme for all the family; country walks, family videos, and a free buffet and party at the end of the week all featured. I am happy to say that the all-age holiday club programme has continued beyond the three-year trial period on into a new ministry there now. We also supported an ecumenical evangelism initiative with considerable support from other church leaders including the bishops of Blackburn and Lancaster, Free Church leaders, and the Roman Catholic Bishop of Salford. Our church hosted a study day that saw the launch of the project. In the lecture room of Blackburn College, local Roman Catholic, Church of England, and Free Church leaders joined together for a series of contemporary apologetics entitled 'Christianity Today'. The local media featured this as an opportunity to question vigorously our Christian faith in the late twentieth century. All of these projects and more were overseen by our Evangelism Action Group (EAG), which was growing in strength and purpose. Some forty people joined our church in those years; some of them are now key leaders of the church in the late 1990s.

The work of the EAG was supported by a similar mission action group. We protested as a church against the closure of the Bramley Mead maternity community hospital; one of our members pioneered a bereavement support service in the district's hospitals; we voiced our protests about the film *The Last Temptation of Christ*. We took part in a Romanian Aid initiative. We protested on behalf of a Romanian pastor, Nestor Popescu, who was languishing in a psychiatric prison hell in Ceausescu's Romania. We challenged our own church bank, the National Westminster, about its Third World debt policy as part of a national Christian Aid campaign. Ecumenically, too, we were active. The West Blackburn churches organized an election forum in time for the 1992 election, which I was invited to chair. The town's MP, Jack Straw, frankly, was outstanding!

Following on from the AIM survey, and encouraged by a member of our church, Professor Graham Ashworth of the 'Tidy Britain' Group, we launched the West Blackburn Grimewatch Action Group. We took part in a road safety campaign. Teams of people from our church, including our Cubs, Scouts, Brownies, and Guides, formed work teams to clear local eyesores of rubbish. We worked closely with the city council. We hosted public meetings where local people could express their feelings on the damage that television cable-laying was doing to roads and pavements. The editor of the local newspaper, who ran an admirable Grimewatch spot daily, spoke at a Green Week we organized. Again, the local media did us proud as a church. Photographs appeared with some regularity as did headlines such as:

'Church mums in good fight'
'Church wages war on grime'
'Plea for Romania'
'TV cable chaos under spotlight'
'Tell us hole truth!'

6. Evangelization

In one sense, the whole final part of this book is about evangelization. As Cardinal Basil Hume reminds us,

> Europe is a whole, but it is made up of a mosaic of peoples. The Church has to speak in languages and in ways appropriate to the cultures of ancient and independent nations, while at the same time remaining aware of a deeper unity, a common heritage, and common problems.[6]

It is no good preaching only half a Gospel. Church growth teachings and all the tinkering with worship patterns we have indulged in across First World local churches in recent decades will be worth little when set against the kind of judgement the Bible teaches us to expect in Matthew 25. Similarly, however, while social action will clearly be of Kingdom value, our Lord will *also* ask us how many new disciples we made, as in Matthew 28. The Gospel is about conversions, nurture, and evangelism, *and* it is about a bias to the poor, feeding the hungry, and liberation.

The truth, of course, as the theologians of liberation vividly remind us, is that the traditional local Church has failed the First World. The process of secularization has seen much of the First World slip increasingly away from the Christian Church. It is barely holding on with its fingertips now in many parts of Europe. What if it is only, for some at least, the old model it is rejecting and not Christ himself? As a voice from Latin America tells us: 'What the modern world is rejecting is the Church built by the clergy of the eighteenth and nineteenth centuries, the Church that refused to face up to the problems of the emergent new world'.[7] In contemporary Britain, less than one in ten people are regular churchgoers. The models, the mind-sets, the priorities we have operated with since at least the last two centuries in Britain's churches have led to the growing gulf between churched and unchurched in the First World. A privatized Christian faith has been far easier to sustain than a serious, critical debate with secular society, its needs, and its thinkers.

The challenge to the New Europe issued by the theologians of liberation is that new local church models are desperately needed to turn the tide and to help win twenty-first-century humankind back to faith in the risen, liberating Christ. The sooner we jettison the old failed models, painful as this will be, the better. As José Comblin again reminds us:

> Evangelization has to be carried out in a context and in terms that atheists understand, or remain on the level of polite conversation. Theology, dogmas, liturgy, and church structures serve only to repel. Only a living experience can command attention and eventually convince; this is now becoming a growing conviction.[8]

Many of today's unchurched may still believe in God or in Christ. But the Gospel has hardly begun to touch their lives, except perhaps at birth, marriage, and another's death. The local church is seen as an optional extra in a lifestyle that has little or no direct reference to God. Atheists, agnostics, and the vast army of the unchurched are unlikely to be convinced by models of the local church that have long ago failed the Gospel; I mean structures that exhibit male chauvinism, anti-intellectualism, and spiritual narcissism.

The Gospel we are to proclaim, and that will shape the model of the Church, is a faith that is concerned about individuals, local communities, cities, nations, and our one world. Such a faith may begin to turn the tide. This is a faith that is expressed in courageous, bold, and at times costly commitment to social change and transformation; a faith that has its contemporary martyrs in the death pits of El Salvador, dying in the torture cells of the rich, lashed by the whips of a Soweto, or fallen on the bloodstained streets of a Poland or a Romania. It is a faith more at ease in, say, the Other Britain than in the Comfortable one. Yet, it is a faith that cares still for *both*; the liberation theologians Boff and Pixley speak of the pastoral needs of *all* sectors of society, including the middle classes: the well-off, the intellectuals, the politicians, those in the communications media, doctors, and professors.[9] The old models of church across the denominations may well survive for decades, yet as the opium of the minorities only. Eventually those models will and must collapse. They have had their day and have failed both the world and Christ. Here's to their funeral. The battle of contemporary evangelization begins with a fight for the soul of the First World's churches.

7. New Humanity

Perhaps one of the most profound insights to emerge from the Second World's experiences of liberation is that of the *solidarity* of all humanity. Solidarity means standing with, suffering with, sometimes bleeding with the poor and marginalized. It means identification like this with the unchurched and devout, atheist or agnostic, expatriates or indigenous, male or female, child or middle-aged or old. Across the ethnic barriers and across those of culture and belief and language, humanity is one. Such solidarity helped to create the New Europe during the Cold War years. International barriers must continue to be superseded; mutual visits bring home still more closely the unity of the one humanity in our divided world. This one humanity is at the heart of the Christian Gospel. Ideologies divide, categorizing people as 'Marxist or Capitalist'; 'Catholic, Orthodox, or Protestant'; 'Muslim or Christian'. These may stop us from hearing each other and can become hindrances to liberation as well as to human friendship and trust. There is a better way.

The theologians of liberation teach us to accept each other in our common humanity, regardless of whether the name of Christ is owned. Jesus showed us the way here. He shared humanity with women and men, poor and rich, priest and sinner, child and aged, prostitute and pious. In his parables, too, he showed us this better way to live, love to the neighbour reaching across creeds, culture, and religious divides. The Good Samaritan did not attempt to convert the Jew he helped! The hungry, naked, and thirsty of Matthew 25 are nowhere described as only Christians. They are simply—no, profoundly—human. She or he who is in need is our neighbour. As we love ourselves and love our God in Christ, so we must seek to love our neighbour with whom we share one humanity. There all true evangelization begins. Again, Basil Hume gets to the heart of the matter: 'There will be no better world without better people. And no better people without growth in genuine love. And there can be no growth in genuine love without faith in God and a true and lasting love of him'.[10]

Not all will respond to the full proclamation of the Christian Gospel. As many do, however, a new humanity emerges. Fear holds some back; wealth others; destitution others still. Many, however, learn to follow the way of Jesus. They mature and grow as human beings into Christ. Christ and the Gospel humanize them. Christ's life, death, and resurrection are experienced as the foretaste of the new humanity. Liberated humanity living life to the full becomes the goal of humankind in Christ. Jesus not only shows us who God is but also how to be true human beings. As Christ humanizes people, *being more* becomes more important than *having more*. That is, human relationships and community friendships mean more than material possessions. As God the

Liberator is revealed, as the Risen Christ is encountered and as the Holy Spirit sets people free and brings whole communities alive, then the new humanity in Christ emerges. Contemporary evangelization must then never lose sight of the goal of the new humanity that the Risen Christ beckons each one of us towards. It must also recognize that not all of those who show the clearest signs of such an encounter with the liberating Christ are to be found in our churches. Let this be said clearly.

8. New Society

Running through so many of the writings of the theologians of liberation is a concern for what we might call a middle or 'Third Way' between Marxism (or Marxist Socialism) and Capitalism. We have seen something of the ways in which Capitalism has compounded the misery of the poor in all three worlds. As Camara bears witness:

> I know how Capitalism works. . . . It's become absolutely clear to me, and to many others in the Third World, that there is no hope of our people being liberated through Capitalism. Of course, there are different kinds of Capitalism; but in every Capitalist system, the concern for profit takes precedence over concern for people.[11]

Until a more humane Capitalism emerges, for example, in a reformed EU Common Agricultural Policy, it remains guilty of this ultimate indictment by Martin Luther King, Jr.: 'We can store our surplus food free of charge in the shrivelled stomachs of the millions of God's children who go to bed hungry at night. We can use our vast resources of wealth to wipe poverty from the earth'.[12]

Marxism too has usually been rejected, except for its analytical methodology, by most contemporary theologians of liberation. The Gospel has been discovered to be a far more potent force for the cause of liberation than has Karl Marx. Liberation is concerned also for the oppressors and for the wealthy as Christ supremely demonstrated. Their co-operation can facilitate and hasten social transformation once they too are truly won for Christ and the vision of the New Society. The theologians of liberation know enough of human nature also to realize that, without the revolution of Christ's transforming love in people's hearts, it will just be George Orwell's 'new pigs in the old beds' all over again.[13] A Third Way is needed. A New Society vision is the preferred way adopted in hope by the theologians of liberation: 'Faith can contribute by marking out new paths to a new society—an alternative to Capitalism and Socialism —a fuller and more humane society, free and liberated, a society of the freed'.[14]

This must be the vision of Europe's network of local churches, too. The best way forward for the First, Second, and Third Worlds is what I suggest might be called a more humane—that is, a more Christian—Capitalism.

A more humane Christian Capitalism in the New Europe is desperately needed as the new millennium approaches; one that is more internationally aware and responsible not least in its foreign and economic policy towards the Third, Second, and First World poor; one that is also environmentally aware and prepared to make sacrifices accordingly; one that builds, through both the State and voluntary sectors, a safety net for Europe's poor. I mean here a net that does not have such gaping holes in it as at present and that does not leave so long a drop to the floor beneath. This will be a Capitalism that is prepared to acknowledge the pain and misery that is caused by the 'usury' and debt on which the whole Capitalist system rests. It will also be a Capitalism that includes some elements of public ownership—primarily of natural resources, commodities, and public services—alongside private ownership of capital. So it will be a 'mixed economy', one more committed to redistributing wealth through an altruistic taxation system.

First World local churches must lobby, vote, pray, and work towards such a new society in the years to come. It will be one more pleasing to Christ than our own can possibly be at present. But this will mean cultivating a vision that looks beyond the next change of government, in whatever country, and knows that a new government and the ones after it—whatever their political hue—will also be *semper reformanda,* or 'always in need of reform'. This too the theology of liberation teaches us. Christians and others need to provide a prophetic critique that views sceptically, but constructively, all the present proffered clichés, policies, and manifestos of those in government and opposition. A new society must be midwifed into life as the twenty-first century approaches.

9. Violence and Non-Violence

Here perhaps is the most vexed of all issues when liberation theology is considered. There have been a few theologians of liberation who have advocated violence and more who have condoned it in resisting unjust régimes and in self-defence. There have been many more still who have continued to argue for the way of non-violence. Some have paid the ultimate price for that stance. As I have already remarked in reflecting on this issue,[15] it is easy enough to sit here in First World comfort and pass judgment on the stance taken by fellow Christians in nightmarish circumstances. To God they answer. To God the death squads and the dictators, the ruling élite and the torturers too must one day answer. Though not a pacifist, my own sympathies lie with the glorious twentieth-century tradition of non-violent resistance that Gandhi initiated in the cause of liberation of India. The film *Gandhi* captured brilliantly the unstoppable power of this movement. Martin Luther King vindicated this form of protest in the US civil rights movement of the 1960s. It has also inspired Solidarity in Poland. The tradition of non-violence was practised—alongside fierce denunciations of the evils of the apartheid system—by Archbishop Desmond Tutu and other church leaders in South Africa. Richard Attenborough's film, *Cry Freedom,* painted for many of us painfully and vividly the context within which the new South Africa was forged. More recently, the emergence of a new South Africa under President Nelson Mandela, who has left the armed struggle behind for the way of forgiveness, has demonstrated again to our world that there *is* a better way.

What relevance does this have for a contemporary First World local church and for its evangelization? Non-violent peaceful protest is the only credible way that First World Christians can contemplate the building of a new society. The way of violence is inexcusable in the First World where access to the ballot box (and so to ascertaining majority views and aspirations) is freely available. That may well be frustrating in practice, but it remains the only ethical option. A contemporary liberation theology for the New Europe must be non-violent both in method and aims. That need not make it toothless or enervated, however, as Helder Camara makes clear, using the startling phrase 'the violence of pacifists':

> No, I don't think there was a particular day when I began to believe in non-violence. It has always been my way of interpreting the Gospel—my temperament if you like. But I don't really like the term non-violence. I much prefer . . . the phrase 'the violence of pacifists'. . . . How can we expect young people to renounce armed violence unless we offer them something strong and effective in exchange—something that can achieve effective results?[16]

10. Contradicting Reality

The heading for this section has its origins in the writings of Jürgen Moltmann. 'Those who hope in Christ', he wrote in words now justly famous, 'can no longer put up with reality as it is, but begin to suffer under it, to contradict it'.[17] The world *is* transformable. Such is the passionate conviction of the theologians of liberation. Far from accepting present realities, they rail at them and then seek to transform them. The grinding of the faces of the poor, mass poverty on a terrifying scale, ignorance of community health, poor sanitation, death squads, and torture cells: these are their enemies and the Gospel's enemies. The

Gospel call is one to transform reality. God is the God who turns life's Good Friday into Easter Day. Again, this means viewing each and every government both with eyes of realism and with eyes of love and vision. Turning from Latin America to Europe, its governments—all of them—can be both reformed and transformed the better to serve the new humanity and new society. Such is the Gospel of hope. Such too is part of the calling of each and every local church. Christians are called to help transform and contradict present reality. This is, in part, what biblical evangelization means.

Romans 13:1-7 enjoins Christians to submit to secular authorities. This is a passage that has been abused, time and time again, by those in power to legitimize and excuse some of the most immoral and repellent régimes in the history of humanity. Do these verses really mean that Christians who trust and respect the Scriptures must never seek to contradict ugly governments? The New Testament scholar John Howard Yoder seems to have given the best answer to this question I have yet come across:

> What is ordained is not a particular government but the concept of a proper government, the principle of government as such. As long as a given government lives up to a certain minimum set of requirements, then that government may properly claim the sanction of divine institution. If, however, a government fails adequately to fulfill the functions assigned to it, it loses its authority. It then becomes the duty of the preacher to teach that this has become an unjust government worthy of rebellion. It can become the duty of Christian citizens to rise up against it, not because they are against the government, but because they are in favour of proper government.[18]

The Christian faith has, in fact, a long and distinguished record of social and political protest, as well as one of sad acquiescence in an unjust status quo. Contradicting reality by challenging governments in the name of a more Christian society and of 'humane Capitalism' must be one of the chief callings of contemporary evangelization. It must also involve the programmes of social action that Christians and many others are already involved in; changing the mood of a situation ranges from creating new attitudes of compassion and care to raising the needs of the Second and Third Worlds high onto the political agenda of the present government—as well as that of the local church. Each loving deed, each act of solidarity with the poor, every Good Samaritan rescue is certainly part of what the theologians of liberation term 'transforming the world' or contradicting its present reality. Our faith is in the God of Easter who always opens up new possibilities.

11. Church and Kingdom

The local church needs to learn from the assertions by the theologians of liberation that God's work, God's Kingdom, is much bigger than what goes on inside the Church itself. How many intercessions, for example, did we sit through during the 1970s and 1980s in First World churches where the suffering Church in the USSR was regularly prayed for, but never the political dissidents or the suffering Jews? How often still our prayers of intercession concentrate on the Church in a particular country or a town but never the government or council of that place. Such prayers expose the level that our vision of God has reached. Our God is still far too small. The information is there in our newspapers, our libraries, our prayer guides, and our television screens. It is just that a faulty theology and a narrow faith blind us to the real extent of the Kingdom.

This topic of Church and Kingdom is complex and difficult. It is also a key one for the future of the First World local churches. In Poland in 1989 it was hardly an issue. The people had seen the liberating God at work and evidences of the Kingdom all around them in social movements of enormous significance. So too have Christians in parts of Latin America, even where socio-political liberation is still a long way off, humanly speaking. In the First World, however, the 'new' model of the Church advocated in these pages in the light of the theology of liberation can never be fully accepted, never mind implemented, until a broader Kingdom vision is attained by far more Christians. My own experience of life has been that of Jacob of old: 'Surely the LORD is in this place, and I was not aware of it. . . . This is none other than the house of God; this is the gate of heaven' (Gen 28:16-17). The God of liberation has led me on over the past two decades to see him in unexpected places way beyond the world of the local church, to love the Church and belong to it as I continue happily to do. So God will show us the scope of the Kingdom, begun on earth but never complete until the best 'new wine' of all is drunk in the life of the age to come.

But there are Christian people who have never broken free of the narrowness that binds them only to their local church and to the outlook of their particular tradition. They have never made the imaginative leap from the Bible of their personal devotions to that breadth of vista that the Bible opens up: 'But will God really dwell on earth? The heavens, even the highest heaven, cannot contain you. How much less this temple I have built' (1 Kgs 8:27). For many Christians in the First World, the world-denying tendency has become engrained over the generations. This cannot be what the Risen Lord intended, as the Gospel of John bears witness:

My prayer is not that you take them out of the world but that you protect them from the evil one. They are not of the world, even as I am not of it. Sanctify them by the truth; your word is truth. As you sent me into the world, I have sent them into the world. (17:15-18)

Some Christians have sadly missed what the Risen Lord is doing beyond their traditions, their narrow selection of Bible verses, their denominational gatherings and—in William Blake's powerful phrase—the 'mind-forged manacles' that hold them. First World Christianity needs to seek God's activity as much in the world as in the local church. The Kingdom of God transcends them both.

12. The Suffering God

In their interpretations of the cross of Jesus, the theologians of liberation have provided the World Church with perhaps the most fruitful new Christian thinking of all. Following again the lead of the German theologian Jürgen Moltmann, God is no longer seen as an abstract potentate, remote and impassible in a realm 'above the clouds'. Instead, the theologians of liberation describe him as the Suffering God who is made known supremely in the cross of Christ the crucified one. The cross tells us that God himself, not just the human nature of Christ, is wounded, bruised, and betrayed by humankind's inhumanity to itself:

For a God who is incapable of suffering is a being who cannot be involved. Suffering and injustice do not affect him. And because he is so completely insensitive, he cannot be shaken or affected by anything. He cannot weep, for he has no tears. But the one who cannot suffer cannot love either. So he is also a loveless being.[19]

Perhaps this is really the only way Christian thinking could develop in its understanding of the God of the Scriptures in the twentieth century. This has been the century—we remember—of First World War trench warfare, of Stalin, Hitler, and Auschwitz and of the Latin American, Cambodian, Rwandan, and Yugoslavian death squads. Moltmann's book *The Crucified God* sought, in part, to rescue the cross from the romantic mystique of silver crucifixes, wooden replicas, and narrow piety. The cross, he argued, must be seen in its real historical context and interpreted in that light too. According to the thinking of the time, Jesus died as a blasphemer, as a rebel, and as someone abandoned by God.[20] In the process, however, he revealed the character of a God very different from the one of traditional piety. He helped to develop, by being crucified, a new understanding of the God we worship.

Crucifixion was sordid. Calvary was a place of torture for the political rebel, the religious blasphemer, the outcasts of society. The victim was pinned helplessly to two bars of wood, as firmly as any butterfly to a pin board, yet still alive . . . for a time. *This* is what the God we worship as Christians has experienced. He *is* the Suffering God made known in Jesus Christ. In and through his Son, God experiences the hell of abandonment and separation. The God we worship has known pain; he has known what it is to be beaten and abused, to bleed and to die. Through the ministry of Jesus, we may dare to say that God 'learned' the pain of rejection, the stresses of conflict, the hurt of misunderstanding, the sadness of having friends deemed loyal run away, and the terrors of torture.

The local church needs to proclaim this Suffering God more than it does. The resources of the vision of a Suffering God can be drawn upon in many and varied areas of pastoral care: in bereavement visiting, protests on behalf of the suffering, intercessions, unemployment counselling, hospital visits, support for prisoners of conscience, hospice chaplaincy, marriage counselling, and dealing with abuse. Graham Monteith, for example, writes about the relevance of this concept of God to the experience of disability:

> God now understands our suffering and our revulsion at the thought of it. He accepts the anger which is vented upon him by those who lose dear ones or find themselves paraplegic after a very active life. . . . The triumphant Christ strides over the realm of despair and suffering, trampling them to the ground, whilst at the same time hanging pathetically from the cross waiting for us to recognise this humiliated figure as the beginning of our salvation.[21]

The traditional models of atonement will continue to speak to people today, not least those of reconciliation, sacrifice, and triumph in defeat. However, the concept of the suffering of God as a model of atonement has come to have increasing meaning to many Christian thinkers as they have reflected on faith for this century and the next. The Suffering God is not the only helpful model of the cross, nor indeed the only valid contemporary insight into the character of the God made known in Christ. It is, however, an enormously valuable one in our world of misery and pain. The theology of liberation has brought it into prominence, and contemporary evangelization will need to have recourse to it again and again.

13. Continuity with Tradition

The theology of liberation is, as this book has argued, a major movement in our day through which God has been speaking to his Church and to our suffering world. Perhaps a new reformation is underway with its roots in the local churches and base communities of every continent. This book has been an attempt to express just how important a movement this is and to communicate at least something of what the Living God may be saying to us through it. Clodovis and Leonardo Boff assess it like this:

> It is . . . a historical theology very much of its time . . . its applicability, although not transhistorical, is not merely transient, a thing of fashion; it covers a historical period, and this period will last for decades, if not centuries . . . it is a whole theology, thought out in terms of today. As a result, its subject matter embraces the whole body of theological investigation . . . it launches an appeal to all theologians of the First, Second, and Third World calling on them to work out the social-liberative dimension of faith.[22]

The theologians of liberation are indeed currently revolutionizing contemporary understandings of the Christian faith, covering 'the whole body of theological investigation'. Church history is being applied afresh to today. The 'historical Jesus' has been rediscovered, not to be neglected alongside 'the Christ of faith'. The resurrection is seen, not as a series of facts or claims to be argued over, but as an event that is both the hope and goal of the new humanity. The doctrine of the Holy Spirit has been creatively interpreted in ways that make both the Bible and the experiences of the contemporary base communities come alive. The Bible itself has been reclaimed for the ordinary believer and clergy, and the specialist theologians are encouraged to sit at their feet and learn. An eschatology that sees God's judgement now as well as in the future has been redirected to transform contemporary evils. Doctrines of the Trinity, Mary, God, Jesus, and the Church are all being creatively redefined in more genuinely biblical ways and always with a focus on contemporary evangelization. Thus the development of a truly contemporary Christian theology is being actively sought, but never losing continuity with the traditional faith. The local church that opens itself to such theology of liberation will soon find it has opened itself to God and to his Word in the Bible. Such a local church will find that it has rediscovered whole parts of the Bible neglected for far too long by any true 'People of the Book'.

There is, of course, a final heading in a contemporary theology of mission: the preferential option for the poor. To this we shall turn after our third glimpse into praxis in a local church in Britain.

14. Third Case Study
Dagnall Street Baptist Church
St. Albans, Hertfordshire, 1992–present

The city of St. Albans has one of the longest Christian heritages in Europe. One of the first European Christian martyrs, Alban, died there in 303 A.D., and the city's magnificent Abbey was built, over many centuries, on the traditional site of his martyrdom. Long before Alban, Roman soldiers colonized the area and named the then occupied town Verulamium. St. Albans remains one of the most fascinating cities in Europe for exploring excavations and relics from the Roman era. Its proximity to London makes it a very popular commuter city, especially with its setting in the gentle countryside of Hertfordshire, with its many picturesque villages. Dagnall Street Baptist Church, St. Albans, is one of the oldest Baptist churches anywhere in the world. Its recorded history goes back more than 350 years. It is also one of the largest Free Churches in the county. The city also has a very constructive ecumenical history, stretching back to the formative years of the ecumenical movement in this century. That was one of the things that especially attracted me to both the church and the city when I accepted the call to minister at Dagnall Street.

In January 1993 I was appointed the new Convenor of Churches Together in St Albans (CTSA). More than a decade of ecumenical involvement in two local churches had convinced me that the one indispensable way forward for contemporary evangelization was to develop a shared praxis in partnership with other Christian churches. 'Better together', indeed. This conviction had been confirmed by the opportunities given to me by the Baptist Union of Great Britain, which I represented on the new ecumenical bodies: Churches Together in England (CTE) and the Council of Churches for Britain and Ireland (CCBI). These include Roman Catholics as full, participating members, unlike the situation in the World Council of Churches. In St. Albans was an opportunity to test my conviction, in a city where some thirty or so different Christian churches had already come together to form the new ecumenical grouping of CTSA.

In October 1992 a significant ecumenical venture in mission began. In the Cross Street Centre, a restaurant and community centre that is a valuable part of Dagnall Street Baptist's ministry, we hosted a public meeting that sought to respond to the needs of homeless people in the city. There were those who claimed that this was not a local problem but really a London one. The evidence of our eyes and of committed Christians working among local homeless and badly housed people told a very different story. Two schemes were explored. One would have seen church halls used across the city on a rotational basis for homeless people to use overnight. The other would be more ambitious but aimed to establish a professionally run night and day shelter in the city. It is not exaggerating to say that this meeting led to a people's movement in our city. There is no other way to describe the phenomenal support the project received from churches, community groups, the city council, the service industries, and all kinds of professionals. A temporary night shelter was established in the former premises of Oxfam in the city, and a learning curve began for many of us, volunteers all. By the end of the three months experiment, the evidence was incontrovertible that there was indeed a desperate need for such a project in our city.

Within the space of a few months, just a year or so after that inaugural meeting, a purpose-built city night shelter—Open Door—was officially opened in the city. This was a truly ecumenical project. Along with professional workers, a network of volunteers, many from our CTSA family, became involved: preparing meals, cleaning, laundering, and getting alongside some of our city's most needy and vulnerable people. Night-time provision expanded into the day as well. Helped by our CTSA media officer—and there can be none better than Peter Crumpler whose book, *Keep in Touch* (Scripture Union 1993), is all about Christian communication— 'Open Door' caught the imagination of the whole city. Newspapers in St. Albans carried a stream of news about the project:

> *'All rally to help city's homeless'*
> *'New shelter for homeless'*
> *'Public meeting about the homeless tomorrow night'*
> *' £150,0000 for homeless base'*
> *'Goodwill and generosity has been the key to the*
> *success of St. Albans' sanctuary for the homeless'*
> *'Ordinary folk's army is a winner'*
> *'Cold night out aids homeless'*
> *'Church backs up plan for homeless'*
> *'Sharing plight of the poor'*
> *'Night shelter is open'*

Another ecumenical project was based on the CCBI Lent programme in 1994 known as 'Have Another Look'. As part of this, CTSA joined forces with the vibrant Abbey community in the city to launch an ambitious evangelistic programme called 'From Lent to Pentecost 1994'. The launch meeting and training events were well attended and resulted in the setting up of some fifty ecumenical Lent groups all over the city. The annual 'Unity at the Cross' service in the Abbey on Good Friday attracted as always hundreds of people. The worship emphasized Christ's own experiences of torture and commended the work of Amnesty International. This was followed by a series of Christian apologetics lectures held that spring in the Abbey Nave that attracted hundreds of people, and on a midweek evening! Nationally-known celebrity speakers explored different aspects of the Christian faith for the 1990s and were supported by a panel of local Christians who helped to answer questions from the floor. Finally, over the 1994 Pentecost weekend, the Abbey was again creatively used. A Saturday Celebration Evening was followed by an all-age programme on Sunday including drama, music making, banners, puppetry, arts and crafts, prayer workshops, and family evensong to conclude the programme. Some of the headlines in the press over those months ran:

'Invitation to take a new look at faith'
'Churches unite for Good Friday services'
'Abbey celebrates Pentecost'
'Churches' campaign a success'

Christian Aid week is well organized ecumenically and incorporates competitions, sponsored walks, and concerts as well as the vital door-to-door collections. A 'Good Neighbour' scheme has been run for many years now with significant ecumenical support. More recently in 1995 youth leaders in Church of England, Free Church, and Roman Catholic churches within CTSA became disturbed about the increasing gulf between young people and the Church. In contemporary Britain it seems that 95 percent of those in their twenties have no contact with any Christian church. The CTSA youth leaders have therefore combined to form an interchurch youth network. Ecumenical youth services have been planned; the pooling of information and some resources is happening; and its ventures include an ecumenical Christmas youth project in solidarity with the poor of Thailand and a Christian rock concert. Local newspapers have again made space for this news, with headlines such as: *'Youth theme for churches'* and *'Churches plan rock concert'*. Evangelization too is better done together.

15. The Preferential Option for the Poor

There are wider issues that affect the liberation of all, whether individuals or nations. I have argued that local churches have a significant part to play in implementing a 'bias to the poor', but governments have a higher responsibility still. There are debates underway in contemporary Britain, for instance, about wide-ranging matters of political and economic policy whose outcomes will, in fact, determine the effectiveness of any policies of bias to the poor in the twenty-first century. If I illustrate this from my own country, I hope that readers elsewhere will see the point about the wider, 'structural' questions that shape the existence of poverty.

There is, for example, the question of the electoral process itself and the case for a move to 'proportional representation' in Britain today. The gap between Comfortable Britain and the Other Britain will never, in my view, be bridged until the ruling government represents the whole electorate and not just the mainly successful parts of it at the last election. Our present system gives all the spoils to the party that gets most of its candidates 'first past the post'. This means in practice that a government voted for by only—say—45 percent of the electorate gets all the spoils of victory and the right to influence and affect life for everyone else for some four to five years. All the Cabinet seats, the lion's share of Parliamentary time, victory in almost all legislation—however controversial—are thus assured. The result of this is that power is kept in the hands of certain sections and interest groups at the expense of all the others. There is an injustice at the heart of our Parliamentary democracy, and the liberation of Britain will be hampered until proportional representation is achieved. Far from giving others lessons in democracy, we should realise that our own political system is seriously flawed. It encourages party spirit and not consensus, divisiveness and not partnership or compromise. The growing gap between the two Britains in the 1990s is the direct tragic consequence of the polarization of society in the post-war years, and I believe that this is, in part, the product of an anachronistic electoral system.

Another issue that bears directly on the state of the poor is the need for an overhaul of the nation's taxation and benefit system. Bridging the gaps between the two Britains will involve a far more wholesale revision of this system than has yet been achieved. The evidence is overwhelming that, while Comfortable Britain has gained during the 1980s and early 1990s, it is the 'Other Britain' that, relatively speaking, has carried the heaviest burdens of taxation. This becomes clear when the whole picture of taxation is considered (including V.A.T. and Council Tax), and not just the changes in 'basic rate' taxation levels on income. Much more research needs to be done to ascertain the impact of the total network of taxation on the various sectors that make up our nation. Pensions, I suggest, need to be seen not as benefits but as earned 'social wages' for our elderly people, realistically linked to the average wage of the rest of the country. The low-paid and those near the poverty line should be 'negatively taxed' in their wage packets or benefit payments. Comfortable Britain needs to be encouraged through the compulsory altruism of the taxation system to see ourselves as belonging to one Britain and to one world. Why aren't more Christians saying these things and saying them loudly?

Other issues under debate at the moment are also, in my view, relevant to the moral demand for a bias to the poor. There is the future of the monarchy, the case for Parliamentary short lists that positively discriminate in favour of women, and the challenge of regenerating the economy and creating wealth with the 'Other Britain' in mind.[23] Prominent among these issues is the need to cultivate a new internationalism. It is with this requirement, applicable to all countries, that I wish to end both this chapter and book.

Liberation for the New Europe is inextricably bound up with developing a new internationalism that embraces the First, Second, and Third Worlds. Once again, Cardinal Basil Hume directs us to the heart of the matter:

> There is a real danger that efforts are being so concentrated on the rebuilding of post-Communist Europe, and on the West's own difficulties, that the grave situation in the developing world will be forgotten. . . . What is needed is not only emergency aid from the wealthier in Europe, but the deep engagement of all Europeans in the welfare of the world's poorest people. It is only by demonstrating a real international solidarity that the whole of Europe can find a way to its moral health. If it shuts out the outside world and attempts to create a separate wealthy bloc, it will risk being suffocated by materialism.[24]

The agenda before humanity in the twenty-first century will need just such a new internationalism if breakthroughs are to be made. Leaders capable of seeing beyond their own narrow national frontiers will be sorely needed. The current evidence suggests that, sadly, they are in very short supply.

A new internationalism for the sake of the poor is also needed among world Baptists, if I may speak finally about the part of the Christian family to which I belong. I have already drawn attention to the significant rôle, with very limited resources, that is being played in New European church life by the European Baptist Federation (EBF).[25] Its scope also embraces parts of the Middle East adjacent to Europe. And the EBF is, of course, just one major constituency of the broader Baptist World Alliance (BWA), whose other regional fellowships include the Asian Baptist Federation, the All-Africa Baptist Fellowship, the Caribbean Baptist Fellowship, the North American Baptist Fellowship, and the Union of Baptists in Latin America. The number of baptized church members in the Baptist World Alliance is 41,000,000 people, belonging to some 153,300 churches. When to this figure are added the children and young people not yet baptized, as well as regular worshippers who are not yet members, a more realistic figure for the size of this world Christian family may well be as many as 100,000,000 people.[26] This would make Baptists the third largest Christian communion in the world, with the added strategic significance of being present in more countries of the world than any other communion, including Roman Catholicism. All this is not a matter of head counting; it is to underline (as I have already remarked) that the Baptist World Alliance is uniquely placed in world Christianity to lobby for, express, and demonstrate a solidarity among the Three Worlds. It also makes more urgent the responsibility of the BWA to listen to voices of Third and Second World Baptist leaders, and increasingly to reflect their experience and vision as the twenty-first century approaches. The theme of inter-connectedness between the various worlds of our small planet, for the sake both of liberation and evangelism, has been central to this study.

The agenda for a new internationalism in the new millennium is obvious already: overcoming hunger and thirst, undermining repression, redirecting money from weapons of death to sources of life, solving debt problems, reforming unjust economic structures, tackling the worldwide oppression of women and children, protecting the environment, and resisting the evils of nationalism and racism. The days of the privileged élite are over or should be: 'Surely it is unchristian and unethical for some to wallow in the soft beds of luxury while others sink in the quicksands of poverty' (Martin Luther King).[27] Unless such changes happen, the danger in the next century is that rich and poor alike will perish together. For we must remember that:

All the flowers of all the tomorrows are in the seeds of today.

Notes

[1]Dom Helder Camara, quoted in José de Broucker, *Dom Helder Camara*, p. 125.

[2]Eduardo Hoornaert, *The Memory of the Christian People* (Burns & Oates, London, 1989).

[3]In José de Broucker, *Dom Helder Camara*, p. 100.

[4]Robert Gurney, *The Face of Pain and Hope, Stories of Diakonia in Europe* (WCC Publications, Geneva, 1995), pp. ix-x.

[5]Ibid., p. 69.

[6]Basil Hume, *Remaking Europe*, p. 78.

[7]José Comblin, *The Holy Spirit and Liberation*, p. 154.

[8]Ibid., p. 18.

[9]C. Boff and J. Pixley, *The Bible, the Church, and the Poor*, p. 228.

[10]Basil Hume, *Remaking Europe*, p. 103.

[11]Helder Camara, in José de Broucker, *Dom Helder Camara*, p. 185.

[12]Martin Luther King, Jr., *Strength to Love* (Collins, Fontana, London, 1969), p. 70.

[13]See George Orwell, *Animal Farm* (Secker and Warburg, London, 1945), ch. X.

[14]Leonardo Boff and Clodovis Boff, *Introducing Liberation Theology*, p. 93.

[15]See above, chapter 6, pp. 126-127.

[16]Helder Camara in de Broucker, *Dom Helder Camara*, p. 179. For a similar approach, see Walter Wink, *Engaging the Powers. Discernment and Resistance in a World of Domination* (Fortress, Minneapolis, 1992).

[17]Jürgen Moltmann, *Theology of Hope*, p. 21.

[18]John Howard Yoder, *The Politics of Jesus*, p. 201.

[19]Jürgen Moltmann, *The Crucified God*, p. 222.

[20]Ibid., pp. 126-159.

[21]W. Graham Monteith, *Disability, Faith, and Acceptance*, pp. 73-74.

[22]Clodovis Boff and Leonardo Boff, *Introducing Liberation Theology*, pp. 91-92.

[23]I considered these issues more fully in two articles published in *The Baptist Times*, 19 October 1995 and 26 October 1995.

[24]Basil Hume, *Remaking Europe*, pp. 46-47.

[25]See above, chapter 8, pp. 169-171.

[26]Statistics are from the *Agenda Book of the General Council Meeting of the Baptist World Alliance* (Hong Kong, 1996).

[27]Martin Luther King, Jr., *Strength to Love*, p. 102.

Index